D1572065

TUTT LIBRARY

A gift to

COLORADO
COLLEGE

WITHDRAWN *from*

The Lorenzo Bennett
Memorial Book Fund

The Expert Cook in Enlightenment France

The Johns Hopkins University Studies in Historical and Political Science
129th Series (2011)

The Expert Cook
in Enlightenment France

SEAN TAKATS

The Johns Hopkins University Press

Baltimore

COLORADO COLLEGE LIBRARY
COLORADO SPRINGS, COLORADO

©2011 The Johns Hopkins University Press
All rights reserved. Published 2011
Printed in the United States of America on acid-free paper
2   4   6   8   9   7   5   3   1

The Johns Hopkins University Press
2715 North Charles Street
Baltimore, Maryland 21218-4363
www.press.jhu.edu

Library of Congress Cataloging-in-Publication Data
Takats, Sean, 1974–
The expert cook in enlightenment France / Sean Takats.
p.   cm. — (The Johns Hopkins University studies in historical and
political science)
Includes bibliographical references and index.
ISBN-13: 978-1-4214-0283-3 (hardcover : alk. paper)
ISBN-10: 1-4214-0283-1 (hardcover : alk. paper)
1. Cooking, French—History—18th century. 2. Cooking—France—History—
18th century. 3. Cooks—France—History—18th century. 4. France—Social life
and customs—18th century. I. Title.
TX719.T253 2011
641.5944—dc22   2011009234

A catalog record for this book is available from the British Library.

*Special discounts are available for bulk purchases of this book. For more information,
please contact Special Sales at 410-516-6936 or specialsales@press.jhu.edu.*

The Johns Hopkins University Press uses environmentally friendly book materials,
including recycled text paper that is composed of at least 30 percent post-consumer
waste, whenever possible.

To those who have found certain traits of history, cuisine, fashion, etc., repugnant: they have forgotten how many works of erudition these topics have spawned and that the most succinct of our articles of this sort will perhaps spare our descendants years of research and volumes of dissertations.

Denis Diderot, "Encyclopédie," in *Encyclopédie, ou Dictionnaire raisonné des sciences, des arts et des métiers* (1751–1772)

He who has no cook has no existence.

Louis-Sébastien Mercier, *Tableau de Paris* (1788)

CONTENTS

It would be a grim enterprise indeed to study French cooks without the occasion to conduct one's own gustatory "field research," in the memorable words of A. J. Liebling. Generous institutional support ensured that I remained exceedingly well fed and otherwise awash in material comfort throughout all phases of research and writing this book. The University of Michigan's history department, Rackham School of Graduate Studies, and International Institute sustained this project in its initial stages. Indiana University's Everett Helm fellowship at the Lilly Library afforded me an essential early look at cookbooks as material artifacts. The Social Science Research Council and the Georges Lurcy Memorial Trust funded extended archival work in France. The Roy Rosenzweig Center for History and New Media provided an extraordinary opportunity to revise this manuscript and to continue my research on early modern France. At George Mason University I have benefited from the generosity of the Allan and Gwen Nelson faculty research fund.

It is a rare pleasure to acknowledge the dozens of fellow scholars who have selflessly contributed to this project. Among them I first and foremost thank Dena Goodman for her constant intellectual support and friendship. It is impossible to imagine this book without the influence of her sharp wit and sage counsel. Laura Lee Downs, Diane Owen Hughes, and Liz Wingrove each substantially refined the methods and argument behind this book while also broadening its scope and relevance. For sharpening my ideas and helping to coax them into publication, I am indebted to fellow conference and workshop panelists Sara Chapman, Richard Clay, Clare Crowston, Colin Jones, Helge Jordheim, Bob Kreiser, Nina Lewallen, Tessie Liu, Morag Martin, Deb Neill, Kate Norberg, Anne Quartararo, Tip Ragan, Catriona Seth, Richard Taws, George Trumbull, Laurent Turcot, and Caroline Warman. Like countless French historians near and far, I owe a special debt of gratitude to the remarkable intellectual stimulation and fellowship of Washington, DC's Old Regime Group, and in particular to Tom

Adams, Katherine Brennan, Tom Brennan, Henriette de Bruyn Kops, Jack Censer, Jim Collins, Mary Gayne, Mack Holt, Sharon Kettering, Bob Kreiser, Chuck Lipp, April Shelford, Don Sutherland, and Allan Tulchin.

I thank the skilled and patient staffs at the Bibliothèque nationale de France, the Centre historique des Archives nationales, the Bibliothèque historique de la ville de Paris, the Lilly Library, the New York Public Library, the Library of Congress, and the National Library of Medicine for their able assistance. Marie-Véronique Vaillant of the Minutier central was particularly helpful in securing access to notarial documents otherwise off limits to researchers. The highly professional staff of the Réunion des musées nationaux and its American affiliate Art Resource made image research and permissions a breeze. Although anything but professional, Lauren and Matthew Miller warmly opened their home to me during follow-up research visits to Paris, and I thank them for their generosity. What good luck to have friends across the street from the Archives nationales!

During the publication process, manuscript readers Kate Norberg and Janine Lanza offered shrewd suggestions for strengthening the book while also supplying welcome encouragement. Editors Henry Tom and Suzanne Flinchbaugh swiftly and painlessly advanced this first-time author's work from proposal to finished product. In the final stage of preparation, copyeditor Peter Dreyer scrupulously rectified innumerable infelicities and faults. Any remaining errors are of course my own.

My debt to my family is more personal but no less important. For their unflagging enthusiasm while I researched and wrote this book, I am grateful to my parents, to my children, and in particular to my wife Sarah. This book is dedicated to her.

The Expert Cook in Enlightenment France

Introduction

The Italians, who style their ideas nicely,
call the introduction *the sauce of a book.*

François Marin, *La Suite des dons de Comus* (1742)

In the final decades of the Old Regime, French cooks achieved universal dominion over the palate. In 1754, the chevalier de Jaucourt lamented the overwhelming
international popularity of French cuisine, claiming that his countrymen had
"found nothing so gratifying as seeing the taste of their cuisine surpass that of
other opulent kingdoms, and to reign without competition from the one end
of the globe to the other."[1] Three years later, in the play *L'Ancienne et nouvelle
cuisine*, one cook characterized another's work as satisfying even "the least delicate palates / from the Antarctic to the Arctic."[2] In his 1773 dictionary of arts and
trades, Philippe Macquer claimed that "in all nations French cooks pass for those
who cook best and whose taste is most delicate with respect to fine dining."[3]
This notion was hardly limited to French imaginations. One Italian observer remarked with disgust, "Nowadays the French reign supreme in the science of fla-
vour, from the North down to the South."[4] In England, indigenous cooks fiercely
opposed the intrusion of French interlopers.[5] And the same faith in the ability
of French cooks circulated across the Atlantic: when one New Yorker witnessed
a few French travelers spontaneously preparing an onion soup, he exclaimed in
vindication that "it was true that all French people were cooks."[6]

Although this mastery usually proved purely imaginary, it arose from cooks'
very real effort to transform themselves from servants into professionals. Operating at a unique intersection of domestic service and occupational expertise,
cooks worked particularly unstable ground. They labored as domestic servants
without the guild oversight that regulated most other urban trades, and unlike in
almost every other occupation, large numbers of both women and men served as
cooks. They toiled in kitchens that were perceived as sites of pollution and decay
threatening the comfort and hygiene of residential space. They were entrusted

with tremendous financial responsibility and yet remained widely suspected of fraud. In the face of this disorganization, cooks audaciously proposed to reconfigure their lowly occupation as a profession. By introducing something they called *la cuisine moderne*, or "modern cooking," during the 1730s, cooks aimed at establishing themselves as expert engineers of taste through the fusion of a new theoretical knowledge with existing mechanical skill. Although largely formulated in cookbooks, *la cuisine moderne*'s most important contribution was not its recipes but rather its new cook: a "taste professional" who along with decorators, architects, and fashion merchants drove France's consumer revolution; a health practitioner who along with doctors, surgeons, dentists, midwives, and pharmacists advanced his professional status by capitalizing on the Enlightenment's new concern for bodily and material happiness over eternal salvation and the life to come. This book is about these cooks and how they sought to establish themselves as a profession and used the tools of the Enlightenment to do so.

When it involved matters beyond the dining table, the civilizing role sought by cooks for the most part inspired pride. According to Antoine de Rivarol, a contemporary commentator, by supplying theater, clothing, taste, manners, language, and a new art of living to the nations around it, France had come to wield over its neighbors "a sort of empire that no other people had ever exercised."[7] Nonetheless, pride in France's achievements was tempered by a persistent undercurrent of anxiety about their nature and, more important, the rising status and power of those individuals behind them. Although founded upon the most sociable and polite of nations, this new French "empire" was unfortunately the empire of marginal characters, including not just cooks but men of letters, seamstresses, and actors. Worse still, it was also often an empire of women, since they were often most closely associated with the consumption and promotion of France's cultural output.[8] Yet even among this questionable company, cooks were viewed as especially disreputable. Detractors worried not just about cooks' international "empire," but also about the "empire" they wielded over those whom they served, exercising scandalously inappropriate dominion over the latter's finances, passions, and bodies.[9] In the process they disrupted social order, redefined aesthetic sensibility, and challenged medical science.

Because of the dubious social standing of those most closely associated with the rapidly expanding sphere of French cultural influence, a curious disjuncture between practitioner and product emerged in the eighteenth century, which has largely persisted. Although their products were exalted, practitioners were denigrated, to the degree that, except for men of letters and a few artists, their names have mostly been lost to history. Major achievements in fashion and cuisine became woven into the very fabric of French national character, but we have forgotten the identities of those responsible for first creating them. These individuals have disappeared because they fit so poorly into established categories of early modern work. On the one hand, in large part through their own efforts, writers and painters successfully elevated themselves to the status of "authors" and "artists," whose work reflected genius and uniqueness. Men of letters in particular capitalized on the rising importance of print, claiming immortality via the enduring quality of their work. On the other hand, urban artisans—like furniture makers, decorators, bakers, and hatters—have remained contained within the history of labor. For these workers, guilds and their records provide the essential analytical framework. However, there was also a third type of practitioner, falling into neither of these two categories. Here we find cooks, who had neither the power to establish themselves as artists nor the institutional support the guilds gave artisans.

Although this book is about cooks, it is not about food. Over the past three decades, scholars from a wide range of disciplines have used French cuisine as a lens through which to analyze European society and culture. Pioneering work by Jean-Louis Flandrin, Philip and Mary Hyman, Stephen Mennell, and Barbara Ketcham Wheaton has established a narrative that traces the remarkable changes in French dining during the Old Regime.[10] In this story, French cuisine during the late seventeenth century underwent dramatic shifts in ingredients, replacing "medieval" spices and profligacy with "natural" herbs and restraint.[11] Sweet and salty flavors were segregated, with sweet moving to the end of the meal. Just a few decades later, *la cuisine moderne* overthrew the existing style, now denigrated as *l'ancienne cuisine*, or "old cooking." With its modular components and renowned sauces more clearly recognizable as precursors to today's French cooking, *la cuisine moderne* promised yet more refinement, and it purported to offer novel health benefits as well. In recent years, a steady stream of new scholarship has continued to flesh out this narrative, and little has emerged to challenge it.[12] Cooks remain entirely absent from this story, and nearly every existing study has focused on food and recipes—or in one case, the restaurant—at the expense of cooks.[13] The material culture of the kitchen, its architecture and its tools, have likewise disappeared from view. We are thus faced with the historical irony that the cooks who created *la cuisine moderne* were ultimately effaced by their own invention.

By focusing on people, and not food, this book not only recovers the eighteenth-century cook but also makes two significant contributions to our understanding of eighteenth-century society. First, it argues that ordinary, "mechanical" people actively participated in the Enlightenment. Despite their low social standing, cooks drew on and contributed to the period's overarching project of systematizing all human knowledge. We must now consider this effort, long associated with the *philosophes*, as significantly more expansive and inclusive. Cooks sought to turn this participation to professional advantage. Thanks to unusually high levels of literacy, they were able to harness the power of print, to position themselves among medical practitioners, to capitalize on the rise of consumption, and to exploit the social anxiety of their masters in a changing world. Second, this book provides a new way of looking at the relationship between labor and gender. Unlike seamstresses, ribbon makers, and other female guild members, female cooks could not exploit the contradictions of Old Regime status and privilege to their own advantage. Indeed, the low status of these women stemmed more from their role as domestic servants than from their sex: male cooks, also servants, operated from an equally weak position. In the face of these seemingly hopeless circumstances, cooks sought to advance their occupation by claiming a novel authority that sprang from the confluence of theoretical knowledge and practical expertise, not from social status.

The following chapters reveal how the humble cook participated in the culture of the Enlightenment and challenged the social structures of the Old Regime. In so doing, cooks made claims that, far from allaying the fears that always dogged them, made such fears even more powerful. As Keith Baker has suggested, politics is about making claims, with political authority "essentially a matter of linguistic authority."[14] Although cooks couched their own argument in the language of taste and the science of the gullet, their history is political. Beneath the smooth surface of the triumphalist narrative of *la cuisine moderne* lies a history of cooks that is fraught with tension. And that tension has far less to do with food than with the social position of cooks, their working conditions, and the claims they made based on their particular skills and the tools of their trade. From these unlikely domestic servants emerged not only a bold challenge to cultural and social order but also the production of some of the eighteenth century's great theoretical works on taste, drawing on the science and medicine of the Enlightenment. Like the *philosophes*, cooks imagined an ideal future where reason and science propelled human society to perfection, and they saw themselves as necessarily contributing to its progress.

To understand what motivated cooks to become active participants in the Enlightenment, this book follows them to where they worked, a unique crossroads that included domestic service, urban trades, and professional medicine, three occupational categories that historians have typically analyzed in entirely

separate spheres. Although excellent studies of domestic service from Cissie Fairchilds, Sarah Maza, Claude Petitfrère, and Jacqueline Sabattier have shed much
light on the complex relationships that existed between servants and masters,
servants' work itself has tended to remain in the shadows.[15] Since servants' productive output was ephemeral and disregarded by contemporaries, it has been
easy to dismiss domestic servants as a disorganized and economically sterile class
whose labor lacked any exchange value.[16] This study seeks to correct this deficit
by restoring servants to the world of work, a particularly fascinating problem,
since servants operated outside many of the conventional boundaries that defined the early modern occupational categories. In stark contrast to other skilled
urban workers, who were generally organized into guilds, servants lacked any
kind of governing corporate body.

According to William H. Sewell, the division between incorporated and unincorporated labor was fundamental, denoting nothing less than the boundary
between order and disorder.[17] As a consequence, most historians have shied away
from venturing beyond the relatively orderly world of guilds. Presumed to lack
economic importance and autonomous social significance, servants have instead
remained largely submerged within narratives of domesticity, with histories of
the family and household taking precedence. If servants have integrated poorly
into histories of labor, the case of cooks only compounds the problem, since
they in turn fit uneasily into histories of domestic service. Cooks' work involved
a degree of expertise absent from other servants' labor, and even their most ar-
dent critics acknowledged that cooks worked with skill. The fact that some cooks
translated their expertise into published cookbooks further complicates the situation. Historians of domestic service have experienced difficulty accounting for
such texts, which although prime examples of the sort of prescriptive literature
that dictated how servants ought to behave, were actually produced by domestic
servants themselves.[18]

The French Revolution often anchors the beginning or the end of studies of
servants and, by extension, French cooking. One typical narrative maintains that
the restaurant arose as a consequence of the Revolution's disruption of domestic service. Their masters guillotined or fleeing the country, cooks supposedly
turned to opening restaurants, simultaneously sounding the death knell of the
era of fine private dining and inaugurating a new age of public gastronomy.[19]
This narrative has recently been questioned, but elite households undoubtedly
suffered catastrophic declines in fortune during the Revolution, forcing servants
(especially males) out of work, particularly during its early years.[20] From 14 July
1789 through 1791, the percentage of male cooks seeking work actually increased,

temporarily reversing a decades-long decline.[21] Perhaps equally damaging to domestic servant cooking were the exigencies of war that followed. Other than exceptional cases like the one with "two immobile fingers" that precluded service in the army, male cooks were swallowed up by the revolutionary armies.[22] The deprivation associated with the height of the Revolution was also hardly conducive to fine dining: the 1795 cookbook *La Cuisinière républicaine* (The Republican Cook) concerned itself more with the basic sustenance offered by potatoes—"the vegetable kingdom offers no plant more healthful, more convenient, and less expensive"—than with the aesthetic and professional concerns that preoccupied its predecessors.[23]

The Revolution had little bearing on the intellectual and cultural contributions of eighteenth-century cooks, however, so this book grants it no special status. Although it dismantled domestic service as practiced under the Old Regime, it in no way limited what cooks were able to achieve, unlike long-standing doubts about the moral and intellectual capacity of servants. Conversely, the Revolution in no way liberated the cook to accomplish what was impossible under the Old Regime. Although the rhetoric of *la cuisine moderne* would resurface in the context of the new institution of the restaurant, the professionalizing impulses of the eighteenth-century cook remained inextricably intertwined with Enlightenment science and culture. The history of French cooks no more requires explanation in terms of the Revolution than the Enlightenment itself does.

Scholars have often sought to differentiate between "professional" and "domestic" cooks, a dichotomy that owes its origins to feminist scholarship and the tendency to view the early modern world of work as strictly divided along gender lines.[24] Studies of artisans and of domestic servants have typically perpetuated this distinction, with the former usually focusing on male-dominated guilds and the latter on female servants. Recent scholarship by Daryl Hafter, Clare Crowston, and Geraldine Sheridan has brilliantly shown how women actively participated as workers and even thrived by exploiting the world of privilege in order to carve out areas of autonomy. But while women workers succeeded by relying on the increasingly backward-looking institutions of the Old Regime, cooks tried something quite different. Instead, they sought to turn the tools of the Enlightenment to professional advantage.[25] These efforts have remained obscure thanks in part to the existence of male culinary guilds under the Old Regime. Practitioners in the incorporated culinary occupations of roasting, pastry making, and catering were effectively exclusively male. Although in practice women played a significant, if minority, role in many of the other formally "male" guilds, they did not do so in the cooking occupations, even in regions where women were otherwise heavily represented.[26]

Male "chefs" in some accounts allegedly vied with female "cooks," even though during the eighteenth century, the use of the word "chef" indicated only the presence of subordinate kitchen staff, not the cook's gender.[27] Most men preparing food were not in fact known as "chefs," but as "cooks." In the case of French cooks working abroad, historians have further complicated this opposition to include a national element: for example, across the Channel, *English* female domestic cooks resented their *French* male professional counterparts.[28] Unfortunately, these distinctions of gender, professionalism, and nationality introduce misleading anachronism into any subsequent narrative, since no such clear distinction existed during the eighteenth century.[29] To be sure, cooks worked at cultural, geographic, and financial extremes: cooking at his master's residences in Paris and Versailles, one male cook might earn wages more than twenty times higher than a woman marooned in a backwater town like Rodez in southern France.[30] Such cases, however, suggest diversity within the occupation rather than bisection. Whether serving in the capital or hinterland, male or female, working alone or in teams, all cooks sustained the same critical overriding occupational constraints. They had no guild or other formal training and certifying institutions, and each cook worked for a single employer, usually living in this master's household and utterly dependent on the master's goodwill. To speak of clearly divided professional and nonprofessional cooks is to impose artificial and anachronistic categories on the past.

Cooks' occupational identity became closely linked to medical practice over the course of the eighteenth century, thanks to a concerted effort to cast cooking as a means of preserving and even improving health. This book restores cooks to a forgotten role as medical practitioners, or at least self-styled ones. Until very recently, the medical history of eighteenth-century France traditionally focused on surgery.[31] The surgeon alone supposedly embodied dynamism, the scientific method, perhaps even modernity itself, in contrast to the allegedly staid physician.[32] In this model, surgeons singlehandedly challenged the traditional "tripartite, corporative, and hierarchical" organization of medicine, which also included physicians and apothecaries.[33] In recent years, however, innovative historians like Nina Gelbart and Colin Jones have begun to investigate a growing number of peripheral actors in the medical world—here, midwives and dentists—who operated at the margins of the core medical world of physicians.[34] But like the surgeons who successfully transitioned from artisans to professionals, these other occupations also usually enjoyed the protection of formal incorporation into guilds. Cooks had no such institutional support, but they nonetheless mounted a spirited effort to style themselves medical practitioners. Rather than simply ignore these claims, contemporary doctors allowed themselves to be drawn into a debate with cooks over their ability to correct and improve health. The outcome of this dispute reveals new aspects of the hardening boundaries of scientific and medical practice during the Enlightenment.

This book is based primarily on archival research in Paris and in several special collections located in libraries in France and the United States. My sources are diverse, because the study of cooks requires an especially multifaceted approach to evidence. When historians have studied other urban occupations, they have tended to turn first to guild records. Cooks do not offer us that luxury, since as servants they left behind no institutional archives. Instead, cooks must usually be approached indirectly from a number of angles and with recourse to a broad range of sources, which may only touch on them tangentially. In order to place the cook at the center of the story of French cuisine, I also necessarily touch on a variety other domains: architecture, consumer culture, and the press, and the history of science and medicine—all situated within the broader context of the Enlightenment. To cast such a wide net, digital resources proved essential. Although this project began while digital history was in its infancy and at a time when online resources were still relatively scarce, it has heavily benefitted from the path-breaking capabilities offered by several early key projects: The Project for American and French Research on the Treasury of the French Language (ARTFL); the electronic indices of the Parisian notary archives (Arno); the electronic catalog of French museum collections (Joconde); and Le Calendrier électronique des spectacles sous l'ancien régime et sous la révolution (CESAR). Without the vast reach of these digital resources, the task of weaving together the disparate evidence necessary to reconstruct the parameters of cooking would have been considerably more difficult, if not impossible.

Over the course of the eighteenth century, cooks produced dozens of cookbooks, which circulated in hundreds of thousands of copies. The Bibliothèque nationale de France, the Gernon collection at Indiana University's Lilly Library, and the Pennell collection at the Library of Congress provided unparalleled opportunities to approach these books as artifacts of cooks' practices, not merely as a means to reconstruct Enlightenment dining. Each cookbook typically includes a lengthy preface, stretching forty pages or longer, which paints a detailed portrait of the author's sense of cooking's cultural and social significance. Cookbooks furnish histories, scientific claims, medical references, and advice for professional development. Even in their overall structure, cookbooks often adopted novel forms of organization in order to differentiate themselves from their competitors and to approach more "natural" forms. And, of course, these cookbooks provide the highest-profile evidence of cooks' voices and their imagined audience of fellow cooks. In addition to cookbooks, I draw on a broad range of other prescriptive literature. Architectural treatises expose the debate over the shifting spatial parameters of the kitchen. Servant-conduct manuals offer insight into the moral economy of domestic service. Medical tracts illuminate the contested boundary between dietetics and cuisine.

Beyond the relatively narrow world of published cooks, I examine a much broader swath of practicing cooks by studying the *affiches*, weekly trade newspapers that circulated throughout eighteenth-century France. Even though mediated and standardized by editors, these documents functioned as mouthpieces for thousands of cooks, not just the handful who published cookbooks. For this study I analyze a sample of 628 employment advertisements drawn from thirty-five years of newspapers in seven French cities: Bordeaux, Cap français (in the Caribbean colony of Saint-Domingue, today Haiti), Metz, Nantes, Paris, Rouen, and Toulouse. Because these advertisements circulated well beyond Paris, we can sketch a more generally urban, as opposed to exclusively Parisian, category of workers. Nonetheless, Paris remains the focus of this book, since it served as the main hub of cooks' networks of circulation, as well as the epicenter of cooks' creative efforts to transform the occupation.

Cooks' own words also turn up in the rich household records swept up in the French Revolution. As the state collected personal papers associated with *émigrés* and the condemned, innumerable domestic accounts also were preserved. I first consulted these archival documents in order to identify wage levels, but I quickly discovered to my surprise that cooks had in fact prepared many of these documents as part of their daily routine. At the Archives nationales de France, I focused on papers from fifteen private households, uncovering a wealth of information regarding cooks' accounting practices, the relationship between cook and master, and the working conditions of the eighteenth-century kitchen. Construction and maintenance records, for example, provide an important counterpoint to the idealized kitchens depicted in architectural manuals. I rely on a sample of 419 records from the notary archives of 1751 and 1761 to situate cooks within their social milieu and material conditions.

In this book, the kinds of evidence that otherwise might serve purely illustrative purposes—a painting, a bawdy story, or a play—instead focus our attention on the limitless array of imagined dangers associated with cooks. Invariably depicted as overfed and oversexed, thieving and scheming, cooks rarely fail to offer rich subject matter. A large corpus of engraved images of cooks circulated in eighteenth-century France, and I draw on the comprehensive collections of these materials preserved in the collection Edmond de Rothschild at the Louvre and in the Département des Estampes et de la photographie at the Bibliothèque nationale de France, as well as paintings housed in a variety of museums. Visual images alone could provide more than enough fodder for a historian to explore the dangers associated with cooks, but I widened my scope of inquiry to include literary representations found in novels and plays. The Département des Arts du spectacle at the Bibliothèque nationale de France hosts an incomparable collection of period plays and performance records. To recover the ways in which cooks' motives were impugned and the rhetoric cooks used to defend themselves, I turned to the legal briefs surrounding *causes célèbres*, highly stylized texts offering starkly defined portraits of the cook as villain or victim.[35] Familiar to scholars of the Enlightenment, sources like Louis-Sébastien Mercier's *Tableau de Paris* and Diderot and d'Alembert's great *Encyclopédie* proved invaluable resources, scooping up cooks in their voracious appetite for the everyday practices of the period.

I open this study with three chapters exploring the material lives and circumstances of cooks. Chapter 1 analyzes the construction of cooks' identity and traces the patterns of their labor. First, I tackle the problem of the cook's identity by examining the eighteenth-century market for cooking services as it figured in the *affiches*. Based on their own self-identification and the qualities demanded by prospective employers, which involved gender, age, moral character, and language, servants negotiated definitions of the ideal cook with their masters. Increasingly, cooks and masters also began to consider expertise, which provided a means of transcending the limitations of the largely physical characteristics that defined the early modern worker. I examine cooks' compensation, monetary and otherwise, which largely distinguished them from other urban workers. To close the chapter, I propose the trajectories that a cook's career might follow. Patterns of hiring and promotion reveal that cooks exercised surprising autonomy in the governance of their own occupation, though they remained sharply constrained by the limits of domestic service.

In Chapter 2, I launch my investigation into the practices and material conditions of cooking by exploring the physical space of the kitchen. Situated at the boundary between servant zones and the master's own living area, the kitchen's design reflected new and growing anxieties about domestic comfort and familial privacy. As residential architecture underwent a dramatic change from disorganized, mixed-use space to individual rooms with specialized functionality, the imagined nuisances and dangers associated with the kitchen rapidly multiplied, with kitchens coming to represent sites of pollution and corruption. Chapter 3 analyzes the cook's tools and associated practices. An inventive panoply of new cooking tools emerged in the early eighteenth century, with minutely special-ized devices often designed for the production of a single dish. Keeping kitchen utensils in good working order was directly linked to health, since poorly main-tained tools were believed to be poisonous. Cooks relied heavily on literacy and numeracy to monitor this maintenance and indeed all their daily practices. But as useful and enlightened as this might appear, cooks' unusual fluency with num-bers and the written word also opened new possibilities for fraud and corruption in the eyes of their eighteenth-century masters.

With the context of cooks' material lives firmly in place, I turn in the book's latter chapters to the audacious project of *la cuisine moderne* and its controversial reception. The great innovation of eighteenth-century cooks was the invention of a theory of the kitchen that would enable them to make broad aesthetic and scientific claims. In Chapter 4, I trace cooks' efforts to insert themselves into the key Enlightenment debate over taste, its origins, and its cultivation. I also explore French cooking's purported shift from secret knowledge, tied closely to the preferences of individual diners, to modular components, endlessly recon-figurable by the cook. With this transformation, cooks effectively seized power over the creation of taste and inverted traditional vectors of cultural transmis-sion. Chapter 5 continues the investigation of *la cuisine moderne* by tracing how cooks sought to redraw the boundaries of domestic service. Brazenly proposing that they serve not only their masters but also doctors, cooks tried to create a new role for themselves as medical practitioners. Physicians and surgeons took cooks' claims to improve constitutions and prolong lives seriously, and they mounted an aggressive campaign to discredit cooks as dire threats to diners' health. The final results were mixed: cooks successfully convinced outsiders that their work involved chemical and medical principles, but they had greater difficulty per-suading the public that they could wield this power responsibly.

Despite the physical and social constraints of domestic service, cooks suc-ceeded in rescuing the kitchen from disdain. They convinced outsiders that cook-ing was a rational and orderly endeavor that could directly and dramatically af-fect the physical well-being of diners. Although cooks contributed entirely new systems of knowledge to the great Enlightenment project of taxonomy and order, they did not enjoy the same level of success as *la cuisine moderne* itself, and their attempt to establish themselves as professionals stalled. Nonetheless, their efforts show us how everyday people participated in the Enlightenment. Cooks demonstrate both the powerful promise of print culture and the limits of who could enjoy its full benefits. They illustrate the gap between the dizzying potential of new systems of knowledge and the crushing reality of the quotidian circumstances of a servant's working life. This striking disjuncture between what cooks said and what they actually did energized the debate around *la cuisine moderne*, and this debate in turn illuminates our understanding of the culture, labor, and science of the Enlightenment.

ONE

Defining the Cook

An excellent cook is worth seeking with care and deserves to be
especially well paid for his efforts.

Louis-Sébastien Mercier, *Tableau de Paris* (1788)

In his influential accounting of the various orders, offices, trades, and professions
of the Third Estate, the jurist Charles Loyseau (1564–1627) meticulously ranked a
comprehensive hierarchy of occupational categories: men of letters, with scientists coming first; faculties of theology, jurisprudence, medicine, and arts; finan-
ciers and merchants; guild artisans, some of them—apothecaries, jewelers, mer-
cers, and drapers—more honorable than the others; and, finally, farm workers.
Even if in practice a variety of forms of unincorporated work chipped away at the
edges of this idealized model, such categories continued to define forms of work
during the Enlightenment.[1] In the eighteenth century, occupational institutions
like guilds remained essential, not only for providing economic organization, but
also for helping to define "social identity, honor, and gender roles," in the words
of one scholar.[2] Yet cooks, and indeed domestic servants in general, had no place
in this orderly world. Loyseau situated *gens de bras*, unskilled laborers he disparaged as "base persons," outside of his neatly tiered system.[3] Here we would find
servant cooks, cast among those brutes operating at the absolute bottom of the
Old Regime's occupational ladder.

Insignificant though their labor might have appeared to a jurist like Loyseau,
cooks hardly lacked for numbers. While it is impossible to state with any precision
the total number of cooks working even in Paris, let alone in France as a whole,
Parisian servants were estimated to range anywhere from 40,000 to 100,000 during the eighteenth century, easily comprising the city's single largest occupational
category at a time when the entire urban population numbered around 600,000
individuals.[4] Within this enormous population of servants, little often separated
the thousands of "cooks" from the far greater number who did "a little cooking"
in the course of their work. There were a handful of cooking-related guilds—

pastry cooks (*pâtissiers*), roasters (*rôtisseurs*), and caterers (*traiteurs*)—but these occupations were both quantitatively and qualitatively inferior to the world of servant cooking. In Paris, between 150 and 200 apprentices entered the pastry cook and roasting guilds each year.[5] Meanwhile the press—just one facet of the overall servant employment market—carried dozens of advertisements posted by servant cooks each month. Even in smaller cities elsewhere in France, servant cooks numbered in the hundreds.[6] If we turn to sources like notary records, we find that servant cooks outnumbered guild cooks in all types of transactions other than apprenticeship contracts, where of course domestic servants were grossly underrepresented.[7] Far more important than this quantitative disparity, however, is the absolute dominion that servant cooks wielded in the public imagination over the theory and practice of cooking. As we shall see in the following chapters, every cookbook published in France was written by a servant cook, and the debate that surrounded food, culture, and the body was inextricably and exclusively bound to domestic service.

The disorder associated with cooks extended beyond their mere exclusion from guild labor. Domestic service was actually viewed by contemporaries as somehow entirely outside the world of work. First, servants were defined, not by the work they did, but by their utter dependency on their masters.[8] This inferior status followed automatically from contemporary understanding of labor, where "skill was considered to be in the worker, not in the job."[9] Second, emerging economic theory branded domestic servants as a "sterile" class that contributed nothing to the productive output of French society.[10] According to Carolyn Steedman, "the servant did work that was not work," in the eyes of contemporaries.[11] Finally, cooks played havoc with contemporary gendered divisions of labor. In contrast to the almost exclusively male guild system, cooks included large numbers of both men and women among their ranks.[12] Thus unlike nearly all other urban trades and even positions of domestic service, no clear lines delineated cooking as an overwhelmingly masculine or feminine pursuit. Cooks thus did not merely operate outside of the contemporary model of occupational labor; they inverted (and in some eyes, perverted) that model.

In stark contrast to the social contempt that dogged cooks and other servants, we encounter Louis-Sébastien Mercier's encouraging advice that an "excellent cook" was "worth seeking." When he wrote, Mercier captured the exuberant mood of the vibrant and fluid market for cooks' services in eighteenth-century France. Servant cooks and their prospective masters sought to fill positions in a wide range of kitchens that cut across geographic, social, and cultural lines. As cooks went about locating employment, they packaged and sold the particular qualities that defined each of them. Through the novel print practice of employment advertisements, cooks and masters alike negotiated a shared definition of the ideal attributes of the cook. Cooks not only imagined themselves to operate far above the fray of disorganized manual labor; they were also compensated accordingly. Thus when we investigate Mercier's recommendation that a good cook also ought to be paid well, we find ample evidence to support his claim. Cooks' wages in the middle of the eighteenth century were extraordinarily high compared to those of other servants, and were often comparable to the earnings of artisans or even of practitioners of liberal professions. Appalled by such lavish pay, critics lambasted cooks and their masters alike, but without any real effect.

Unlike more public artisans, cooks and their labor largely disappeared into private residential spaces. Consequently, we must follow cooks there in order to learn anything more about their work. By examining private archival documents such as records of household transactions known as *livres de compte*, we can trace a variety of typical trajectories taken by the career of a cook. Such artifacts offer a window, not just into the wages paid to cooks, but also into the circumstances of the hiring (and firing) of servants. A cook's place of origin, age, and requests for loans or pay raises were noteworthy data for eighteenth-century record keepers, and when a continuous series of documents has survived, we can occasionally follow the arc of a cook's career from novice to expert. Though they lacked a guild, cooks actively structured their work around similar principles, sometimes recapitulating guild practices, but in many other ways crafting novel work identities that found no real analog in the incorporated world.

What Was a Cook?

One of the most basic challenges in the study of the "cook" is the definition of the word itself. In Enlightenment France, a dizzying number of titles or positions involved cooking. To be sure, many cooks saw themselves as just that: "cooks" (*cuisiniers* or *cuisinières*). Yet some servants who cooked or sought jobs that involved cooking never identified themselves as "cooks." For example, a servant who washed laundry, cleaned house, and did "a bit of cooking" might have labeled herself simply as a *domestique* or *servante*. Because no clear occupational boundaries distinguished "cooks" from those who did "a bit of cooking," confusion often arose in the hiring process. When one woman sought to engage a cook in 1783, she despaired of finding an actual cook among the multitude of servants who presented themselves looking for employment, noting, "I only want a cook and have had a hard time finding one."[13] Meanwhile, at the opposite end of this range of talent, some cooks might also consider their skills too refined or special-ized to fall under the general rubric of "cook." Kitchen servants who worked in teams of differentiated workers often assumed titles that reflected their specific activities and their relative positions within a large kitchen's hierarchy: *maître d'hôtel, chef de cuisine, aide de cuisine, garçon de cuisine, enfant de cuisine,* and *servante de cuisine,* to name a few.

Nomenclature aside, what kinds of generalizations can we make about the identity of the eighteenth-century cook? Most households that hired a cook en-gaged a lone woman. Sometimes she worked as a general-purpose servant, and cooking only comprised a portion of her duties. In other cases, this woman might occupy herself solely with the kitchen, a role that sharply distinguished her from other servants. Despite differences in gender and in the status of the masters they served, the responsibilities of this single female cook had much in common with those of the male maître d'hôtel, or household steward, who often oversaw the large and complicated kitchen staffs of the most rarefied of households. From the late seventeenth century through the eighteenth, prescriptive literature iden-tified these individuals, whether male or female, as effectively the planners and organizers of the kitchen's functions.[14] According to one conduct manual, the maître d'hôtel possessed "the organization and the foresight to secure the neces-sary provisions in the proper time and season."[15] Mercier enumerates the tasks of the maître d'hôtel as including "the planning of the table, the choice and the purchase of comestibles, to know where to find them, to know how to keep them ready to be properly consumed, and to preserve them from the weather and any loss."[16] The maître d'hôtel was also charged with maintaining order among his subordinate staff, since "he appeases quarrels and will not tolerate cooks mis-treating their subordinates."[17] One seventeenth-century manual suggested that his most desirable quality was "fidelity," ensuring honest use of the master's re-sources, while a contemporary guide said the same of a woman cook, who ought to be "wise and of good conscience" in her accounts.[18] Seventy years later, con-duct manuals continued to cite fidelity as the maître d'hôtel's "first duty."[19]

In the wealthiest of households, a chef de cuisine, or head cook, worked under the maître d'hôtel and was charged with the actual execution of meals and the coordination of kitchen staff. This role as a leader of subordinate staff ultimately gave rise to the original distinction between "chef" and "cook," since in principle the title *chef* indicated a cook's role as the leader of a team.[20] In practice, how-ever, titles like cook and chef were already interchangeable in eighteenth-century France. The chef de cuisine might command an extensive staff but remained subordinate to the maître d'hôtel. According to one conduct manual, the cook needed always to have "dinner and supper ready at the times specified by the lord or his maître d'hôtel." But the cook was in charge in the kitchen and had to "know how to order and make himself obeyed by his assistants and boys."[21] Just as "chef" and "cook" were often conflated, clear distinctions between maître d'hôtel and chef de cuisine did not always exist. In fact, the functions of both were often performed by a single person. A maître d'hôtel might himself cook and work directly over his assistants. Conversely, a chef de cuisine might perform the functions of the maître d'hôtel. Conduct manuals remained a bit vague on the role of either servant in the composition of meals, recommending that menus include items "according to the whim of the maître d'hôtel or the cook."[22] A maître d'hôtel needed "to determine each evening the table service for the following day," according to Claude Fleury.[23] Yet this task could just as easily fall to the cook, as in the case of one household where the cook was instructed to plan each dinner one day in advance.[24] Other archival evidence suggests that the two terms were often regarded as virtually interchangeable. Kitchen receipts, for example, could list the same individual alternately as either chef de cuisine or maître d'hôtel.[25]

Continuing downward in the model cooking hierarchy, the *aide de cuisine*, or kitchen assistant, worked immediately under the cook and was likely to succeed to the head cook's position in the event of a vacancy. Next in line were the kitchen boys (*garçons de cuisine* or *enfants de cuisine*) who were generally the most junior members of the kitchen team. In many cases, they were the sons or younger brothers of other cooks. Prescriptive literature made little distinction between kitchen assistants and kitchen boys, suggesting only that both act "according to the orders given to them by their chef."[26] Wage records from the eighteenth century suggest a profound gulf between the two, however, with kitchen assistants often earning nearly as much as the head cook, while kitchen boys received a far smaller salary. Finally, a very wealthy household might have an entirely separate staff to prepare and serve pastries, desserts, and fruit, with its own chef, assistants, and kitchen boys. This was called *l'office* and was subordinate to either the maître d'hôtel or the chef de cuisine, working in concert with the kitchen.

Market Definitions

Prescriptive literature portrays only the ideal kitchen staff. A more accurate picture of the cook emerges from the way cooks described themselves. Beginning in the 1760s, cooks began to place advertisements offering their labor in the *affiches*, regional newspapers published in a wide range of France's cities and towns.[27] By the 1770s they offered their services in newspapers across the kingdom.[28] By then the *affiches* had become a space where both cooks and their prospective masters could negotiate the terms and boundaries of servant cooking. Here cooks aggressively promoted their various, self-identified qualities, ranging from pleasing physical appearance to expert technical prowess. Whether seeking solitary employment in a middling family's kitchen or trying to secure a coveted slot in an elite household's cooking team, cooks relied on the same medium of printed advertisements to locate work. Prospective masters advertised in turn for cooks, outlining their requirements, which might include good moral behavior and a documented record of faithful service. By posting and responding to advertisements, cooks and their potential employers interacted on a surprisingly level playing field. Masters found themselves negotiating with servants over matters of taste, the qualities of the cook, and the conditions of service.[29]

Affiches were not the only marketplace for cooks' services. Other important conduits (both informal and formal) for seeking employment clearly existed. Social networks, including family, facilitated the hiring process, and nepotism was anything but rare among large kitchen staffs. Cooks also implicitly advertised their skills any time their masters hosted guests, often to the chagrin of their employers. Flush with the acclaim of such an occasion, a cook might resign his position, confident of his own marketability.[30] Finally, scattered evidence suggests that there was something like an employment agency for domestic servants in France during the second half of the eighteenth century.[31] Yet given the difficulties of tracing these alternative circuits of work, the *affiches* provide our best and most reliable window into the labor market for cooks, encompassing a continuum ranging from experienced maîtres d'hôtel to neophytes, and a geographic range that extended throughout France and beyond.

Age, Size, and Looks

Eighteenth-century job seekers were not shy about promoting their appearance, and nor were masters slow to indicate precisely what they sought in terms of a cook's looks. Among her physical characteristics, a cook's age was probably her single most important quality, and about three-quarters of all employment advertisements for cooks made some mention of age.[32] While many of these ads sought only cooks of a vaguely defined age, well over half specified the cook's age in years, requesting cooks of ages ranging from seventeen to sixty.[33] In general, the very young and very old were shunned, the former because they were perceived to lack the maturity of more experienced domestics, and the latter because they might lack the vigor necessary to fulfill their duties. Somewhere in between these extremes, masters aimed for a comfortable balance; they wanted cooks of "a mature age" (*un âge mûr*), who were thought more likely to possess the requisite bearing and experience to keep them out of trouble.

A cook's physical size was less important. Because a full-time cook remained largely concealed in the kitchen, his stature theoretically mattered less than with more conspicuous servants like valets. It is thus unsurprising that the vast majority of advertisements seeking cooks do not specify a desired height. When a woman named Dasse placed an advertisement seeking to hire two servants, she specified only the desired height of the man who would shave, dress hair, and serve at the table. The cook was only desired to be aged around fifty and single.[34] For a few masters, however, servants' height was something of an obsession, which could extend even to include cooks. The lawyer Delville, for example, sought three servants of differing heights: one who was five feet seven or eight inches tall to work in the kitchen, serve at table, and shave; one who was at least five feet six to polish floors and shave; and one who was five feet eight, knew the city of Paris well, and could polish floors.[35] One master hoped to find a servant between five feet three and five feet four inches tall who knew how to read and write and who understood gardening and cooking.[36] These last dimensions were evidently in high demand, since a week later, another master looked for someone of the same height, "around forty years old, who knows how to style hair, polish floors, and do a bit of cooking.[37] Either prospective master may have found himself in luck, since later that month "a young man of 25 years, height 5 feet 3 to 4 inches, who knows how to read, write, polish floors, and prepare a good *cuisine bourgeoise*" placed an ad in the same newspaper.[38] As this last advertisement suggests, some cooks very occasionally indicated their own size. One "young man . . . who knows how to cook well" claimed a height of five feet five inches. Another "young man" described himself as of "a good height."[39] A couple of cooks described their own size as "advantageous."[40] Even cooks with numerous cooking qualifications would sometimes provide their height. A thirty-eight-year-old former cook and maître d'hôtel advertised his height of five feet four inches.[41] An especially qualified fellow in Metz identified himself as "a good cook knowing pastry making, desserts, aged 26 years, height 5 feet 8 inches and having good certificates."[42] Likewise, a "boy of 33 years, knowing cooking, pastry making, desserts, and a bit of everything" gave a height of five feet five.[43]

Both men and women also highlighted their physical condition and the quality of their appearance. One woman described herself as "robust," while another man claimed to be "very robust."[44] A twenty-four-year-old woman described herself as "big and well-made."[45] In general, however, cooks were less likely than other servants to be prized for their looks, thanks to their relative invisibility within the household. In contrast to the invisibility associated with the kitchen, a chambermaid might advertise her "very interesting looks."[46] Underscoring the distinction between those who worked inside and outside the kitchen, one Bordelais advertisement requested "a servant who knows how to serve, speak well, and with agreeable looks and another who knows how to serve at the table and work in the kitchen."[47] The overwhelming preference for "mature" cooks stands at odds with the popular image of the nubile, naïve young female cook. Belying the fantasy of the cook as seductress or seduced, the looks of most kitchen workers simply were not important.

Gender

Cooks placing their own ads in the *affiches* invariably indicated their gender, and masters seeking to hire nearly always indicated the gender of the desired cook, with their advertisements splitting nearly evenly among those looking for female cooks versus male cooks.[48] Only in extraordinary circumstances would a master place a notice expressing the willingness to hire a cook of either sex.[49] But the apparently rigid gender dichotomy displayed by the *affiches* conceals far greater ambiguity in the hiring process, where female and male cooks could be considered interchangeable. When discussing the prospect of hiring a new cook, Bernard de Bonnard asked his wife Sophie, "Would you like a male cook better? It seems as though that would be more expensive."[50] While indeed a male cook would have cost more to engage, this prospective master made no strong qualitative distinction between the two: as cooks, either would have served the household's purposes. Louis-Sébastien Mercier likewise suggests that male and female cooks were equally capable of turning out the sort of delicacies enjoyed in elite households.[51] Because women cooks could substitute for men (and at a lower cost), they broadened the market for skilled cooks' services.

The specification of a male or female cook marked cooking as unique from other jobs advertised in the *affiches*, where the occupation's gender was largely fixed: gardeners were invariably men, governesses women, and so on. Indeed, all servant work was so divided, with a single exception: cooks.[52] No clear boundary separated the team of male cooks serving a minister at one end of the spectrum from the woman cooking alone at the other. Kitchen staffs of every imaginable size and configuration existed between these extremes, and cooks often worked in staffs of mixed gender. For example, one household sought to hire a female cook to oversee "two or three [female] servants and several [male] domestic workers, who are numerous." The prospective masters further guaranteed that they would grant this woman "superiority in all domestic affairs."[53] Nicolas Rétif de la Bretonne dramatized such a relationship in an erotic story: a master provided a servant to his cook, instructing her, "You are for us, and this woman is for you. It is up to you to direct her, and she must obey you."[54] Women also sometimes worked under male cooks. A 1771 advertisement, for example, requests the services of a woman "who would know a bit of cooking in order to help as the [male] cook needs."[55] In the Dreneux household of the 1760s, a kitchen girl named Louison Barre worked under the direction of a male cook.[56] This evidence suggests that women in such circumstances performed more skilled work than the simple sweeping and washing prescribed by conduct manuals.[57] Cooking thus functioned as a uniquely destabilizing occupation when it came to gender.

I do not mean to obscure the existence of gender gradients that correlated to wealth and shifted over time. In general, it is evident that many more men than women worked as cooks in wealthy households with large kitchen staffs. Nonetheless, over the course of the eighteenth century, increasing numbers of women chiseled away at this numerical advantage, in some cases displacing men whose services had become too expensive.[58] Thus, in 1781, Bernard de Bonnard and Sophie Silvestre ultimately decided to replace their male cook with a woman.[59] No rigid barrier separated women from men who worked in the kitchen, and any attempt to divide servant cooking into distinct masculine and feminine spheres would encounter the impossible task of trying to account for time, geography, social status, and a master's own personal preference. Within domestic service, the critical boundary was not located in gender, but rather in the power differential between cooks of all kinds and other servants. Cooks invariably assumed a position near or at the top of the household hierarchy of servants, overseeing domestic chores, paying wages, and, of course, regulating access to food.

Family Situation

Most masters sought to hire servants without spouses or children, who might drain household resources or otherwise be burdensome. Usually, they conveyed this through the terms used to describe the potential cook. Employers looking to hire a woman typically asked for a *fille* (girl), though this term was hardly restricted to cooks of a young age. What masters actually sought was an unmarried woman. One such advertisement asked for a "woman or girl of thirty-five or forty years."[60] Another asked for "a widow or a girl of thirty to forty years."[61] A third asked for "a girl or a widow of thirty to thirty-five years."[62] Few advertisements in the *affiches* looked for married cooks. While the rare master sought a married servant couple, there were far more married couples looking for work, suggesting the difficulty such servants faced finding employment.[63] In these married couples, the cook was usually a woman, but in about a quarter of the cases, married male cooks sought employment for both themselves and their wives. For example, one man proposed to work as maître d'hôtel while his wife served as chambermaid.[64] Another prospecting cook noted that he was married to a woman who knew how "to style hair and work in fashion."[65]

Based on a close reading of prescriptive literature, one historian has argued that masters shied away from hiring married servants because of their presumed "divided loyalties."[66] Yet at least in some cases masters actively tried to hire married couples, perhaps in an effort to avoid the destabilizing influence of unmarried servants. In 1775, a certain Madame Girard sought to hire a "good servant who knows how to brush a horse and drive a carriage whose wife is a good cook."[67] In 1781, an abbé Aleaume looked for "a widowed or married gardener, whose daughter or wife is a good cook: they will live together in the countryside."[68] Another advertisement appeared to leave open the possibility of engaging a husband and wife, seeking "for a tranquil house, first a married porter without children; second a [female] cook of a certain age."[69] When Jean Forcade hired his porter in January 1740, he did not realize the man was married. Upon this discovery, he decided to take the porter's wife on as his cook.[70] This occasional willingness to seek out or accept married couples suggests that spouses did not invariably represent a potential drain on the household, especially if both worked as servants. Children, in contrast, posed a more unavoidable threat, since they would almost certainly offer little more than an extra mouth to feed. In the *affiches*, masters regularly looked to hire cooks "without children," and cooks for their part were quick to note their lack of children. Outside the *affiches*, however, we do find that households occasionally engaged cooks with children, and in some cases these children also worked in the kitchens. Jean Forcade's cook, for example, began her service with a one-year-old daughter in tow, and in time the daughter began to assist her mother.[71]

Moral Character

Over a third of all cooks' employment advertisements mentioned morals.[72] Servants seeking employment eagerly asserted their moral qualifications, and masters likewise demanded guarantees of sound character. Advertisements regularly promised the possession of certificates attesting to the job-seeker's probity. In other cases, a cook might rely on her public reputation, claiming that she was "known" (*connue*) in the community. In July 1773, for example, "a known person" sought a position as a cook in Bordeaux.[73] Such public knowledge of a person's character could bolster a cook's letters of recommendation, as in the case of one cook who pointed out that he both had "good references" and was "known."[74] Likewise, one woman seeking a position as a cook added to her claim of "good lifestyle and morals" the fact that she was "known."[75] Morals could overshadow all qualifications, particularly in the case of women.[76] A twenty-two-year-old "girl" seeking a position of a cook first noted that she came with "good recommendations and [was] known in this city." Only afterward did she mention that she knew cooking and pastry making well.[77] One childless couple sought to hire a cook, as long as she had good morals and was not a drunk.[78]

In contrast, men might point to their origins as a sign of their character. A thirty-year-old man claimed to be "well-born" in his advertisement seeking a "position analogous to his talents," which in addition to cooking included reading, writing, delivering mail, driving a carriage, brushing horses, and a bit of hairstyling for men and women.[79] Another "well-born" man vowed that he could read, write, count, and cook.[80] Such demands for morality could extend the other way, albeit in limited fashion. Many cooks expressed their desire to work in a "good house," which could imply a degree of wealth and status, while a very small percentage of masters promised work in a good house. Other cooks looked for work in a "tranquil house," which might demand less work.[81] These last examples underscore just how divorced the stereotype of the morally decrepit cook was from the reality of the job market. Whatever fantasies circulated about cooks' vices, masters kept hiring them.

Expertise: Skills and Experience

Servants' advertisements commonly promised good moral behavior, but under certain conditions, cooks did not feel the need to provide it, especially if they could claim a high level of technical expertise, when the guarantee of morals was considerably less important. Compare, for example, the following two typical advertisements:

> A single man of a mature age, knowing how to read, write, shave, comb, and
> if necessary how to do a bit of cooking, would like to be placed as a servant.
> He is known by several people in this city and will give guarantees on his life
> and morals.[82]

A [female] cook who knows pastry making well would like to find a good house.[83]

In the first advertisement, the servant claims a wide variety of skills, including cooking, a hard-sell approach that was not unusual in the *affiches*.[84] The servant also emphasizes his standing in the community and stresses his good character. Servants like this one, who claimed only to be able to perform "a bit of cooking," posted about one out of six advertisements for cooking services.[85] Their notices usually stress their diverse qualifications, perhaps conveying a certain desperation. In stark contrast, the cook of the second advertisement emphasizes her skill, and she is looking for a "good house."

Cooks with specialized skills like pastry making or roasting tended to post especially confident advertisements. In Metz, a "good cook, roaster, and pastry maker" sought a position of cook.[86] In Paris, a cook with the same three skills looked for "a stable position."[87] In Bordeaux, a woman characterized herself as "a very good cook, very competent in pastry" and left her qualifications at that.[88] In 1779, yet another cook who described herself as "knowing how to make pastry" wanted to find "a solid position."[89] In none of these examples did the cooks mention good morals or make other claims about their character. Moreover, they boldly stated the specific type of position they sought. On the other side of the hiring equation, masters placing advertisements were similarly unlikely to mention character if they sought a highly skilled cook. One master looked for "a very good cook for the city" without any concern for morals.[90]

By providing a qualitative description of the cooking to be performed, cooks and masters who placed advertisements could indicate the desired level of technical expertise. Beginning in the 1770s, cooks began to declare themselves capable of preparing a *cuisine bourgeoise*, a type of cooking based on the latest styles but adapted for a more modest budget. Thereafter, the phrase *cuisine bourgeoise* occurs in about one out of every eight employment advertisements for cooks, appearing with equal frequency among ads placed by masters and by cooks. It also traveled widely, with cooks claiming expertise in preparing a *cuisine bourgeoise* whether they worked in Paris or in provincial cities like Rouen and Bordeaux. The increasing popularity of the phrase paralleled the proliferation of copies of Menon's wildly successful cookbook *La Cuisinière bourgeoise*, first published in 1746.[91] As its title implied, this cookbook promised a type of cooking aimed, not only at a more middling audience, but also for execution by women cooks (*cuisinière* being the feminine form of "cook"). This style of cooking retained its association with female cooks, and women were more than twice as likely as men to claim to know how to prepare a *cuisine bourgeoise.*[92] Like other specialized cooking skills, knowledge of *la cuisine bourgeoise* alone occasionally sufficed for job qualifications. In May 1785, one cook wrote only, "a girl presents herself who knows how to prepare a *cuisine bourgeoise.*"[93] In 1789, another woman confidently wrote, "A woman aged fifty years, who knows how to prepare a good *cuisine bourgeoise,* would like to be placed."[94]

It was not especially unusual for cooks to speak languages in addition to French. One man who could speak Italian sought a position in Paris, the provinces, or "even to travel." A forty-year-old servant who could do a bit of cooking claimed to speak German, Italian, English, and French. These polyglot cooks often pointed to past travel, suggesting that they had learned their languages while voyaging with previous masters. A thirty-five-year-old German searching for a position as a cook claimed that he had "traveled a lot" and could speak French and English. Foreign languages and backgrounds could translate into knowledge of foreign cuisine, with many cooks boasting they could practice multiple styles. One woman not only stated that she had traveled abroad and spoke English, she also claimed she knew well "how to prepare French and English cuisine." Another cook likewise stated he could work "English-style and French-style." A thirty-five-year-old woman, "arriving from Russia," declared that she could cook and make pastries in both Russian and French styles. A German cook "who speaks French" claimed knowledge of both German and French cooking and pastry making.[95] These claims also evince the broadening tastes reflected by French cookbooks, which in the mid-eighteenth century began to include increasing numbers of foreign recipes.[96] Cooks advertised such skills in order to secure employment in households that had a particular need. A German woman in Paris sought a position as a cook in a German household.[97] A young man who described himself as a "good cook, roaster, and pastry maker" argued that he could not only speak French and German but could even write in both languages.[98]

A cook's degree of experience could also help to indicate her level of expertise. Here technical skill tended to shaded into moral character, since experience could be judged either by the quality of the houses in which a cook had served or by the length of service. One cook indicated that he had served "twelve years in two good houses."[99] Another claimed that he had "worked in the best houses."[100] A former maître d'hôtel noted that he had worked for "people of distinction."[101] Cooks and masters alike also offered the ability to manage a staff as a badge of valuable experience. One advertisement sought "a man able to cook well for five or six people, intelligent and active enough to engage in all the details of a house whose servants would be subordinate to him."[102] Another looked for a woman of thirty-five to forty years age "to oversee . . . the kitchen and all the servants" in a château.[103] A third requested "a good [female] cook capable of managing a household."[104] Cooks with this level of experience rarely offered promises of their good character. Instead their skills and their previous employment in households of status allowed them to seek positions with confidence.

Compensation

Wage labor was in many ways more closely associated with domestic service than with any other kind of work. Indeed, Michael Sonenscher has suggested that servants were the only true wage laborers in Old Regime France, since the French word for wages, *gages*, originated in this "engagement" of domestics.[105] Jacqueline Sabattier has similarly argued that the wage relationship comprised the essential contractual and legal basis of domestic service.[106] Yet despite the fundamental relationship between domestic service and wages, historians have generally shied away from making any such comparison. Fifty years ago J. J. Hecht warned "how hazardous must be any attempt to compare wage data for servants."[107] More recently, Sabattier has suggested that historians' attempts to calculate general wages for servants are in vain.[108] Even the study of wages in the general population remains "a problem that has long preoccupied economic historians," without any conclusive resolution, Jean Sgard notes.[109] In the case of cooks, we can attribute these difficulties to a lack of data. Aside from the examples given above, hard numbers regarding remuneration appear relatively infrequently in the pages of the *affiches*. If records from private household accounts provide a somewhat more satisfying scattering of data points, we are still left with a sample limited to a relatively narrow range of wealthy households. Beyond a lack of data, however, a deeper problem arises when historians try to compare wages among different types of servants. Cooks, porters, chambermaids, and lackeys all performed vastly different tasks and were compensated quite differently.

According to Sabattier, these varying skills and wages suggest a degree of correlation between what a servant did and what she earned. Sabattier proposes a broad category of those servants earning 100 to 150 livres annually, comprised of those with little in the way of skills. Earning more were "specialized personnel," which included most cooks. Finally, "the great servants, men of confidence" could earn above 1,000 livres a year.[110] Outside of domestic service, how did these wages compare to the earnings of the general population? Sgard's characterization of wages begins with the lowest category of 100 to 300 livres, where we find "workers" including laborers and servants. According to Sgard, 300 to 1,000 livres per year constituted a "professional" salary, earned by specialized workers, mid-level business clerks, and teachers. Above 1,000 livres Sgard finds university instructors and low-level royal officials.[111] Sgard's intent is to provide, not precise salaries, but rather "an economic and social context" for a given level of wages.[112]

Just as the diversity of cooking complicates gender categorization, it also frustrates efforts to classify the occupation according to wage levels. Cooks earned salaries that cut across all of both Sabattier's and Sgard's groupings. Most cooks were promised "wages proportional to [their] talents."[113] The vague promise of "honest" compensation frequently appeared, with masters promising cooks "honest wages," an "honest salary," or an "honest outcome."[114] Other masters promised just a "good salary."[115] Cooks less commonly mentioned payment, and when they did they asked only for "modest wages."[116] Beyond these vague gestures, about one in twelve advertisements mentioned precise wages, in marked contrast to the general silence of the *affiches* regarding specific pay.[117] Here wages ranged widely, from the 120 livres offered to "a good cook" to the lavish 600 livres promised to the highly skilled woman willing to cross the Channel to cook for an English family.[118] In 1783, an advertisement suggested that a servant who knew "well enough how to cook" could earn wages of 150 livres and more "if she becomes attached to her mistress."[119] In January 1785, an intelligent and mature girl who could prepare *une cuisine bourgeoise* was likewise offered 150 livres.[120] Mercier pegged female cooks' wages at precisely this level, but also suggested that their pay could rise still higher, noting that "it is the least one can give."[121] In Rétif de la Bretonne's salacious tale of "The Pretty Cook," the naïve Paule at first earns 200 livres per year but soon receives a raise to 500 from her lecherous master.[122] Wages offered to male cooks tended to be slightly higher. In January 1785, one advertisement promised 200 livres to a male servant who knew how to cook.[123] One master offered a "good cook" willing to work in Bayonne wages of 200 livres.[124] Even wages for subordinate kitchen staff make an appearance in the *affiches*, with 150 livres offered to a kitchen boy in 1793.[125]

Although many of the wages for cooks listed in the *affiches* belong in the poorest category, other evidence suggests that cooks often earned a relatively high income. Cooks were invariably perceived as earning high wages, with contemporary depictions of cooks suggesting that they were grossly overpaid. Voltaire noted that a cook could earn 1,500 livres, which he described as 500 more than a tutor and 1,000 more than a personal secretary.[126] In his *Tableau de Paris*, Louis-Sébastien Mercier claimed an even broader disparity, asserting that the best cooks earned four times as much as tutors.[127] If cooks' earnings reveal anything about their esteem in the eyes of masters—and contemporaries certainly opined that they did—cooks could easily equal or even outrank surgeons. In the Coigny household, the maître d'hôtel, Pajos, and the surgeon, Houssier, both earned 1,000 livres per year.[128] When they worked abroad, French cooks were notorious for their lofty wages, typically earning more than anyone else among the domestic staff.[129]

Prescriptive literature confirms cooks' high pay, with one conduct manual recommending a salary of 500 livres for a maître d'hôtel as early as the end of the seventeenth century.[130] While this particular work did not necessarily purport to represent typical wages—the author undoubtedly skewed his figures toward elite households and in any case only provided general guidelines—what is most striking about his figures is the *relative* level of cooks' wages when compared to those of other domestic servants. For example, at 500 livres, the maître d'hôtel was the highest-paid servant in the entire household. At 300 livres, the cook was surpassed or matched by only two servants working outside the kitchen: the head of the stables and the master's secretary. The result of such extraordinarily high wages was to tilt the overall expenditure on servants heavily in favor of the kitchen staff. In this conduct manual's model household, the kitchen servants accounted for one-third of the total wages paid to servants, despite comprising fewer than a quarter of the domestics employed.

Over the course of the eighteenth century, cooks' wages climbed still higher compared to those of other servants. In contrast to the fairly static wages of unskilled servants like chambermaids, cooks' wages (especially among men) rose dramatically, suggesting that contemporaries increasingly prized and rewarded cooks' services.[131] This acceleration was most profound during the middle of the eighteenth century, when cooks began to promote *la cuisine moderne*. Cooks working in the finest households could earn over 1,000 livres per year in addition to room and board. Louis XVI's finance minister Charles-Alexandre de Calonne paid his maître d'hôtel and chef de cuisine 1,000 and 800 livres, respectively.[132] Madame de Kerry paid her own maître d'hôtel and cook 1,200 and 800 livres.[133] The prince de Lambesc paid his same two servants 1,200 and 1,000 livres.[134]

In these wealthiest of households, only the most skilled and experienced cooks received such elevated wages; kitchen boys and dishwashers did not experience similar benefits. In the Coigny household during the 1730s, 1740s, and 1750s, for example, the maître d'hôtel earned an annual salary of 1,000 livres, while his kitchen boys received just 100. Around the same time, the prince de Lambesc engaged his chef de cuisine at 800 livres, plus an additional 150 livres for wine, while he paid his kitchen boys just 120 livres. We can detect some upward movement at the lower end of the spectrum: de Kerry's kitchen boy Vicare earned 300 livres in the late 1770s, or more than double what kitchen boys made a few decades earlier. Yet for the most part a wide gulf separated the best paid cooks from their subordinate staff. The prince de Lambesc continued to engage his kitchen boys at just 72 livres per year through the late 1780s, an appallingly low sum approaching just 5 sols per day and well below the average wage for a common laborer.[135]

Whether high or low, a cook's wages were only one component of her compensation. Masters generally lodged their cooks, often in the kitchen itself or in a nearby room. Meals were also provided to servants, though with cooks such generosity was hardly optional. In some cases, cooks received a cash wine allowance. In the de Lambesc household, the maître d'hôtel and chef de cuisine each collected 150 livres per year for wine, while the *aides de cuisine* received 100 livres and the *garçon de cuisine* 72 livres.[136] Compensation frequently included clothing. A couple living in the countryside outside Rouen promised in addition that their cook would be "dressed, but not liveried."[137] In 1785, a Monsieur Bony likewise guaranteed that his prospective cook "will be dressed."[138] Other references to compensation were considerably more vague: a Monsieur Delville promised the servant he sought "profits" in addition to his wages. In this case, Delville may have obliquely referred to the controversial (and illegal) practice of saving and reselling the kitchen's leftover grease and scraps.[139] Monsieur Barraut similarly promised "profits" to the "young person" he aimed to hire "to sew, wash, comb, and do a bit of cooking."[140] Another master promised "lodging, food, and even extraordinary gratifications."[141] When cooks were made to travel or when the master was away, they might also receive extra money to pay for their own meals, perhaps 30 sols per day.[142] If cooks fell ill, they could expect some degree of medical treatment at their masters' expense. In August 1771, *président à mortier* of the parlement of Paris, Omer Joly de Fleury, paid for a doctor to visit and treat his cook, and in 1773, a surgeon billed him for treating a kitchen boy.[143] Among other things, the poor boy's decidedly harrowing treatment involved three visits, a "vomiting purgative," and a further "ordinary" purging two days later. According to Mercier, such care was anything but unusual: he told of a master who, on discovering that his cook had fallen ill, rushed to procure a doctor to cure him. So happy was the master that he kissed the doctor in Mercier's presence and paid him amply.[144]

Career Trajectories

Like other domestic servants, cooks circulated in geographic networks as they moved from country to city or from household to household. Paris was at the

center of these networks, and contemporaries generally agreed that the best cooks
practiced their art there. Indeed it became something of a commonplace to mention the "skilled cooks of Paris" in any discussion of cuisine.[145] The assertion of
Parisian supremacy was hardly novel to the eighteenth century: as early as 1652,
La Varenne's cookbook *Le Cuisinier françois* (The French Cook) had declared
Paris to rule "eminently over the other provinces of the kingdom" in matters of
taste.[146] But Paris's cooks were hardly all Parisian in origin, as both fictional accounts and archival sources reveal.[147] Paule, Rétif de la Bretonne's "Pretty Cook,"
notes that she entered into service after her "arrival in Paris."[148] The old cook
from the verse *La Maltôte des cuisinières* claimed that at age fifteen she had come
"alone to Paris from Abbeville," a distance of well over a hundred miles.[149] In the
real-life kitchen of the de Lambesc household, Hugues Volant, a forty-year-old
chef de cuisine, traced his origins to "Marly, near Versailles," about fifteen miles
from Paris. In the same kitchen, François Lemerle had come over sixty miles from
Fremont to work in Paris, ultimately rising to be maître d'hôtel.[150]

The migration of cooks from country to city provoked considerably anxiety,
as the 1779 engraving *La Cuisinière nouvellement arrivée* (fig. 1.1) makes abundantly clear. This image depicts a young woman dressed nominally in the style
of a cook, complete with traditional cook's bonnet and a market sack in tow.
However, the engraving's caption—"Cook newly arrived from the provinces and
who begins to assume the elegant airs of Paris"—invites a closer inspection of her
attire. According to the accompanying description: "A skirt without decoration
and a canvas apron are still the remnants of the simplicity of her station. But already the fine tissue shawl is embellished and revealing, and her hairstyle appears
to be accompanied by an earring and a wisp of hair over her ear. Thus gradually
her coquettishness will extend from her head to her feet."[151]

Indeed, the feet in question already sported dainty shoes, complete with a
vertiginous heel. If not for the leg of lamb jutting from her market sack (pro-
truding at a decidedly suggestive angle, no less), this woman's line of work might
have remained in doubt. By juxtaposing provincial innocence with the corrupting influence of Paris, the artist evoked the image of a dangerously ambitious and
promiscuous cook.

If Paris sat at the center of cooks' networks of labor, other cities functioned as
regional nodes. Olwen Hufton has suggested that these cities in turn drew superior cooks from particular regions: "In Paris the best cooks were said to be from
Carcassonne . . . . In Lyon cooks came from the Beaujolais and the Lyonnais; in
Bordeaux from the Périgord; in Strasbourg from the Île de France."[152] According
to Fernand Braudel, Paris's best cooks came from Languedoc.[153] Louis-Sébastien

Fig. 1.1. Paris transforms a naïve provincial into a sophisticated cook. *Cuisinière nouvellement arrivée de Province* (1779). Engraving by Pierre-Adrien Le Beau (ca. 1740–ca. 1796) after Pierre-Thomas Le Clerc, in *Galerie des modes et costumes français* (Paris: Esnauts & Rapilly, 1779–1781), 1: pl. 11. Photo: Print Collection, Miriam and Ira D. Wallach Division of Art, Prints, and Photographs, The New York Public Library, Astor, Lenox, and Tilden Foundations.

Mercier provided his own characterization of the provincial origins of cooks, though with decidedly different regional preferences. He claimed that women cooks from Picardy had the finest taste, followed by those from Orléans and Flanders. Those hailing from Burgundy were the most faithful, and from Normandy came "by all accounts the worst of all."[154] Although opinions differed as to where the best cooks originated, the impression of mobility remains constant: cooks moved, and the good ones were worth seeking out, even if from a long way away. Moreover, although the majority of servants may have moved in relatively narrow regional circuits, the variety of claims about the geographic origins of the best cooks suggests that these servants also circulated in much wider networks.

Cooks did not always make a single move from the provinces to a regional city. Instead, many cooks continued to migrate throughout their careers, and even on reaching Paris, they might ultimately depart once again. As early as 1660, one cookbook described the "young people who run from town to town in order to imitate this beautiful science" of cooking.[155] Some cooks also joined their masters in their seasonal peregrinations between town and country. A woman in Rouen sought a chambermaid who could work as a cook "when one goes to pass several months in the countryside."[156] Cooks also relied on masters to get them where they needed or wanted to go. A thirty-five-year-old cook from Plombières looked for a master "who would go there to take the baths."[157] A young man in Bordeaux wanted to cook for a master intending to go to Paris.[158] Whether out of wanderlust or desperation, many cooks were adamant about their desire to travel, often far afield.[159] A woman of twenty-four sought a position with a mistress as either a cook, a seamstress, or a chambermaid. Above all, however, she wanted to leave Bordeaux, "and even go to America, if the opportunity presented itself."[160] One man who could do a bit of cooking wanted a position with "a lord or other, in order to travel by land or by sea."[161] A well-qualified cook sought a place "in Paris, in the provinces, or abroad."[162] Masters for their part also offered to take cooks abroad. A 1763 advertisement sought, for example, "a cook who knows how to make bread, for a ship going to St. Domingue."[163] Moreover, a healthy market for French cooks operated across the Channel.[164] The duke of Newcastle maintained a lively correspondence with the British ambassador in Paris, who regularly sent him cooks and information about the state of *la cuisine moderne* during the 1750s.[165] Foreign employers also placed ads in the French *affiches*, seeking to bring French cooks abroad.[166] In these advertisements, we witness the motivations and circumstances that facilitated the expansion of cooks' imagined influence both within France and beyond.

Hiring

Once we move beyond the employment advertisements explored above, the precise conditions of the hiring process are largely elusive, and little direct evidence survives to document them. In some cases, servants were promised work at a future date by potential employers. A signed note to one servant guaranteed "a position in eighteen months—and if I have no vacancies at that point to take her as a supernumerary with pay."[167] Personal correspondence also occasionally offers a rare glimpse into the conditions surrounding the hiring of a cook. When Sophie Silvestre and Bernard de Bonnard set out to engage a new cook, they worried endlessly about finding a suitable candidate. In one letter, Sophie noted that she had just met with a cook who had "the air of a good girl." Sophie wanted to hire her right away; otherwise, she was certain the cook would find another position.[168] Louis-Sébastien Mercier shared the sentiment that a good cook was a real find, since one might have to sift through as many as ninety candidates to find her.[169]

Cooks played a regular role in the vetting and hiring of subordinate kitchen staff, as persistent warnings against such practices suggest. In a conduct manual aimed at servants, the abbé Pierre Collet said that cooks should not take on apprentices, since "in their first efforts they waste and lose many things." This was especially alarming, since cooks would likely ignore any loss that only affected their masters.[170] At least one mistress explicitly echoed Collet's advice: Madame de Kerry warned her own cook in October 1787 against making changes to the kitchen staff without informing her. She instructed him instead to notify her when he was "unhappy with his boys." Despite such warnings, archival evidence indicates that cooks frequently influenced the hiring decisions for their kitchens. One Huré was hired in 1783 to work as a roaster "on the recommendation" of Olivier, the chef de cuisine. In the same household, a kitchen boy was likewise engaged on Olivier's "certification."[171] Vincent La Chapelle in fact encouraged this sort of behavior in his cookbook *Le Cuisinier moderne* (The Modern Cook), cautioning cooks not to be caught ill-prepared for a major event by reason of having lacked the "desire to take on assistants." La Chapelle maintained that "it is up to the maître d'hôtel to choose good officers both for the kitchen and for the *office*," and evidence suggests that cooks followed his advice.[172] For major holidays like Easter, Pentecost, and Assumption, Joly de Fleury's cook hired additional staff, along with renting extra equipment.[173] For occasions as momentous as the Assembly of Notables charged with saving France from financial ruin in the spring of 1787, Controller-general Calonne's cook engaged extra assistants.[174]

Cooks looking for employment could rely on family networks, which played an essential role in staffing kitchens. Siblings often worked side by side, and parents engaged their children as de facto apprentices. On 1 August 1743, the Coigny household hired two brothers, one to work as *enfant de cuisine*, the lowest formally defined position in this particular kitchen, and the other to serve as *enfant d'office*, occupying much the same role preparing sweets and desserts. In June 1749, the former brother was promoted to *aide de cuisine*, doubling his wages from 100 livres to 200. When in the spring of 1752 the latter brother was promoted to *aide d'office*, a third brother was engaged to fill the now-vacant position of *enfant d'office*. In 1750, the *aide de cuisine*, perhaps dissatisfied with his salary (he had unsuccessfully requested a raise to 300 livres), departed the Coigny household. Because he did not stay long enough to collect his final wages, he instead left this task to his siblings, who continued to work together at least until 1759. In other cases, the head of the kitchen more or less packed the kitchen staff with his own children. Maître d'hôtel and chef de cuisine La Borde hired one of his sons to work as kitchen assistant in 1757, and took on another to serve as kitchen boy in 1758.[175] The autonomy displayed by such hiring had deeper social implications as well, since one of chief benefits afforded to guild masters was the ability to offer employment to family members.[176] Cooks' hiring practices thus neatly replicated the privileges jealously guarded by corporations. While cooks' children might also work as kitchen servants, they rarely if ever apprenticed with guild cooks. Indeed, while apprenticeship records reveal a host of trades into which servant cooks' sons entered—jeweler, rug maker, glazier, wigmaker, and engraver, to name a few—no evidence suggests they ever joined the cooking guilds.[177] The lack of a generational career trajectory from servant to guild cook strongly suggests that such public cooking did not represent a significant social or economic step up from domestic service, and it further underscores the disjuncture between servant cooking and the culinary guilds.

Training and Promotion

Novice cooks could not expect to learn much from cookbooks, which for all their novel talk of theory and practice still presupposed a great deal of existing skill and knowledge.[178] Personal instruction from an experienced cook instead remained the most important path toward acquiring expertise. According to one contemporary characterization, "cooking was a labyrinth" dominated by a "small number of people noted for their talent," who in turn trained students.[179] With no institutional options for training, assuming a supporting role in an established kitchen was the surest way to learn how to cook.[180] Thus one young man in 1779 placed an advertisement seeking "a place under a cook." In 1783, a household sought a kitchen boy "to work under a good cook."[181] Such a description of his future supervisor hinted at the possibility of the boy cultivating a degree of expertise. If necessary, a cook might have to move from kitchen to kitchen to acquire the requisite skills.[182] Even experienced cooks searched for subordinate positions: one man who already knew how to cook and make pastries desired to work as a second cook or kitchen assistant. Another man who described himself as "acquainted with cooking" sought a position as a kitchen assistant.[183] Even in the absence of an instructor, evidence suggests that cooks were expected to learn on the job. When one master prepared to hire a new cook, he sought only a woman who knew the basics and had good "principles of cooking."

> Give her a teacher, if necessary, but in the name of my appetite, of health, and of the pleasure so natural of eating healthy and well-prepared things, that she know at least how to make a good soup, cook a boiled joint just right, choose meat, roast a leg of lamb and a chicken, cook fresh eggs, and make a white sauce. The rest will come later.[184]

These skills formed the necessary foundation in any cook he might hire.

As we have seen, wealthier households would employ a kitchen staff that included a number of servants, while families of middling means engaged a single dedicated cook or perhaps a general-purpose servant who did some cooking. Both types of kitchens illustrate the dynamics of training and promotion particular to cooking. Two patterns of advancement emerge: vertical promotion within a single household and lateral promotion by shifting among masters. By working in a single household, a cook could wait for a senior position to open within that kitchen and thus move up the chain of command. Alternatively, by moving from one household to another—for example, by leaving a high-status master for another of lesser means—a cook could enjoy a relative increase in status and compensation.

Whenever an upper-level position became available, lower kitchen staff typically moved up in rank. Unfortunately, though there was frequent turnover among the subordinate positions—dishwashers and kitchen boys came and went—top spots only rarely opened. A retirement or a firing could free a position, but often one was vacated only when its holder died. In such circumstances, everyone working below could profit. For example, the death of maître d'hôtel Plocq in May 1749 set in motion a cascade of promotions, with each member of his kitchen staff ascending the ladder: within a week, chef de cuisine Cabrol had become maître d'hôtel; Allegre rose from kitchen assistant to chef de cuisine; and Hallée, the kitchen boy, became the new kitchen assistant. Each of these promotions also carried a significant increase in income. Both Hallée and Allegre received an additional 100 livres per year, with Hallée's wages doubling from 100 to 200 livres and Allegre's increasing from 500 to 600 livres. Cabrol's wages went from 800 to 1,000 livres. A similar wave of promotions occurred in 1775 in the prince de Lambesc's kitchen. Chef de cuisine Duval rose to be maître d'hôtel, while his kitchen assistant, Gerin, assumed Duval's former position. When the duc de Biron's cook, Crosnier, retired in 1753, his assistant immediately took his place.[185] Because cooks could work for years as assistants at relatively modest wages only to receive a sudden promotion on the death of the maître d'hôtel, kitchen titles and wages function as a relatively inexact measure of a cooks' skill or even experience. Yet such an environment forced cooks to work at all levels in a kitchen, a system that the cookbook author Vincent La Chapelle praised as essential for producing a capable maître d'hôtel, who ideally had passed through all of the positions he would himself supervise as manager of the household's kitchen.[186]

Cooks also gained by working in elite households—even if they never advanced within their own kitchen's hierarchy—because a cook's status was inextricably linked to the prestige of the household that engaged him. François Marin rose to be maître d'hôtel to the maréchal de Soubise based on the reputation he had cultivated as cook to the duchesse de Gèvres.[187] One self-described "good cook" who had been maître d'hôtel for "people of distinction" confidently sought a position in Paris or in a château in the provinces.[188] This cook had already reached the acme of his occupation, but other, less accomplished cooks could potentially rise in rank if they transferred to another household. This lateral form of promotion allowed skilled cooks to assume senior positions without waiting for a post to open up above them. One cook seeking work in Bordeaux described the situation succinctly: "a young man of good living and morals, well recommended, having done a good apprenticeship in cooking, desires a position as kitchen assistant in a good house or cook in a bourgeois house."[189] While his skills merited only a supporting position in a "good house," he believed himself fully qualified to serve as a full cook in a lesser household. Moving abroad often provided the ultimate form of lateral promotion. By relocating to another country where French cooking was especially prized, cooks could gain an instant increase in income and responsibility. In 1789, a couple offered 600 livres in wages to a female cook willing to relocate to London, where she would be responsible for serving as many as fifteen to twenty people.[190]

This form of relative promotion by shifting households provoked disdain from some cooks. Pierre Lamireau bitterly complained that the cook succeeding him was "only an assistant" from the kitchen of the baron d'Holbach.[191] For her part, Lamireau's mistress must have felt fortunate to find a replacement who had lately been responsible for hosting a weekly salon and preparing some of the most lavish feasts of the Old Regime.[192] From the perspective of the newly hired cook, such a move also made very good sense: d'Holbach was by then already in his sixties—and indeed, would die within three years—and the possibility of the assistant of gaining promotion within that household may have seemed increasingly remote. Tantalizing evidence also suggests that hiring a star cook was perceived to burnish the master's reputation. Masters showcased their own sensibility by hosting exquisite dinners prepared by their cooks. "Infantry, cavalry, and navy officers, people of the church, nobility, of the court, finance and commerce, all work only in order to host a table with the most splendor and delicacy," Mercier observed. "One only looks for more lucrative employment in order one day to give feasts to one's neighbors, acquaintances, parents, and friends. He who has no cook has no existence."[193]

The potential social benefits of an excellent cook were most attractive to those seeking entry into elite society. "More distinguished [cooks] are often to be found in the houses of lawyers and bankers than in those of people of quality; one thing is certain—they pay better," the duke of Albemarle explained to the duke of Newcastle.[194] With such importance placed on fine dining, Mercier could easily joke, "A cook is the necessary man, and without a cook what real advantage would the rich have over the poor?"[195]

Escaping the Kitchen

Although the *affiches* suggest heavy turnover among cooks, little evidence indicates the immediate cause. Private household accounts often leave us only a simple "departed" (*sorti*) in the household wage register, providing no clue as to who made the decision to terminate service or why. In just one household, for example, no fewer than seven cooks made their appearance in the space of just two years.[196] We can only speculate as to what precipitated this instability. Occasionally, however, a bit more detail seeps into the records, especially when the circumstances of departure were especially noteworthy. In 1748, Hugues Volant did not merely leave service: his master's register indicates that Volant was fired.[197] In 1750, the kitchen assistant Hallée left after unsuccessfully demanding a 50 percent raise—perhaps the very audacity of his request merited recording.

During the same year, the kitchen boy Champagne also asked to be released from service. When yet another *aide de cuisine* quit in 1752 after only three months' service, the maître d'hôtel did not bother to seek a permanent replacement, instead just hiring "a man while waiting for a suitable assistant to be found."[198] Mercier characterized this behavior as driven more by cooks than by masters, complaining that cooks left households "painlessly and without remorse in order to enter another where they will not attach themselves any further."[199]

Cooks also left when household circumstances changed, and crisis in the master's life could spell catastrophe for a cook, underscoring the tenuous nature of domestic service. A sudden downturn of fortune, for example, could result in drastic reduction of the kitchen staff. When Controller-General of France Calonne was sacked after the disastrous 1787 Assembly of Notables, for example, his cook Olivier tasted a share of his master's fate, losing his extraordinarily lucrative position.[200] And when masters died, their kitchen staffs were frequently liquidated, since surviving relatives typically lacked either the means or inclination to retain them. As a result, cooks frequently pointed to the death of their masters as the only reason for their sudden availability. One cook declared that he had left his master only upon his death, and another noted that he had just "lost a master that he served for twenty-four years." A third cook claimed that he had been put "out of service by the death of his master."[201]

Old age also drove cooks from the kitchen. The problems of the elderly perplexed and preoccupied Enlightenment thinkers.[202] Servants and other urban laborers often could barely sustain themselves while actively working and earning, leaving little margin for survival once age or injuries began to take their toll.[203] Time was particularly unkind to those who spent years of their lives consigned to the kitchen, whatever the preference expressed in the *affiches* for "mature" cooks. What happened to cooks when they could no longer tolerate life in the kitchen? For domestic servants in general, the notion of retirement was pure fantasy, notwithstanding a 1750 proposal to establish a retirement home and regular pensions for domestics.[204] But while the outlook for other servants was generally grim, many cooks were fortunate enough to enjoy the support of a pension in their old age.

During the 1750s, for example, the duc de Biron's former cook, Crosnier, received 200 livres per year "granted to him ... for his support." Martin who worked in the Brienne kitchen appears to have enjoyed a pension of 300 livres after 1788. In both cases, the cooks received pensions equivalent to half of their previous wages. The prince de Lambesc's maître d'hôtel Duval received a pension of 500 livres, after having earned 1,200 livres per year.[205] Jean-Baptiste Queval benefited from a lifetime pension of 150 livres from the estate of his former mistress, Madame de Berville, having served thirty-three years in her household (and later in her daughter's).[206] Masters sometimes remembered their cooks in their wills: in 1771, the prince de Carignan's executors searched for his former chef de cuisine to offer him his inheritance.[207] The cook had worked for the prince for just two years. Evidence also suggests that cooks accumulated substantial savings, thanks to their relatively high incomes. At his marriage in 1733, Maître d'hôtel Lemerle already possessed a fortune of three thousand livres, and he continued to work in the same household for another twenty years, earning as much as 650 livres per year. When the cook Nicolas Claude Paradis died in 1751, he left nearly 10,000 livres.[208] In 1779, a cook pointed to his *rente* of 400 livres when he sought a position as concierge along with his wife, a seamstress.[209]

Older cooks frequently sought to escape kitchens for calmer work, typically as concierges or porters. On the same day in 1781, two different aged cooks posted advertisements in the same newspaper seeking alternative employment. The first, "a former cook of around sixty years" looked for a position as either a porter in Paris or a concierge in the countryside. The second man, also aged around sixty, sought a position as a porter, even though he knew "a bit of cooking." Another older man who knew cooking well wanted to escape, not just the kitchen, but perhaps also the city: he requested a position as concierge "around Paris or more distant." A thirty-eight-year-old cook who had been "at the head of a good house" wanted to become a concierge. The death of a master could provide the pretext to leave cooking. A fifty-year-old cook who noted that he had just lost his master decided to escape the kitchen either by managing the other servants "at the head of the house" or by becoming a porter or concierge. Another man put out of service by the death of his master preferred to become a porter, although he knew how to prepare *une cuisine bourgeoise*. Masters recognized the desire to escape busy kitchens and often promised a quiet post: in 1779, one advertisement searched for a skilled female cook in her early forties who would be willing to leave a "big kitchen" for "a more tranquil life serving only retired people." Another advertisement promised "a tranquil house where there are never suppers for the masters" to a fifty-year-old male cook who had several years of service with a single master.[210]

Health concerns, often linked to the physical space of the kitchen, motivated cooks to leave the occupation. In 1789, a cook wrote that "his health requires him to quit this position." He sought instead to become "maître d'hôtel, dessert cook, or something similar."[211] According to Louis-Sébastien Mercier, male cooks all had "their taste burned by the age of fifty." And even if Mercier claimed that women "at this age still cook well," other evidence suggests that cooking was viewed as a relatively taxing occupation, particularly given the conditions of the kitchen.[212] In the 1757 play *L'Ancienne et nouvelle cuisine*, one character joked about "the effects of a few charcoal vapors" on the mental faculties of an old cook.[213] Another, very real cook proposed a new kind of stove to "protect himself against the accidents to which charcoal vapors frequently exposed him."[214] According to one contemporary study of workers' illnesses, such vapors posed the greatest threat to cooks' health, not physical exertion.[215] Whether or not the vapors were ultimately to blame, many cooks simply worked until their deaths.[216]

The eighteenth-century "cook" comprised a broad range of qualities, skills, and experience. While good morals remained the essential qualification for all servants, a cook's particular expertise could allow her to command higher wages and better conditions without constantly defending her own character. Although life in the kitchen might prove difficult and even fatal, it remained considerably more lucrative and secure than many other occupations, especially in comparison to domestic service in general. Clare Crowston has suggested that in spite of its limitations, women's work could afford "opportunities denied to male workers."[217] Cooks similarly benefited from opportunities denied to other servants. In the way they hired subordinates, established hierarchies within domestic service, and positioned themselves as technically and morally competent, cooks mimicked many practices long associated only with guilds. But however much cooks recapitulated guild organization, they also superseded or circumvented traditional patterns of work, enjoying advantages unknown to guild workers. Though laboring in disorderly and dangerous kitchens, cooks established an occupational expertise that could be cultivated and promoted independent of any formal institution.

TWO

Corrupting Spaces

You must never descend into the kitchen if you wish
to eat with pleasure intact.

Louis-Sébastien Mercier, *Tableau de Paris* (1788)

Most architects prior to the eighteenth century did not regard the kitchen as meriting any particular attention. Seventeenth-century architectural manuals offered only slim and often contradictory advice on little more than the most basic aspects of kitchen design. Yet a century later, dictionaries described the kitchen as quite literally forming the structural foundation of the residence, and architects agreed that no other space better showcased their skills. Architectural treatises during the eighteenth century offered exhaustive advice on such details as the kitchen's spatial location and orientation, its ventilation and drainage, its communication to interior and exterior spaces, the materials used in its construction, and even minutiae like preferred color schemes and aesthetic styles. Why did the kitchen suddenly become so important to eighteenth-century designers? The answer lies largely in the adoption of new ideas about hygiene and growing sense that the kitchen constituted a potential site of corruption.

The kitchen of the Enlightenment was a dreadful place, at least in the minds of those who cared to think about it. Utterly unlike today's idealized site of familial bonding and delicious smells, the eighteenth-century kitchen was characterized by filth and decay. Emitting foul vapors and relentless clangor, it assaulted the senses with its odors and sounds, its sooty smoke spoiling household furniture and endangering health. When the architect Nicolas Le Camus de Mézières revealed his state-of-the-art kitchen in 1780, he sought to cure the space by gearing its design toward cleanliness above all other considerations. The architect enumerated such features as smooth and straight whitewashed walls, a sloped floor for drainage, and windows that would ventilate the space without introducing dust and dirt. Le Camus de Mézières urged meticulous attention to closing holes against rats and mice in the storage pantry, and he prescribed a regular cleaning regimen to ensure a healthful environment. The architect devoted more pages to the kitchen than to any other area of the house, and he was hardly alone in his belief that the kitchen was the most important interior space, at least from the perspective of the challenges its design posed. Likewise, this architect's obsession with kitchen cleanliness was anything but unique. Rather, his description represented the apotheosis of decades of efforts to impose hygiene on a space that had come to be understood through the lens of pathology.[1]

When it came to the kitchen, actual building practices did not widely diverge from architectural theory. Eighteenth-century construction plans and maintenance records describe kitchens that largely conform to the vision set out in Le Camus de Mézières's text and those of like-minded contemporary architects. Setting aside for a moment the contentious question of the kitchen's location, the typical kitchen's aesthetic was sober. Flagstone floors and high, vaulted ceilings framed its main room in heavy masonry, which had the advantages of both fire-resistance and easy cleaning.[2] Occasionally, the kitchen's floors were tiled in terra-cotta or the ceilings plastered, alternatives that similarly provided durable surfaces that lent themselves to washing.[3] To facilitate overall cleaning, the kitchen's stone floor sloped gently toward a drain cut through an exterior wall.[4] Wide doorways allowed servants to enter and exit the kitchen with ease, and, when possible, tall casement windows provided ample light and ventilation.[5] Walls, doors, and window framing painted white or gray helped to brighten the room.[6]

The kitchen's most prominent and newest architectural feature was the stove, an invention of the late seventeenth century that increasingly appeared in new construction and renovations over the course of the eighteenth century.[7] Typically positioned under a window, the device could accommodate up to ten or more cooking vessels at once. Perhaps painted red, this stove could provide one of the only visual highlights among the kitchen's otherwise muted whites and grays. Near the stove (and often at right angles, forming an L), an open stone hearth dominated the space of the kitchen. Here large cuts of meat roasted and pots simmered over charcoal and wood fires. Shelves and hooks embedded in the walls throughout the kitchen helped to organize meticulously burnished copper and iron cookware and utensils.[8] In the center of the room, one or more large wooden tables provided a surface for chopping and other food preparation, and a masonry sink typically stood in the corner for washing (and perhaps also supplied water through a faucet).[9] These features inevitably shifted to accommodate the overall dimensions and orientation of the residence, but the general form outlined here would have been familiar to any architect or cook in the eighteenth century.[10]

While little in this description may strike today's reader as particularly con-troversial, the eighteenth-century kitchen's design was in fact the outcome of a vigorous and decades-long debate centered on its spatial configuration and inte-gration into the rest of the residence. Until the middle of the seventeenth century, French architects had usually situated the kitchen either at ground level in an ad-jacent wing or underground beneath the *corps de logis*, or main living area, which contained spaces like the master's bedroom, dining room, and salon. Of these two options, early seventeenth-century architects expressed no clear preference. Pierre Le Muet, for example, placed kitchens in a wide variety of locations dur-ing the 1620s: on the ground floor, the second floor, in basements, and in remote wings far from living areas.[11] Removing the kitchen to a distant wing reduced the risks associated with fire and lessened the impact of noise and odors, but such a design required a large footprint that consumed valuable ground-level space. Locating the kitchen below the *corps de logis*, on the other hand, saved space and typically allowed for easier and faster communication between kitchen and din-ing areas, but it also introduced problems of drainage and ventilation.[12] Le Muet's contemporary Louis Savot recommended the installation of tall and well-built chimneys to protect upper floors from kitchen smoke, but still expressed no clear preference for the location of the kitchen itself. Savot most clearly articulated the reasons for his contemporaries' and his own lack of interest in the kitchen: such areas were "of little concern," since they remained "out of sight of visitors" and were "destined only for servants' comfort."[13]

Ambivalence about the kitchen's location began to fade around the middle of the seventeenth century, when most architects started to advocate a specific location, although at least one architect declined to take a stand even as late as 1691.[14] Some designers proposed an alternative to the options of the wing or sub-terranean kitchen, instead elevating the kitchen to ground level but still keeping it below the residence's main living apartment, which was raised to the second floor.[15] This arrangement of preserving space on the ground floor for servants' areas or shops was dubbed "Roman" in design, while wing or basement kitchens were labeled "French" configurations, a contrast that reflects the degree to which classical ideals influenced architectural fashion and constituted the benchmark against which any new style was judged.[16] But after just two decades of popular-ity, the so-called Roman configuration came under attack. In 1673, the architect François Blondel rejected the Roman kitchen outright, suggesting that his read-ers abandon the practice of placing kitchens beneath any living areas.[17] According to Blondel, a kitchen's "noise" and "bad odor" would disturb the occupants of any rooms above. Worst of all, residents might dine directly over such a kitchen, and Blondel found "nothing as disagreeable as the smell of the kitchen and meats while meals are served."[18] Roman kitchens fell out of favor as the "modern" took precedence over the "ancient" in aesthetics and literature. Thus the Quarrel of the Ancients and Moderns, the literary debate that captivated French and other European thinkers at the close of the seventeenth century, penetrated even into the details of kitchen design.[19]

Space Planning

Blondel's concerns about the communication of odors and noise among interior spaces anticipated the eighteenth century's fascination with *la distribution,* or space planning.[20] Beginning in the 1720s, architects began to promote space planning in a series of architectural treatises, and they found ample opportunity to put the new theory into practice with the building boom in Paris that followed Louis XIV's death. As the political and cultural center of gravity shifted from Versailles to Paris during the Regency, elites raced to revive old residences and construct new ones.[21] The result was not only a radically transformed cityscape but also a revolutionary conceptualization of interior space. In these new and renovated sites, *la distribution* became detached from its original broad meaning of "arrangement" or "allocation" and now came to convey a specifically architectural meaning, involving a holistic approach to the layout of the entire residential space. For example, it required that all zones of the residence be "properly situated" and "placed according to their uses" with a close understanding of the relationships among structures and the people who occupied them.[22] These residential areas, in turn, were precisely subdivided into specialized rooms intended for particular purposes. In a self-conscious rejection of the sort of polyvalent spaces that had defined earlier residential design, architects proposed a dizzying array of antechambers, libraries, offices, and boudoirs. In the process, the dining rooms and salons emerged where much of the cultural and intellectual exchange of the Enlightenment transpired.[23] The implementation of *la distribution* thus had the not insubstantial effect of redrawing not only the urban landscape but the social and cultural topography of eighteenth-century France.

Practitioners of *la distribution* were quick to note both its novelty and its modernity. Skilled implementation of *la distribution* purportedly demonstrated the superiority of modern, eighteenth-century architecture over ancient Greek and Roman antecedents. According to one contemporary architect, in the organization of interior space, he and his colleagues had finally "surpassed the Ancients."[24] Ancient architecture did not lose all appeal, but it now remained prized solely for its external form, with architects encouraged only to emulate ancient exteriors.[25] The organization of interior space was an entirely different matter and was touted as a clear triumph of moderns over ancients. As in many other domains, the word *moderne* itself came to assume totemic qualities. Charles-Étienne Briseux and Charles-Antoine Jombert championed *la distribution* in treatises titled *L'Architecture moderne,* published in 1728 and 1764. Jacques-François Blondel's *De la distribution des maisons de plaisance et de la décoration des édifices en général* (On the Distribution of Follies and the Decoration of Buildings in General) declared on its title page that it was an "Architectural Treatise in the Modern Taste." And if *la distribution* was especially modern, it was also particularly French; "*la distribution* in France is pushed to the highest degree of perfection," Blondel claimed.[26] To be sure, architectural labels such as "ancient" and "modern" were hardly mutually exclusive. In the hands of a skilled architect, *la distribution* could potentially complement classical Roman and Greek orders.[27] Classical design could supply external aesthetic beauty while *la distribution* improved communication among spaces and their functions. Moreover, it must be noted that modern architecture involved less a rejection of classical forms than of the more recent vulgar gothic antecedents. In the realm of architecture, to be modern was to be tasteful; the *moderne,* the philosophe Jean Le Rond d'Alembert asserted, was "not in absolute opposition to that which is old, but to that which was in bad taste."[28]

If the kitchen had served as the prototype of *la distribution,* it also came to pose space planning's greatest challenge. The earliest indication of this new interest in the layout of the kitchen and its internal functions appeared in Sebastian Leblond's 1710 "De la nouvelle manière de distribuer les plans." To some extent, Leblond's work functioned as a bridge between the indifference of the seventeenth century and the eighteenth century's obsession, and the author occasionally describes servant areas as lost or wasted space. But Leblond also ushered in a new age of concern about the kitchen's location, seeking to eliminate the construction of basement kitchens, which were in his opinion expensive, offensive to the senses, and even dangerous.[29] Following Leblond, eighteenth-century architectural treatises agreed that in the implementation of *la distribution,* no single zone better indicated an architect's talent than the kitchen. Charles-Étienne Briseux wrote in 1728 that it was "in this section principally that one knows whether an architect is skilled in *la distribution.*"[30] Four decades later, the author of *L'Architecture moderne* agreed, suggesting that an architect's kitchen offered the best example of whether *la distribution* was "understood well."[31]

Comfort

La distribution sought to redefine the integration of the kitchen into domestic space, and over the course of the eighteenth century, architects used the kitchen as a foil for the new anxieties that emerged around the configuration of residential interiors. As Blondel's concerns about the kitchen's noise and odors suggest, the main goal behind space planning was the emerging ideal of comfort, known in French as *la commodité*, which came also to govern residential architectural design.[32] *La commodité* is a rather broad term, which could also translate as "convenience," and the architect's litany of complaints about the kitchen's "inconveniences" stood in stark contrast to the emerging ideals of residential comfort. Perhaps unsurprisingly, the comfort in question was that of masters, not servants, but this emphasis did not in any way diminish the importance of servant space. In the seventeenth century, servant space had been "of little concern," but now the design of servant space had a direct and overwhelming impact on the comfort of masters. In the eighteenth century's new, comprehensive approach to residential architecture, no single servant space jeopardized comfort more than the kitchen.

The kitchen's two main assaults on domestic comfort were its noise and its odors. Unlike urban street noise, which could be avoided through careful orientation of the *corps de logis*, kitchen noise posed a more pervasive threat, at odds with residential tranquility. Domestics performed much of their work in open courtyards, and without sufficient isolation, masters would be "inconvenienced by noise."[33] Kitchens too close to the *corps de logis* left their masters "ceaselessly inconvenienced by the noise made by domestics and the people working to prepare food there."[34] Annotations to a 1722 plan for the Palais de Bourbon note the "care taken" in placing the bedroom above rooms other than the kitchen, "in order to avoid . . . the noise and odor" of that space.[35] Closely linked to the kitchen's location was its communication with other residential spaces. Although at least one architectural historian has characterized kitchen staircases as a "novel feature of domestic comfort," they were regarded in the eighteenth century as conduits that might convey kitchen nuisances directly into the residence's living areas.[36] Basement kitchens, for example, left masters "extremely inconvenienced by the noise made by domestics going up and down."[37] In response, Briseux proposed specially designed staircases leading to the kitchen that would prevent masters from being "interrupted" by the noise of servants ascending and descending kitchen stairs, but it is not clear whether such a design was ever implemented.[38] Concerns about the kitchen's noise were hardly limited to architects: prescriptive literature urged cooks to limit noise, and one conduct manual suggested that chief among the tasks of the cook was to prevent, "as much as he can, the noise and tumult in the kitchen."[39] Literary representations likewise depicted the kitchen as a noisy space. In one popular account of a kitchen brawl, the dispute was settled only after the "noise of their racket" reached the master's ears, prompting him to investigate "what was happening in his house."[40]

Kitchen sounds were surpassed in intensity only by odors. If today we equate the kitchen's aromas with welcome domesticity, in the eighteenth century, they were generally regarded as a fetid miasma. "Worst was the kitchen," declares Alain Corbin in his history of odors, and contemporary descriptions of kitchens more than bear out this assertion.[41] *L'Architecture françoise* (1673) bemoaned "the odor of the kitchen and meats."[42] Leblond attacked kitchen stenches, arguing that they invaded the entire domestic space.[43] Kitchen smoke posed a particularly intractable problem. Kitchens reeked of "the odor of charcoal, which could be communicated to the apartments," Blondel declared.[44] Even when all other chimneys went cold, kitchens continued to belch smoke year round.[45] Whether the kitchen sat in the basement or on the ground floor was increasingly irrelevant; if the kitchen was "too close, the bad odor which it continuously exhales, joined to the harmful odor of charcoal and the smoke of dishes, penetrates the apartments, where it spoils and blackens paintings and gilding."[46] This last concern, that smoke would destroy furnishings, was a typical refrain in eighteenth-century architectural advice.[47]

Contemporary scientific experiments reinforced the notion that the food in the kitchen was especially likely to produce a foul stench, with observers noting the "putrid and cadaverous odor" produced by wet and rotting meat, though fish was the worst offender.[48] When providing advice on how to remove the "infected odor" of fish that was "a bit off," one cook suggested working outside: "There I let all of this unbearable odor evaporate; then I throw this water far away. It smells very bad."[49] Unfortunately, such actions merely transmitted the fish's odor to the air circulating through the residence, as Le Camus de Mézières lamented.[50] Louis-Sébastien Mercier conceded that the street filth of Paris was "necessarily black," thanks to particles of iron flaking off of carriage wheels, "but the water flowing from kitchens renders it stinking."[51] A 1786 guide to healthful living counseled readers to make certain that "the air you breathe is clear, pure, and calm. Flee that which is laden with a bad smell or the emanations of a cesspool."[52] One could hardly write a more fitting description of the eighteenth-century kitchen.

Privacy

Even more insidious than the kitchen's effluvia was its human pollution. In the eyes of contemporaries, even a glimpse of the kitchen's workers was particularly troubling sight. At the same time, kitchens played host to an especially dense population of servants, whose own roving gaze threatened to invade domestic privacy and disrupt comfort. In addition to their cooks, kitchens often filled with a "crowd" of other household domestics jostling to take their meals, while outsiders added to the fray as porters arrived with deliveries.[53] One historian describes the kitchen as a site where cooks could woo servants of other households, a scene that masters might enjoy depicted in a genre painting but certainly not in the flesh.[54] Architects accordingly aimed to place the kitchen out of view of its masters and likewise its masters away from the eyes of those who worked in the kitchen. For example, Leblond suggested using the *corps de logis* as a barrier between the entrance courtyard and the garden since "there one is less exposed to the noise of the street and to the sight of domestics and strangers because one is not obliged to cross a courtyard to go to the garden."[55] Here Leblond lumped servants, street noise, and strangers into one threatening category: all such foreign pollutants jeopardized domestic tranquility. These alien elements threatened to invade and corrupt the private space of the household, just as kitchen fumes damaged art and furnishings.

To curb the human pollution associated with the kitchen, some architects sought to limit the movement of its staff, designing a residential space where "domestics [could] do their service without troubling their masters."[56] Blondel proposed a particularly restrictive kitchen where cooks were physically unable to mingle with nonservants: "I have only placed doors at the extremities of its façade, in order to allow less freedom to the kitchen staff on the side of the terrace where it is situated, and which lies in view of the château. I preferred to limit them to the exits on the courtyard, which is intended for them."[57]

Here the architect exposed the fundamental opposition between kitchen and domestic comfort: only by turning its back to the *corps de logis* and hiding its workers and suppliers from sight would the kitchen not threaten the comfort of those on the other side. A similar design by another architect gave the kitchen "an exit on the street, detached and distinct from the main entrance."[58] By restricting access to the rest of the *hôtel*, architects concealed the spectacle of cooks going about their labors. Masters and their guests could come and go without encountering the kitchen's pollution, human or otherwise.

In an extreme fantasy of screening the kitchen from sight, Jean-François de

Bastide imagined a kitchen that remained entirely invisible. In his 1753 novel *La Petite Maison*, Bastide depicts a guest sitting down to dinner only to be surprised to find servants strangely absent:

> "But where are the servants?" asked Mélite. "Why this air of mystery?"
>
> "They never come in here," he answered, "and I thought that it would be wise to dismiss them for the day. They gossip, and would give you a reputation—I respect you too much."[59]

The host had engineered his house to become a site of unbridled seduction, hidden from the wandering eyes and wagging tongues of servants, a feat that required no small amount of ingenuity. When the time came for dessert, "the table dropped down into the kitchen in the cellar, and from above, a new table descended to take its place. It promptly filled the gap left in the flooring, protected by a balustrade of gilded iron."[60] Thanks to this elaborate contraption, dishes came and went without human intervention, underscoring the disjuncture of servant and master space. Bastide's fanciful invention reflected the very real fascination with technical solutions to the problem of privacy. According to the architectural historian Michel Gallet, such "ingenious devices introduced into the house were an expression of a twofold anxiety: to alleviate the drudgery of servants, but also to avoid their presence as far as possible by multiplying the means of serving oneself with the least effort."[61]

As Bastide's scene suggests, the kitchen served as the focal point in the project of organizing interior space into clearly delineated servant and master zones. In theory, the *corps de logis* included the master's living spaces, such as salon, bedrooms, dining areas, and library, among others. In practice, such labeling often lacked precision, and the "master's space" was understood as simply wherever the master happened to be. For example, any "passages frequented by the masters" were effectively privileged space, according to Blondel.[62] Conversely, servants could taint an area merely by occupying it, injecting further ambiguity into the division of master and servant spaces. Courtyards, for example, were "dirtied" or "crowded" by servants working in them.[63] Thus the division of space had at least as much to do with the separation of masters from servants as it did with architectural design. By strengthening and redefining the relationships between the *corps de logis* and its dependent spaces, eighteenth-century architects explicitly sought to regulate interactions between masters and servants.

Executing what amounted to a disappearing act required substantial foresight, but the potential benefits of shielding masters from servants were immense. "It is by this arrangement that one finds the comforts of life, which naturally brings us to cherish what is good for us, and to avoid all which can harm us," Blondel averred.[64] To guarantee masters' comfort, architects aimed to separate them from their servants, essentially dividing residential space into zones of comfort and discomfort.[65] In effect, the boundary between domestic space and the external inconveniences of urban life was joined by an additional internal division between servant space and master space. Architects claimed that such a division would also facilitate servants' work. Blondel, for example, sought to join "good taste and elegance to the ease of service of domestics."[66] Unfortunately, the goal of isolating the kitchen from the *corps de logis* potentially raised as many problems as it solved. As kitchens moved farther away, ever-increasing numbers of servants were often required to bring food to the table, frequently relying on cumbersome covered dishes as they passed outside even during inclement weather.[67] But more important, a more remote kitchen was an unsupervised kitchen, and this lack of oversight invited a host of problems.

In principle, cooks filled the role of overseer, monitoring the security of kitchen space and its valuable contents and guarding against theft by other servants. Leblond suggested that the cook's bedroom be situated nearby in order to supervise "the dishes and other effects with which [the cook] has been charged."[68] Blondel concurred, arguing that the cook needed to sleep near the kitchen, ideally in an adjacent bedroom.[69] In larger dwellings, a cook might have a special bedroom near the kitchen and distinct from other servants' rooms. In the Hôtel Pompadour at Versailles, for example, the cook slept in a ground floor bedroom adjacent to the main kitchen. Tucked cozily (or perhaps precariously) behind the main hearth, he could easily supervise the kitchen at all hours (fig. 2.1).[70] If limited space prevented the placement of a bedroom next to the kitchen, the cook might sleep in the mezzanine above.[71] In smaller residences, cooks often slept inside the kitchen itself. Construction records for one apartment in the Tuileries, for example, locate the cook's bed in the redesigned kitchen.[72] When Bernard de Bonnard dreamed of reconfiguring his Paris apartment, he planned to move the kitchen to the ground floor and have his cook sleep there.[73] Architects admired these sorts of configurations, urging builders "as much possible" to situate the head cook's lodging "near his work."[74] Such an arrangement supposedly ensured the safety of both "their provisions and their utensils."[75] Since most servants were required to take their meals communally in or near the kitchen, a nearby cook could also oversee other household staff.[76]

In practice, proximity between the cook's bedroom and workspace encouraged the notion in the popular imagination that the kitchen provided a remote and safe haven for cooks to commit fraud and otherwise act disreputably. Removed

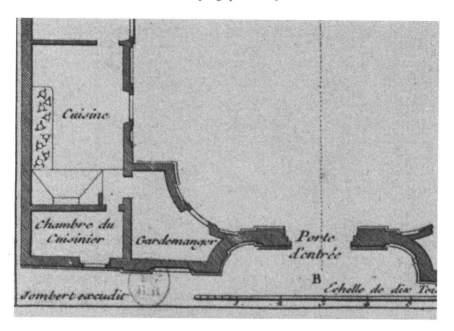

Fig. 2.1.   Detail of the Hôtel Pompadour's ground floor. Situated directly behind the hearth and stove, this cook's bedroom allowed easy supervision of the kitchen (and no shortage of heat). Jacques-François Blondel, *Architecture françoise* (Paris: Charles-Antoine Jombert, 1752), *distribution* XII, pl. 1. Photo: Bibliothèque nationale de France.

from the moralizing oversight of their masters, cooks could rapidly degenerate into criminals, each risking, in the words of one conduct manual, "his soul for a pound of sugar, a piece of meat, a trifle." The same guide warned "the more difficult it is for the master to recognize [cooks'] swindling, the more criminal they become," suggesting the unique dangers posed by a distant kitchen.[77] Safe from their masters' gaze, cooks could purportedly profit from audacious schemes. Louis-Sébastien Mercier relates an account of one cook actually selling access to his mistress's kitchen for twenty-seven livres per month.[78] And even if cooks did not actually sell food on the side, they could give it away to their friends. In Alain-René Lesage's delightful early eighteenth-century picaresque novel *Gil Blas*, the title character first encounters his new master's maître d'hôtel and cook in the act of despoiling the household provisions: "The maître d'hôtel was with five or six friends who were gorging themselves on hams, beef tongues, and other salted meats, which made them drink cup after cup." The cook, meanwhile, treats other outsiders to wine and rabbit and partridge pâtés. Gil is dumbfounded: "I thought I was in a house abandoned to pillage; however, that was nothing. I had only seen a trifle compared to what I had not yet discovered."[79] Thus however desirable for reasons of privacy, the physical isolation of the kitchen also stoked fears about cooks. Away from the master's watchful eyes, the kitchen descended into disorder, and servants ran wild.

The Seductress

In the fevered imagination of contemporaries, the ungoverned kitchen encouraged not just theft but sexual promiscuity. Anyone viewing François Boucher's popular 1735 genre painting *La Cuisinière* ("The Cook"), for example, encountered a cook all but in flagrante delicto (fig. 2.2); she stands before a seated man, who embraces her, one arm grasping her neck and the other tugging at her hand and apron. Around the couple, the kitchen is in wild disarray. Vegetables and overturned cooking vessels litter the floor, and a cat has seized and begun to devour a game bird intended for the master's table. With his breeches pushed up and his stocking sagging, the man's bare knee wraps around the cook's leg. Although the cook appears to lean away from the man, she smiles down obligingly on him, oblivious to the eggs cradled precariously in her arms. With an egg already cracked and leaking at her feet—beside a cucumber, no less—Boucher none too subtly suggests to his painting's viewers that this cook has already been corrupted.

Since kitchens were already believed to be decidedly unpleasant spaces, the very disarray of Boucher's kitchen helped to sell audiences on its authenticity. Describing an engraved version of Boucher's painting, a contemporary advertisement asserted that the chaotic scene "accurately represents the interior of a kitchen."[80] The kitchen's disorder stemmed in part from its particular relationship to exterior space. Because kitchens necessarily remained open to the outside world—for deliveries, waste removal, and ventilation—they permitted a level of spatial promiscuity that engendered disrepute. Strangers could and did invade the kitchen space, and images like Boucher's *La Cuisinière* fanned fears of infiltration.[81] While the identity of *La Cuisinière*'s young man is open to a variety of interpretations, his dress clearly indicates that he is not a cook. As new architectural designs increasingly walled off the kitchen from the rest of the residence, cooks were understood to have nearly unfettered reign in the disgusting sites left behind. At the same time, the kitchen was increasingly disconnected from the rest of residence, potentially enabling the admission of outsiders. Open to the external world and with its back turned to its putative masters, the space of the kitchen played an essential role in the fantasy of the cook's seductive powers.[82]

Fig. 2.2. A cook receives a visitor, her kitchen in wild disarray. François Boucher, *La Cuisinière* (1735). Musée Cognacq-Jay. Photo: Réunion des Musées Nationaux / Art Resource, NY / Bulloz.

Though the original painting left almost immediately for London with its new English owner, *La Cuisinière* enjoyed significant and enduring popularity in France, and the image was reproduced in various engravings, which circulated widely (fig. 2.3).[83] One such reproduction was selling "with great success," *Mercure de France* reported in April 1735. Further mention of the same engraving in June 1737 and again in June 1738 suggests that avid buyers continued to purchase prints of *La Cuisinière* for several years.[84] These prints not only widely disseminated this particular image of the kitchen as a site of debauchery; they also amplified its message through captions added to help "explain" the image, a common practice with engravings of genre paintings. Here the captions highlighted the image's sexual innuendo, with one noting the threat to the cook's eggs posed by what it called "the lecher." Another engraved version underlined the seductive and corrupting influence of the kitchen by recasting the image's woman as a vendor who found herself in the wrong place. It sternly warned, "Little girl, take care!" Both focused attention on the eggs carried by the cook, which represented both the master's possessions and the cook's own purity. The licentious behavior encouraged by the kitchen therefore also jeopardized the master's property.

The juxtaposition of erotic imagery with moral instruction in engravings of *La Cuisinière* was not especially unusual for the period. According to the art historian Anne Schroder, during the eighteenth century, "moralizing subjects coexisted with erotic themes; one did not supplant the other."[85] But if we compare the engravings of *La Cuisinière* with a reproduction of *La Belle Villageoise* ("The Beautiful Villager")—the original paintings were displayed as companion pieces—we find surprising differences. *La Belle Villageoise*'s verse declares,

> Happy children, happy mother
> In your humble hovel content with necessity
> The simplest object fulfills your desires
> The wise man rightly prefers
> To the pomp of court, to the charms of Kíthira
> The innocence of your pleasures.[86]

Although this engraving's verse also delivers a sexually charged message, it (along with the image itself) lacks the elements of money and seduction displayed by *La Cuisinière*. Unlike the cook, who is complicit in the seduction, the villager merely functions as the object of the viewer's desire. No groping male is present, no money is at stake, and the village woman is not tainted by the kitchen's corruption in the manner of *La Cuisinière*.

The cook's seductive powers frequently shaded her culinary skills, and by

conflating sexual and dietary appetites, cooks could be made to appear especially alluring to those who chanced upon them in their kitchens. An otherwise
unremarkable engraving of a cook chopping onions is accompanied by a decidedly salacious caption: "I really only want to believe that you are / Knowledgeable in the appetizing art of preparing dishes / But I feel much more appetite for
you / Than for the dish you are making."[87] In another engraving, a decrepit old
man is driven to desire by the sight of a young cook, here labeled a "wench," with
the caption explaining: "Your feeble resistance and naughty looks / Recall in the
heart of this gallant geezer, / The taste of pleasures that age denies him" (fig. 2.4).[88]
In popular depictions of the cook, sex appeal could even overcome the dinginess
of the kitchen, with the space augmenting the cook's beauty rather than detract-
ing from it. In the 1755 play *L'Ancienne et nouvelle cuisine*, one character spies the
cook and exclaims, "She's coming back. By the gods, she is beautiful! This steam
is increasing her charms."[89]

The purported sexual magnetism of the cook inspired concern in fictional accounts like Rétif de la Bretonne's "The Pretty Cook," in which a master instructs
his young cook Paule to avoid potentially dishonorable contact with other servants: "You are good-looking, and I believe you know it. I advise you not to be
familiar with the servants of the opposite sex. From this moment I declare that
you are above them, and I expect them to obey you in all respects that are not
contrary to my orders or Madame's. But no *familiarity*! You understand, I think,
what this word means?"

It turns out, of course, that the master's intentions are anything but noble. He
has hatched his own prurient scheme to exploit the cook. Rétif de la Bretonne
adds the twist of (perhaps pretended) naïveté to the familiar caricature of the
scheming cook. "I was too new to see anything there that ought to have raised my
suspicions," Paule reflects, after her master more than doubles her wages to five
hundred livres a year. She ultimately marries her former master, however, suggesting that cooks could successfully capitalize on their charms for undeserved
social and economic gain.[90]

Masters took these fears to heart. Bernard de Bonnard urged his cook to pad-
lock her own rooms to protect herself from unwanted advances. At the same
time, he denied her any other keys in order to limit her access to the rest of the
residence.[91] Although they were commonly depicted as objects of desire, cooks'
own sexual appetites were also legendary. One broadsheet tells of Geneviève Pi-
cola, a cook in the Marais who married three husbands at the same time, weaving
a tangled web of lies to keep their existence secret from one another: "she knew
her job well," alternately identifying the men as her cousins, parents, and friends.

LA BELLE CUISINIERE

F. Boucher pinxit.

P. Aveline Sculp.

Vos œufs s'échapent Mathurine?
Ce présage est mauvais pour nous,

Ce grivois dans votre cuisine?
Pourroit bien vous les casser tous.

à Paris chez Drouais peintre du Roy rue de Richelieu au Bout Royal.

Fig. 2.3. François Boucher's *La Cuisinière* was reproduced in multiple engravings and sold for years. *Above*, Pierre-Alexandre Aveline after Boucher, *La Belle Cuisinière* (Paris: Drouais, ca. 1735). *Opposite*, Duverbret after François Boucher, *L'Infortunée Pourvoieuse* (*The Luckless Purveyoress*) (Paris: ca. 1735). Photos: Réunion des Musées Nationaux / Art Resource, NY / Thierry Le Mage.

F. Boucher Pinx.

P. Duverbret Sculp.

L'INFORTUNÉE POURVOIEUSE

Suson, si sur votre Chemin   *Je prédis sans être Devin*

Vous rencontrez encor quelqu'un, qui vous lutine   *Que vous ne porterez point d'œufs à la Cuisine,*

Fillette doit toujours veiller.   *Sur ses Œufs en son tablier.*

Fig. 2.4. Fantasies of licentious behavior. Jacob Van Schuppen, *La Cuisinière*, engraved by Louis Surugue (1686?–1762). Photo: Bibliothèque nationale de France.

When she dies, however, the husbands discover one anothers' existence and come to blows gathered in mourning around her body. Laughing at their predicament, Geneviève's employer resolves the conflict—the moral being that masters must police their kitchens.[92]

The seductive threat posed by cooks also infiltrated legal proceedings, which in turn further captivated the public imagination. As Sarah Maza has shown in her study of eighteenth-century causes célèbres, lawsuits could illustrate broader social categories like gender, rank, and authority.[93] These causes célèbres tended to cluster around particularly contentious issues, and the fears widely associated with cooks were no exception. Jean Forcade died in September 1754, leaving the vast majority of his wealth, not to his surviving family members, but to his cook's daughter. In his will, Forcade promised the daughter the vast sum of 80,000 livres—at a time when a laborer might earn just one livre per day—in addition to whatever other assets he had already bestowed upon her prior to his death. In contrast, the man's own relatives stood to inherit relatively paltry sums. His two illegitimate sons would receive just 6,000 livres each. Worse still, Forcade's nephew would inherit remaining assets only in the unlikely event of any surplus. Excluded by the will altogether, Forcade's sister (and the nephew's mother) Marie Forcade vigorously contested her brother's last wishes.

In a published legal brief, the sister claimed that Jean Forcade had been recklessly intimate with his cook, who enjoyed "the greatest familiarity with him."[94] So close were the two that the cook's own husband had allegedly threatened her and Jean Forcade, for which he received a prison sentence. Even more alarming than the suggested indiscretions between Jean Forcade and his cook were intimations that the cook had exploited her own daughter in order to compromise her master. Marie Forcade claimed that from the age of thirteen or fourteen, her brother had summoned his cook's daughter from the convent in order to sleep in the bedroom adjoining his, an arrangement that the cook had "had the indecency to tolerate."[95] Because the adjoining bedroom ordinarily belonged to Marie Forcade's son-in-law, this displacement was doubly insulting. Marie Forcade argued that, thanks to the cook's machinations, her daughter had escaped the kitchen and penetrated into her master's family's own personal living spaces.

Her brother had always recorded "all that concerned" the cook's daughter in a register titled "Servant Book," Marie Forcade said, thus clearly circumscribing his dealings with her within the confines of the master-servant relationship.[96] In her own trial brief, the cook's daughter asserted that she had regularly eaten at her master's table like a member of the family. Marie Forcade denied this, declaring that the daughter "ate in the kitchen with the servants." Indeed, according to Marie Forcade, the daughter had been "always raised in Forcade's kitchen by her mother, whom she helped in her functions as a servant as soon as her age permitted." To escape the kitchen and to eat instead at the master's table implied a level of equality that Marie Forcade could not countenance.[97] Such a perversion of family order jeopardized far more than just the household; the behavior of the cook and her daughter threatened the very fabric of social order. "Is there anything more invalid than a clause [in a will] that injures good moral conduct and compromises all of society?" Marie Forcade asked. "What sort of empire could a cook, a porter, and their fourteen-year-old daughter wield over the will of their master?"[98] By playing on popular conceptions of the dangers associated with cooks, especially their alleged powers of seduction, Marie Forcade hoped to sway public opinion to her side.

Corruption

The same isolation that encouraged fantasies of seduction also potentially allowed the kitchen to degenerate into a genuinely toxic site. Contemporaries vilified a range of artisanal workspaces as dangerous emitters of fumes, miasmas, exhalations, and effluvia. The kitchen was no exception.[99] Cast in the popular imagination as a hellish workshop permeated by poisonous vapors, the kitchen was reported by medical experts to pose a mortal threat to those exposed to them.[100] The *Gazette de santé* ("Health Gazette") frequently reminded readers of the dangers of charcoal fumes.[101] In response to these concerns, one cook devised a stove specifically designed to eliminate the health risk of such vapors.[102] Cooks were sometimes imagined actually to benefit from their exposure to the kitchen. According to one doctor, cooks devoured food's nutritious qualities merely by breathing the kitchen's air, laden with airborne "vapors and quintessence," while their masters in consequence starved. He pointed to the cook's robust figure as evidence of this phenomenon: "the cook is nearly always the fattest and best-fed creature in the house."[103] Lending some weight to this claim, Mercier once noted that a bystander "could practically feed himself on the thick fumes" pouring out of household kitchens on to the street.[104]

Though cooks might be imagined to be immune to its dangers, others were not. As the kitchen's noise, odors, and crowds shaded into putrefaction and pollution, an entirely new fear emerged: the kitchen as a site of corruption. Prior to the eighteenth century, the kitchen may have been perceived as loud and malodorous, but certainly not as diseased. François Blondel had cautioned in 1673 against the construction of kitchens below the *corps de logis*, for example, because they could offend the sensibility of those present above, not because they threatened anyone's health. Architects in general had for a long time likewise remained nearly silent on the relationship of health and kitchen design.[105] In 1710, however, the idea of an infectious space surfaced when Leblond employed it to argue for the elimination of any underground kitchen, regardless of the rest of the residence's design. To be sure, kitchens continued to imperil the noses and ears of their masters, but now they posed the new danger of corruption. Because underground kitchens "lacked air, [their] humidity corrupted meats," according to the architect. Wastewater could not drain from them easily, and it too "became corrupted and infected meats."[106] Later architectural treatises amplified Leblond's fears: *L'Architecture moderne* worried, for example, that underground kitchens "spoiled meats and infected everything one wanted to store there," which emphasized the kitchen's corrupting influence whether or not inconvenient odors and noises communicated beyond the kitchen's walls.[107] Thus whereas seventeenth-century basement kitchens had merely annoyed the occupants of overhead rooms, their eighteenth-century successors risked contaminating the food itself.

Ancient Hippocratic notions of hygiene informed architectural design, and the kitchen's dank and dark conditions were blamed for contributing to its insalubrity.[108] Improper lighting and ventilation encouraged foul conditions, according to eighteenth-century architects. Heat was a frequent worry. Architects recommended a northern exposure, which was "favorable" for kitchens and would "prevent heat from corrupting meats."[109] They also kept pantries "turned to the north." away from sunlight, whose heat would likewise "spoil meats."[110] While too much sun was to be avoided, so was excessive darkness, which could introduce its own dangers into the kitchen. Kitchens without sizeable windows were especially at risk: "because they were only illuminated by skylights and lacked air, [their] humidity corrupted meat."[111] To combat this danger, Le Camus de Mézières deemed it "essential that this room be well lit, that the chimney and stoves receive direct light."[112] Blondel's ideal kitchen included "extremely high windows" that illuminated the room from both sides.[113] Such recommendations were rarely followed, and many kitchens had only a single window. Even after a 1757 renovation, one kitchen in the Tuileries "only received daylight from the public stair."[114] Construction records indicate that at least some builders sought to comply with the latest advice by adding windows to existing kitchens. For example, late eighteenth-century renovations to one Paris residence called for the "piercing of a bay casement window on the street to ventilate and illuminate said kitchen."[115]

Like exposure to the sun, a kitchen's relationship with water ideally aimed for a happy medium between too little and too much. All kitchens required an ample water supply for food preparation and cleaning, and, according to one architect, "the greatest convenience a kitchen could enjoy is to have water in abundance."[116] Another architectural manual urged builders to situate a kitchen's washroom "in the vicinity of a well or fountain, in order always to have water in abundance."[117] A third suggested that each kitchen ought to have "a tap with a basin underneath to receive water and also to wash fish."[118] Unfortunately, according to the latest scientific thinking, most water entered the kitchen already fouled.[119] To combat these impurities, some Paris kitchens cleaned their water by passing it through filters of sand. By 1750, these devices had become, at least in the self-serving words of one engineer, "indispensable for purifying water destined for drinking and for preparing food."[120] Yet while sand could remove most silt and other macroscopic deposits, it supplied only an imperfect solution. The same engineer suggested the addition of a sponge-based filtration system in order to remove further impurities. Even so, some water proved irredeemably foul. Well water, when filtered through a sponge, left behind "a rather thick and sticky slime—sensible to the finger and to the eye—like an egg white."[121]

Whatever the risks involved in its supply, the problem of water disposal posed the greater danger. Water flowing from kitchens was, in architectural parlance, "greasy, unclean, and of bad odor."[122] Architects concentrated their attention particularly on subterranean kitchen wastewater, which "having no escape other than cesspools and sumps, becomes corrupted and infects the kitchen."[123] Any of these drainage systems generated complaints. *L'Architecture moderne* lamented "the stench of cesspools and sumps that one was obliged to install in the vicinity of the basement for the drainage of kitchen water."[124] To some degree, situating kitchens on the ground floor could alleviate most drainage problems and reduce the risk of infection. Here water could exit through any hole in the wall, a simple system that was easy to implement. In the 1770s, the maréchal de Mirepoix's *hôtel* on rue Saint Domingue had a ground-level kitchen with a drainage system consisting of a "a cut and hollowed-out flagstone to drain water in a gutter passing through the thickness of the back wall; in front of this hole is an iron grate." Builders needed only to provide some kind of appropriate destination, and either a courtyard or the public street would suffice. Kitchens that happened to be situated above the ground floor could likewise easily drain outside, the one located on the second floor of 36 rue du faubourg Saint Honoré, where wastewater flowed through a pipe leading down from its washing stone.[125] In all of these cases, gravity did the work.

Although architects initially confined their worries to basement kitchens, even ground floor kitchens eventually developed the potential to become corrupt, thanks to their association with the generation of filth and waste. As early as 1710, for example, Leblond grouped the kitchen with the stables at the ends of a residence's wings, allowing them both to face the street. By arranging kitchen and stables together, the architect underscored their shared nature as breeding grounds of filth, arguing that the "best placement of the stables and kitchen is at the extremity of the wings and on the street, in order to muck out the former without passing through the main courtyard." Such an orientation "drained away horse urine," he argued, just as kitchen sinks discharged the kitchen's "water and filth."[126] Waste from both kitchen and stables thus posed analogous problems, to which Leblond offered the same solution: isolation from the interior living space in favor of proximity to the dumping site of the public street. As with noise, odors, and other pollution, such isolation of the kitchen would prove a relatively popular strategy, with a later architectural manual describing the arrangement "ideal . . . for the ease of draining water and for convenience of service."[127] The net effect on the urban environment, however, was grim. A treatise on Paris streets noted that the kitchen's greasy discharge contributed to the problem of "infected" mud.[128]

If a residence happened to occupy a large plot of land, Leblond proposed that the kitchen open onto a smaller courtyard distinct from the main entrance. This kitchen might share the smaller courtyard with the stables in order to ensure that "the main courtyard is never dirtied or crowded." Better yet, on the largest of sites, the kitchen could have its own exclusive courtyard, resulting in an "extremely convenient" arrangement.[129] Given the intractable problem of kitchen waste—contemporary receipts track expenses related to "trash removed from the courtyard"—this configuration quickly gained popularity, with other eighteenth-century French architects embracing Leblond's approach.[130] In 1728, Briseux offered very nearly the same advice as Leblond, counseling readers, "When one can place them at will, it is suitable to put them at the end of the wings on the street, but if the site was extremely large, it would be necessary to make a courtyard for the kitchen and office, where they could be situated as one wished."[131] Blondel likewise encouraged the use of separate courtyards to solve drainage problems. They ensured that "the evacuation of dirty water and other waste coming from the kitchen" transpired far from the *corps de logis*.[132] Another architectural manual counseled readers to situate residences on "a sufficiently spacious property to make an individual courtyard for the kitchen where one can procure all the advantages it needs."[133] By 1780, Le Camus de Mézières was recommending that every kitchen drain "immediately outside, otherwise humidity and odor would be disagreeable."[134]

Hygiene

To cure the kitchen's ills, human and otherwise, Le Camus de Mézières prescribed a comprehensive regimen of hygiene. In his 1780 *Le Génie d'architecture* (The Genius of Architecture), the architect recommended a regular cycle of washing to ensure cleanliness, and the nearby servant's dining area required washing "at least once per week." Cleanliness was the single most important quality of a kitchen, since it "seems to announce the excellence of its dishes." But cleanliness required careful architectural design and constant vigilance. Otherwise, the kitchen and its dependent spaces left unchecked would rapidly degenerate into a "refuge for filth." Moving beyond the basic precepts of *la distribution*, which alone could not fully solve the problem of corruption, Le Camus de Mézières devoted painstaking attention to every detail of the kitchen's form. For example, he worried that imperfections in kitchen walls would otherwise become "stores of filth" and thus recommended that they be "white-washed" and "straight and even." He suggested that work tables detach from the wall to allow for easy and frequent cleaning. Tightly fitting doors would keep rats and mice at bay. Specially designed windows opened only at the top. According to Le Camus de Mézières, "several reasons require this: first, heat always rises, and through this means steam dissipates more easily; second, if the casements opened at the bottom, they would ruin dishes [cooking] on the stove, create dust, and stir up filth." Because floors could become especially grimy, the architect recommended that they gently slope to allow for drainage. Such floors ensured that "water flows easily outside, and that everything dries quickly." Paving stones further reduced risks of slippage and "the saddest accidents" that came from greasy or wet floors. Even provisions for fire safety simultaneously provided opportunities for improved cleanliness.[135]

Cleanliness required order, but with the kitchen separated from the *corps de logis*, how could one ensure that servants remained under control? Le Camus de Mézières proposed to harness the immutable appeal of classical aesthetics to halt the kitchen's otherwise inevitable slide into disorder and chaos. The kitchen's basic contours should follow the Tuscan order, a style characterized by broad and unfluted columns with unadorned capitals.[136] According to one contemporary definition, the Tuscan order was only used in buildings "which require much solidity, like the gates of fortresses, bridges, arsenals, jails, etc.,"[137] but Le Camus de Mézières asserted that it "announces, through its sense of force, the idea of a well-founded kitchen."[138] Moreover, it also masculinized kitchen space: "By its proportions, the Tuscan order proclaims force and solidity; it symbolizes a muscular and robust man."[139] More feminine styles like Ionic and Corinthian were utterly inappropriate, and even the Doric order, representing "a man of noble and becoming height," lacked sufficient force.[140] That Le Camus de Mézières equated masculinity with strength and solidity is not especially surprising, but the interest he showed in imposing these characteristics on kitchens suggests that he found these areas especially in need of the masculinizing architectural influence. Like cleanliness, masculinity was an essential sign of a uncorrupted kitchen.

The intended recipients of message of the kitchen's clean and manly design were the servants who worked there. Le Camus de Mézières implicitly expected servants to possess the requisite sensibility to understand his message. For him, a properly executed architectural form broadcast a universally effective sentiment. Le Camus de Mézières based his argument on the premise "that particular sensations are aroused by particular forms and that these can be manipulated and arranged to specific effect—that there is indeed a science of the sensations," Robin Middleton writes. Sensitive to the powerful architectural forms surrounding them, cooks would bow to the will of their masters. Through the application of this science, Le Camus de Mézières sought to eliminate corruption at its source.[141]

Le Camus de Mézières's architectural treatise reveals why kitchen corruption remained a persistent threat: notwithstanding the best efforts of France's most talented architects, kitchens ultimately could not be tamed by *la distribution* alone. As architects attempted to impose order on the totality of domestic space, household kitchens emerged as ever more critical sites of social contestation. Efforts to purify domestic space sought to divide servants from masters and to eliminate all signs of the former from the space of the latter. With servants and masters occupying separate spheres, however, the kitchen became increasingly susceptible to corruption. The perils of infection and decay demanded ever greater oversight, without which kitchens would jeopardize both moral and physiological health. At the kitchen's center stood the corrupt and corrupting cook, whom contemporaries viewed as an integral part of the kitchen's problems, even if this seductress also remained charged with taming its ills.

THREE

Pots and Pens

You will make an inventory of the kitchen's equipment that you
will put on the last pages of this book. It is understood that
anything lost will be replaced.

Madame de Kerry to her cook

Nicolas de Larmessin's *Habit de cuisinier* (fig. 3.1), an engraving made around
1695, portrays a cook cloaked in a dazzling array of dishes and utensils. Although
enjoying a temporary respite from the confines of the kitchen, the cook is trapped
inside the clanging accoutrements of his labor. Pots and pans encase his body like
a suit of armor, forks and spoons dangle from his breeches, and knives buckle his
shoes. A sash of sausages drapes across his chest, and a ham swings from his belt.
Wielding an enormous frying pan and crowned by a suckling pig, de Larmessin's
cook stands poised and ready to serve.[1]

Although this cook was just one of de Larmessin's many engravings of artisans, each decked out in the tools of his trade, the image of a cook literally
composed of his tools was a popular conceit adopted by other early modern artists. An earlier, sixteenth-century pen-and-ink drawing follows the exercise to its
logical conclusion, with kitchen tools comprising even the cook's face.[2] A later,
eighteenth-century print *Architecture vivante: La cuisinière* likewise portrays a
cook built from the tools of her kitchen. A fiery hearth constitutes her torso,
and the sort of strong architectural column advocated by Le Camus de Mézières
stands in for her legs. Like de Larmessin's cook, she carries a long-handled pan
intended for use in a hearth, but perched atop her head, she sports a broom, a
bucket, and a towel, signaling the cleaning chores more typically associated with
women cooks. In each of these fanciful renderings, the artist's selection of cooking equipment reveals an especially mechanical understanding of cooks' work.
Each of the tools depicted corresponds to one of the physical processes of preparing a meal (or cleaning up after it). We see in de Larmessin's engraving, for
example, a meal's complete cycle of preparation: ingredients (sausages, a joint

Fig. 3.1. The tools make the cook. Nicolas de Larmessin II, *Habit de cuisinier* (ca. 1695).
Photo: Bibliothèque nationale de France.

of meat), the tools used to process them (pans, knives), and finally the finished product (a roast suckling pig, a display of fruit). The cook has been reduced to the sum of his tools, and any evidence of the individual's own talents is absent. Viewing these images, we sense that the utensil, not the bearer, transforms the raw into the cooked.

At odds with this representation of the cook as embodiment of his tools, a new, competing vision emerged over the course of the eighteenth century. This image focused less on cooking utensils than on a decidedly different implement. The cook in Pierre-Louis Dumesnil's painting *La Cuisinière* (fig. 3.2) stands in stark contrast to the equipment-laden seventeenth-century cook portrayed by de Larmessin. This mid-eighteenth-century cook holds just one tool: a pen. She is leaning over a kitchen work table to prepare her kitchen accounts, and as she writes, more papers spill from an open drawer. Nowhere do we see her cooking utensils. The pen, the table, and a few scattered food items suffice to indicate the writer's occupation. As with the image of the cook-as-tools, the writing cook likewise widely circulated in a variety of eighteenth-century media, including visual images, verse, and the theater. While it requires no great leap of the imagination to identify de Larmessin's utensil-encumbered character as a cook, the occupation of *La Cuisinière* might remain considerably more ambiguous for today's observer. Instead, for the eighteenth-century viewer, the mere act of writing strongly signaled that this woman was a cook.[3]

These two competing representations suggest the complexity of the occupation of cooking. On the one hand, cooks used a large and growing array of utensils and gadgets. The variety of these tools in turn conveys the increasing intricacy of cooking. On the other hand, writing had assumed a central role in the activities of the kitchen including, among other tasks, the preparation of inventories to keep track of these utensils. When Madame de Kerry ordered her cook to make an inventory of the kitchen's equipment, she explicitly linked these two key aspects of the cook's activity.[4] The eighteenth-century cook needed not only to prepare food but also to write about it.

Pots: *La batterie de cuisine*

The tools worn by Larmessin's cook date from the late seventeenth century, but they would have been at home in any eighteenth-century kitchen, since the tools of the past were not so much replaced as they were augmented by increasingly specialized utensils. Most of the gear displayed by *Le Cuisinier* and the other such fancifully rendered cooks was known as *la batterie de cuisine*, a name taken from

Fig. 3.2. The cook wields her most important utensil: the pen. Pierre-Louis Dumes-nil the Younger, *La Cuisinière,* engraved by Claude-Augustin Duflos in 1762. Note the papers spilling from the table drawer. Photo: Bibliothèque nationale de France.

the beaten (*battu*) copper cooking vessels that constituted the bulk of a kitchen's equipment. During the eighteenth century, the batterie de cuisine came increasingly to include utensils of other metals, notably iron, but copper continued to prevail.[5] As a raw material, copper was expensive, and usage examples from contemporary dictionaries describe its "purchase" and declare it "beautiful," underscoring its role in signifying the quality and wealth of a kitchen. Although their owners tended to see eighteenth-century kitchens as revolting, they were expensively outfitted.

When the maréchale de Mirepoix's cook, Garache, compiled an inventory of his kitchen's tools on 22 April 1780, he began with "a table and its drawer," perhaps the very surface on which he was writing, and probably much like the one used by the cook of *La Cuisinière.* Such a table would have been useful for storing the paper needed for drafting receipts and for composing the kitchen's daily and monthly reports.[6] Tables with drawers figure in other images of the kitchen, like Étienne Jeaurat's 1752 genre painting *L'Éplucheuse de salade* (The Salad Picker).[7] Tables also regularly appear in architectural diagrams of kitchens, often placed in the center of the room, and the architect Le Camus de Mézières insisted on having them.[8] In 1785, the prince de Lambesc's cook, St. Martin, ordered several tables, one to go beside the door of his kitchen.[9] A butcher block and a mortar and pestle were to be found near Garache's worktable, and his kitchen also contained water barrels and a linen cupboard. After recording various baskets, he turned to the batterie de cuisine, starting with the ironware. Dozens of iron pots, pans, their lids, and their spoons hung from hooks or rested on shelves arranged around the kitchen's perimeter. The cook then itemized the kitchen's heavy iron utensils, which included tools used at the hearth and stove, a roasting spit and its dripping pan, knives and sieves. Garache then counted the more expensive copper utensils, which ranged in size from large cauldrons to tiny pâté molds. Finally, he went into the pantry to note a few remaining items.[10]

Cooks in the Mirepoix household compiled such inventories three times in the course of a decade, in 1777, 1780 and 1788, but these documents also served an ongoing purpose between complete overhauls, since cooks frequently annotated them to indicate losses and additions to their arsenals.[11] For example, penciled annotations to the 1780 report reveal that pots and spoons periodically became unusable or went missing.[12] At other times, cooks appended acquisitions to the inventory, noting the purchase of new pie dishes or sieves for quenelles, flour, and bouillon.[13] Because cooks were responsible for the integrity of their kitchens' equipment, creating and maintaining inventories of valuable tools was essential. Madame de Kerry warned her cook that he was responsible for kitchen equipment and that anything lost would have to be replaced.[14] As the title of another kitchen inventory makes quite clear, the kitchen equipment was "left in the care" of the cook.[15] Servants came and went in these households, and inventories kept by cooks helped to guarantee the integrity of the kitchen's equipment.

In her study of eighteenth-century material culture, Annik Pardailhé-Galabrun invites us to "imagine those shining copper pots, with their warm, bright colors, lining the walls."[16] A single copper cooking vessel could cost the equivalent of several days of a cook's wages, and the combined value of even a relatively modest kitchen's pots and pans could easily equal several months' pay or more. In 1761, for example, a cobbler's modest kitchen equipment sold for over 300 livres, a year's wages for a laborer.[17] Despite their cost, cooking utensils were nearly universally owned even at geographic and social extremes, and often in surprising diversity. Whereas in the homes of artisans, one found only a few iron utensils and copper cooking vessels, a middle-class kitchen was likely to contain "a rich batterie de cuisine dominated by copper and tin."[18] Urban areas had no monopoly on cooking utensils, which were found in abundance in rural house-holds; a single farm kitchen might contain dozens of tools with a combined value of over six hundred livres.[19] The kitchen equipment of the elite was often notable for its sheer quantity. To cite only one example, Charles-Alexandre de Calonne, controller-general of finances from 1783 to 1787, owned more than five hundred pieces of cooking equipment.[20]

By the mid eighteenth century, a bewildering range of short-handled pots and pans, pie dishes, fish kettles, and skimmers had joined the venerable type of long-handled pan wielded by Larmessin's cook.[21] Cooking equipment owed much of this diversification to the rising popularity of the kitchen stove, a relatively recent innovation in the period. The ancient stone hearth had made it possible to use only a relatively simple set of cauldrons and roasting spits, but each of the new stove's heating plates could support a separate cooking vessel, and some of them even assumed the distinct outline of the vessel they would heat. Long oval plates, for example, were designed for fish poachers. Fashionable new foods also often necessitated novel equipment. The preparation of *poupetons*, slices of veal stuffed with minced meat, required a unique tool, the *poupetonnière*. Cooks poached most fish in *poissonières*, but thanks to its odd shape the turbot merited prepa-ration in a specialized *turbotière*. Small copper molds allowed cooks to create fanciful edible displays, and one kitchen had at least eighteen of them. Kitchens acquired specialized sieves for particular uses, and differentiation was the order of the day.[22]

A lively market in utensils sprang up around estate sales, which became closely associated with used kitchen equipment. A broad swath of society owned enough kitchen equipment to merit advertisement and sale, with people like apothecaries and sculptors among those whose estate advertisements included a full batterie de cuisine.[23] A diverse array of kitchen tools was considered so unexceptional that a French dictionary used the example "the entire estate inventory consisted only of several little kitchen utensils."[24] Indeed, the nearly absurd idea of *not* having any kitchen utensils allowed Mercier to joke that the impoverished estates of men of letters offered "neither laces, nor diamonds, nor even batterie de cuisine."[25] In the rare event of an estate sale containing few cooking utensils, advertisements were careful to steer buyers elsewhere, and two such notices began with a warning that their sales would contain little in the way of kitchen gear.[26]

Kitchen tools were so ubiquitous that vending them alongside luxury goods occasionally raised eyebrows. Mercier described the awkward scene of copper-smiths gathered to purchase kitchen utensils at an estate sale, finding themselves waiting along with those who had come to buy the deceased's luxury items, like upscale Boulle furniture. To avoid such uncomfortable situations, kitchen effects were almost always sold first. Mercier made light of this practice, noting, "In estate sales . . . one begins ordinarily with the batterie de cuisine, the deceased no longer needing it."[27] The duchesse du Maine's estate notice promised the sale of the batterie de cuisine from nine o'clock in the morning until one in the afternoon. Only after three o'clock would chandeliers, bronzes, porcelains, jewelry and lacquered items be available for purchase.[28] The late Monsieur Mauclere's batterie de cuisine similarly went on sale the morning of 8 February 1773, with the following eight days reserved for the rest of his belongings.[29] Occasionally, the batterie de cuisine would warrant its own separate sale.[30]

Many estate sales sold the batterie de cuisine along with other household items that, though of some value, also attracted the wrong crowd. A royal officer's estate sale began with a "beautiful batterie de cuisine, sand-filtered and other fountains, iron stove grates, earthenware and cast pans." Another sale included the kitchen's linens along with its "considerable" batterie de cuisine. A third combined the batterie with ceramics. Servant furnishings often joined the batterie de cuisine on the auction block, underscoring the volatile conditions of domestic servitude. Among other effects, estate sales regularly featured "servant beds" for sale along with the batterie de cuisine.[31] Along with almost certain unemployment, the death of a cook's master typically meant the dispersion of a cook's tools and furniture, which were counted among the possessions of the master, not the cook.[32]

Notably absent from those selling a batterie de cuisine were cooks themselves, who simply did not acquire kitchen utensils in any substantial quantity. Cooks seldom even possessed many cooking tools for their own personal use. Jean-René Vaverel, cook to the intendant of Bordeaux, had only sixteen livres worth of cooking utensils at his death. Marthe-Louise Petit, widow of one cook and remarried to another, owned a batterie de cuisine worth less than nine livres at her death. Cooks' own holdings of cooking utensils thus tended to be very small and certainly not on a scale of even a modest bourgeois kitchen. They did, however, purchase cooking utensils on behalf of their masters for use in the workplace. In 1783, one cook bought for his kitchen two earthenware pots, six earthenware pans, and twelve wooden spoons. On 19 October 1787, another cook purchased a grater for 1 livre 12 sols. Cooks also had to replace any tools lost or broken under their supervision.[33]

Despite their intrinsic value, kitchen tools and their ownership constituted a particularly inconspicuous form of consumption. The extent of a household's batterie de cuisine could be judged only indirectly by the variety of dishes gracing its owner's table. Furthermore, even the most discerning diner could never be sure whether his host actually owned the implement used to prepare a given dish. If a certain tool was especially infrequently used, the cook might opt to borrow it for the occasional feast.[34] For example, Omer Joly de Fleury's cook rented a batterie de cuisine three times to celebrate holidays in 1770, paying five to six livres each time. Records for his Pentecost feast indicate the rental of specialty items including a *turbotière, tourtière, poissonière,* and *brochetière.* Even in kitchens as lavishly equipped as Controller-General Calonne's, cooks sometimes rented equipment.[35]

Maintenance

In an era before stainless steel and Teflon, the expense of the batterie de cuisine continued long past its initial purchase. All metallic cooking implements required frequent maintenance to protect their cooking surfaces from corrosion. This need for continual repair may help to explain the enduring value of used kitchen tools: whether a utensil was newly manufactured or fifteen years old, it could be brought into good working order through regular attention. Until the mid eighteenth century, copper was the unquestioned metal of choice for kitchen tools. In addition to conducting heat efficiently, copper is especially malleable and thus permits extremely flexible designs. Yet copper was expensive and— more troublingly—potentially dangerous. Copper surfaces easily corrode, and contact with any type of food or liquid produces poisonous verdigris.[36] Verdigris had long been recognized as a health risk, but during the eighteenth century concerns arose regarding the tiny but steady doses potentially delivered by cooking utensils.[37] By 1750, worry about the dangers of verdigris reached a fever pitch, with one alarmist treatise remarking, "There is no man, however uneducated, who does not recognize the danger of verdigris, a terrifying poison."[38] Judicial memoranda traded blows over the dangers of copper, and one writer condemned verdigris for spoiling ladies' teeth, though conventional wisdom usually blamed Paris's foul air.[39]

To prevent direct contact between food and copper, coppersmiths had traditionally coated and recoated cooking vessels' surfaces with tin. This process, known as *rétamage,* often occurred in the coppersmith's workshop—a plate from Diderot and d'Alembert's *Encyclopédie* illustrates a coppersmith at work tinning a pan—though itinerant tinners also performed the service on site (see fig. 3.3).[40] Resurfacing tools with tin provided only temporary protection, because, as the tin wore away, even tiny fissures could unleash an invisible and tasteless poison. Efforts to prevent this problem could take a disturbing turn, with one coppersmith ominously offering to coat copper kitchen fountains and taps with a thick layer of lead to avoid the buildup of verdigris.[41] An increasingly popular (and considerably safer) solution required abandoning copper altogether, and chemists and doctors widely supported a complete elimination of copper cooking vessels.[42] In 1740 the "very ingenious worker and excellent citizen" Prémery obtained a royal privilege to use iron rather than copper to make his kitchen utensils, creating a batterie de cuisine that was, in his words, "very healthful, lighter, and less expensive."[43] Even so, his utensils still required tinning; otherwise rust would discolor foods. Discoloration aside, proponents of iron cookware claimed that iron oxide was at worst harmless, while a few even suggested that rust could actually convey significant health benefits. One judicial *mémoire* championing the case of iron cooking vessels cited the robust constitutions of workers in iron mines, noting that they "enjoyed a perfect health," quite unlike miners of other metals.[44]

Economic factors also conspired against the continuing use of copper utensils, because price increases during the eighteenth century elevated them above the reach of poorer consumers.[45] Yet despite its higher costs and the emerging consensus in favor of iron, copper did not by any means disappear from kitchens. During the 1750s and 1760s, the *Encyclopédie* continued to define most cooking vessels as made of copper.[46] Even the largest batteries de cuisine still consisted almost entirely of copper pieces.[47] A dialogue in Louis-Sébastien Mercier's 1776 novel *Jezennemours* laments that despite the well-known danger of verdigris, copper utensils remained in three-quarters of residences.[48] Even wealthy masters continued to purchase new copper utensils for their kitchens; in April 1770, Joly de Fleury bought a new "casserole weighing three pounds four ounces in copper."[49] As always, these dishes remained only as safe as their thin protective layers of tin.

Much to the alarm of contemporaries, the responsibility of using and maintaining properly tinned utensils rested in the hands of cooks. According to one scholar, "kitchen utensils were undoubtedly objects of expertise, and hence arguably mysterious," but it was not at all clear that cooks were prepared to master their complexity.[50] One observer lamented "the carelessness of servants and cooks, who reject recently tinned dishes because of the bad taste which comes from the material used to attach tin to copper."[51] He claimed the danger was even greater for wealthier diners more isolated from their own kitchens, because they

Fig. 3.3. The coppersmith makes a house call. François Boucher, *Chaudronier, chaudronier,* engraved by Simon-François Ravenet, in *Les Cris de Paris* (ca. 1737). Photo: Réunion des Musées Nationaux / Art Resource, NY / Thierry Le Mage.

rarely saw the state of their cooking vessels.[52] An eighteenth-century physician likewise remarked that verdigris especially threatened the "low and humid kitchens such as one sees in the great houses of the capital."[53] Cooks might be tempted to use the services of unscrupulous craftsmen, who cut corners by using toxic lead instead of tin.[54] Urging them to follow safe maintenance practices, the engineer Joseph Amy commanded cooks, "Therefore obey or leave."[55] Fortunately for historians, most cooks did obey, and in the process they accumulated countless receipts for tinning that communicate something of the operation's frequency, along with the size and composition of their batteries de cuisine. Because each metal surface that came into contact with food required tin, almost every kitchen tool appears at some point in these maintenance records.

Fluctuating monthly repair numbers suggest that some tools required repair more often than others. A tool used only rarely required infrequent maintenance since its protective layer of tin did not experience much wear. As a result, the figures indicated in tinning receipts reflect only a fraction of the total number of kitchen tools held by each kitchen. For example, though the Kerry kitchen repaired just 44 pieces in January 1788, an inventory dating from the preceding October indicates ownership of 141 pieces which would ordinarily require tinning.[56] Likewise, the Mirepoix kitchen generally repaired 30 to 50 pieces per month, but its inventory indicates around 120 pieces requiring regular service.[57] In a few cases, these tinning jobs included astronomical numbers of pieces. For example, Calonne's cook regularly ordered the repair of more than 200 tools; in a single month, he ordered nearly 500 pieces tinned.[58] At the other end of the spectrum, more modest kitchens tinned just a handful of utensils from time to time. In the Dreneux household, for example, an order might include only seven items.[59] Between these extremes, a typical monthly repair job for a prosperous Paris household contained 30 to 40 pieces. One such order included twenty pans, six pan lids, five pots with their lids, three skimming spoons, two cooking spoons, two pie dishes, and one platter.[60] The cost of such maintenance was hardly trivial: prices per piece of *rétamage* doubled, from 8 sols in 1770 to 15 sols in the late 1780s. Thus even a smaller batterie de cuisine such as Joly de Fleury's required substantial investment. In a seven-month period, he paid 55 livres to his coppersmith Rey for repairs, rental, and new equipment purchases; his January 1770 bill alone ran to 16 livres.[61] Beyond basic tinning, some kitchen tools occasionally required more extensive repairs, such as the soldering of a kettle spout or the attachment of new pot handles.[62] In all cases responsibility ultimately rested with the cook.

Pens: *Le livre de compte*

To track the maintenance of kitchen equipment, cooks relied on a decidedly different utensil that was nonetheless essential to their work: the pen. Overwhelming evidence suggests that few kitchens could function without the written records that managed inventories, purchases, and wages. Contemporary representations of cooks frequently depict individuals actively engaged in the process of bookkeeping, and Dumesnil's painting of *La Cuisinière* preparing her *mémoire* examined above (fig. 3.2) is by no means an anomaly. For example, in the play *La Dinde du Mans*, the character of the cook makes her first appearance when she arrives in her master's study to deliver her regular account for review and reimbursement.[63] In the verse *La Maltôte des cuisinières*, the two women's stratagems for defrauding their masters likewise rely on the manipulation of accounts and receipts. The notion of the writing and calculating cook permeates contemporary prescriptive literature, and domestic conduct manuals simply assumed that cooks knew bookkeeping.[64]

The vast majority of these documents record daily food and fuel expenses, an intensive task, which generated massive amounts of paperwork. Some historians have described bookkeeping only as a job of the maître d'hôtel, a more senior servant position found in only in the wealthiest of households, but the archives reveal that ordinary cooks composed the vast majority of kitchen accounts.[65] Indeed, even in households served by maîtres d'hôtel, cooks often still produced their own accounting records.[66] The eighteenth-century cook was a prodigious writer, calculating daily expenses and drafting regular formal reports. Despite their number, these documents have largely escaped historians' notice, and until now no one has considered them as artifacts of the practices of cooking.[67] Yet through bookkeeping, kitchens became important sites of writing and calculation.[68]

In the simplest of cases, kitchen accounts might consist of a few loose sheets of paper summarizing recent expenses.[69] Each of these *mémoires* summarized a discrete period of the kitchen's costs, typically ranging from a week to a month in length. At the other end of the spectrum, we find highly organized bound volumes of accounts covering a year or more of transactions.[70] Known as *livres de compte* or *livres de raison*, these registers often had preprinted lines to aid entry and calculation of expenses. Whatever the physical format, these documents all reflect a highly consistent set of practices. First, at a regular interval each cook prepared a formal account of her expenses, using supply receipts, maintenance costs, and sometimes the wage records of subordinate kitchen staff. By condensing these disparate sources into a single report, the cook created a unified and concise account of the state of the kitchen's finances. Next, the cook submitted this report to her master for review. Finally, the master would approve the document and disburse funds to cover the kitchen's expenditures.

Cooks left an extensive paper trail documenting the daily purchases necessary to supply their kitchens. A cook would typically purchase from a number of purveyors, and in some households the total number of kitchen suppliers could run to a dozen or more. Meat, bread, and vegetables came, respectively, from a butcher, baker, and greengrocer. A creamery supplied eggs and milk. Some items like oysters were sold (and even shucked on site by the bushel) by specialized vendors.[71] In addition to food supplies, cooks purchased wine for their masters and for consumption by other servants.[72] They bought wood and charcoal to fuel their stoves.[73] Cooks paid for maintenance to the kitchen's equipment, utensils, locks, and windows, and, if necessary, they hired workers to do odd jobs such as tidy up the grass of the kitchen courtyard.[74] Kitchen accounts also helped to track more unusual expenses, like those associated with guests or special events. Joly de Fleury's cook Audiger compiled summary spending reports for each of the major Catholic feast days. For example, in 1770, he documented the outlay of nearly 1,000 livres each for the Easter and Pentecost celebrations.[75] Ponsignon, pastry cook to Controller-General of Finances Calonne, oversaw the provisioning of a decidedly more extraordinary function, the convening of the Assembly of Notables. Though the Assembly failed to act decisively in the face of France's looming fiscal crisis, it was hardly for lack of stimulants. Ponsignon's records show that in one month alone, the assembled body consumed 160 pounds of coffee and more than 500 pounds of sugar.[76]

Most of these supplies and services were purchased on credit, and each purveyor issued invoices for future payment, either for a single purchase or for sales made over a longer period, typically one month. The seller drafted the invoice, and the resulting spelling, punctuation, and even arithmetic were extremely variable and subject to the merchant's own level of education and skill. As with any transaction between buyer and seller, this paperwork allowed both cook and purveyor to keep track of credit and debt for the purpose of settling accounts. For cooks, however, these documents served an additional function: they provided the evidentiary basis for kitchen accounting, which in turn preserved a paper trail allowing cooks' masters to monitor and audit kitchen expenditures.

In addition to safeguarding copies of invoices, cooks maintained their own concurrent registers of daily expenses, enabling their masters instantly to determine how money was being spent. These daily entries contained commonplace purchases such as bread and meat, as well as luxuries like foie gras, truffles, and gruyère and parmesan cheese.[77] Rather than present their masters with a stack of diverse receipts scrawled by a variety of merchants, cooks condensed all the expenses into a single account for their masters' review. For example, the duchess of Fitz-James's cook, Gÿ, consolidated each day's costs in a register listing each purchase (fig. 3.4). As she completed each page, Gÿ would calculate a running total at the bottom:

On the 28th [of September 1785]	[livres]	[sols]
bread	1	14
eight and a half pounds of meat	4	5
a chicken	1	16
three artichokes		18
spinach		8
gruyère		7
capers		2
cauliflower		12
milk		3
frogs		6
carrots		6
onions		8
herbs		3
On the 29th [of September 1785]		
bread	1	3
milk		3
eleven and a half pounds of meat	5	15
a fat chicken	2	15
six eggs		15
three artichokes		15
white beans		6
herbs		6
six frogs		6
half a hen and noodle soup from the *restaurateur*	4	2
	27	14

All cooks used the same accounting method. For example, the maréchale de Mirepoix's cook, Geux, similarly prepared a single *mémoire* each month to summarize his expenses, tabulating each day's petty expenses chronologically:

On the 4th [February 1788]	[livres]	[sols]
truffles	10	
veal sweetbreads and brains	4	
white wine	2	8
double and simple cream	3	
chocolate	4	
dishwasher	1	4
ice	1	2

In this last example, we see how the cook's costs for supplies could mingle with labor expenses—a dishwasher had been hired to help in the kitchen. After itemizing each day's expenses, Geux then appended monthly receipts from his major suppliers, who had each provided their own running tallies. For the month of February 1788, these receipts included purchases from his butcher, fruit and vegetable supplier, roaster, *charcutier*, coppersmith, grocer, and oyster vendor. Working from his records of daily petty purchases and the monthly receipts from major suppliers, Geux neatly drafted his account on a large folio sheet of paper. When finished, he folded it in half and inserted his suppliers' receipts. Each month, he prepared his kitchen's *mémoire* in the same fashion.[78]

In addition to weekly or monthly reports, cooks also prepared annual summaries for their masters. These documents identified any lingering debts to suppliers and provided a synopsis of annual spending patterns, and they could also form the basis of annual budget planning. The prince de Lambesc's cook, for example, was expected in 1775 to adhere to an annual budget of 30,000 livres.[79] These yearly assessments even monitored the number of *gras* (fat) and *maigre* (lean) days. On *gras* days, the Catholic Church allowed the consumption of meat; on *maigre* days, it was proscribed. Since fish typically cost far more than meat, budgets required adjustment accordingly. And since the number *gras* and *maigre* days fluctuated from year to year based on the liturgical calendar, cooks needed to calibrate their spending to compensate for the variation.

To monitor the daily cycle of purchases, cooks often computed precise rates of consumption. For example, in some households, masters were particularly keen to monitor spending on meat. Madame de Kerry demanded that her cook provide a daily tally of the weight of meat consumed, and the cooks who served the comtesse d'Artois likewise calculated the amount of meat purchased and eaten each week.[80] After noting the weekly total, the cook who served d'Artois then reckoned both the amount consumed each *gras* day and the portion per person.[81] With its "Observation on the consumption of butcher's meat," this particular cook's registers reveal something of the complexity of the required arithmetic:

> The consumption this week is 32 pounds ...
>   32 pounds divided by ~~five~~ four days makes ~~6 pounds 6 ounces per day~~ 8 pounds per day.
>   There are five people in the kitchen and Felix makes 6, therefore this is one pound eight ounces per person.[82]

Here the cook's arithmetic included division, an operation well beyond the simple addition and subtraction ordinarily involved in basic daily accounting. These calculations helped to determine the broader cost of maintaining the household: by figuring the total expense of his mistress's servants, this cook helped her to know how much her retinue cost. In practice, cooks' accounts assumed a variety of forms; in all cases, however, it was a time-consuming task.[83] In a letter, one cook apologized to his wife for being busy with "the accounts that [my mistress] demands of me for tomorrow."[84] The size of many of these reports also suggests the long hours involved in their preparation, with one cook's monthly account running no fewer than thirteen pages.

Literacy and Numeracy

How did cooks learn to keep accounts? Little evidence suggests any kind of formal schooling, but at least one primer purported to teach the necessary skills. The handbook *Le Livre nécessaire à touttes* [sic] *sortes de personnes* (1776) promoted just the sort of chronological accounting system used to produce of kitchen accounts illustrated above by such cooks as Gÿ and Geux.[85] In the section entitled "Manner of Correctly Composing and Writing the Expenses of Each Day of the Week," the author teaches the basic accounting of kitchen expenses (fig. 3.5). In the sample account, we see the individual expenses of each weekday: Wednesday's purchases, for example, include a *tête de veau*, a rack of mutton, four pigeons, a pheasant, six quails, a pound of roquefort, and two bottles of champagne. Clearly, no one was suffering in this fictional household, and it comes as no surprise when a character named "Mr. Good Taste" makes his appearance a few pages later.[86]

The type and cost of the sample purchases suggest that servant cooks may have constituted one audience for this particular lesson, though it bears not-

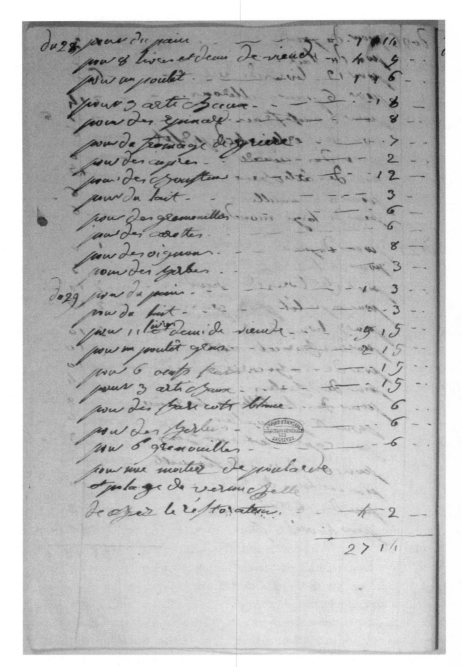

Fig. 3.4. Monthly register kept by Gÿ, cook to the duchesse de Fitz-James, with signatures attesting to the account's accuracy. AN T 186/44 (1785). Photos by author.

du 30 pour du pain — — — — — 1 3 - -

pour du lait — — — — — — 3 - -

pour 10 livres de viande — — — 5 - - -

pour 6 pain d'oeillerons — — — 2 15 - -

pour de la chicorée — — — — 10 - -

pour des haricots vert — — — 10 - -

pour une livre de beure — — — 1 4 -

pour des grenouilles — — — — 6 -

pour 3 oeufs frais — — — — 7 6

Je soussigné reconnois avoir reçu de Madame
la Duchesse de Fitzjames par les mains de Monsieur
Farré la somme de quatre vingt cinq livres dix sept
six deniers faisant avec trois cent soixante seize livres
quinze sols payés le premier de ce mois celle de quatre
cent soixante deux livres cinq sols six deniers pour
le contenu au présent mémoire suivant l'achat de
Mad. Dame Duchesse de Fitzjames sur mon livre
de dépense du 1er 8bre 1785, dont quittance, fait à
Paris ce 4 8bre 1785.

approuvé le débet cydessus faisant 462

12	08	6
27	14	0
31	18	0
30	14	0
41	07	0
33	03	6
42	11	0
38	12	0
34	18	0
46	07	0
36	16	0
32	16	0
53	02	6
462	**05**	**6**

Dixneuf pieces au Chapitre cinq du
Compte arrêté le 1er avril 1786.

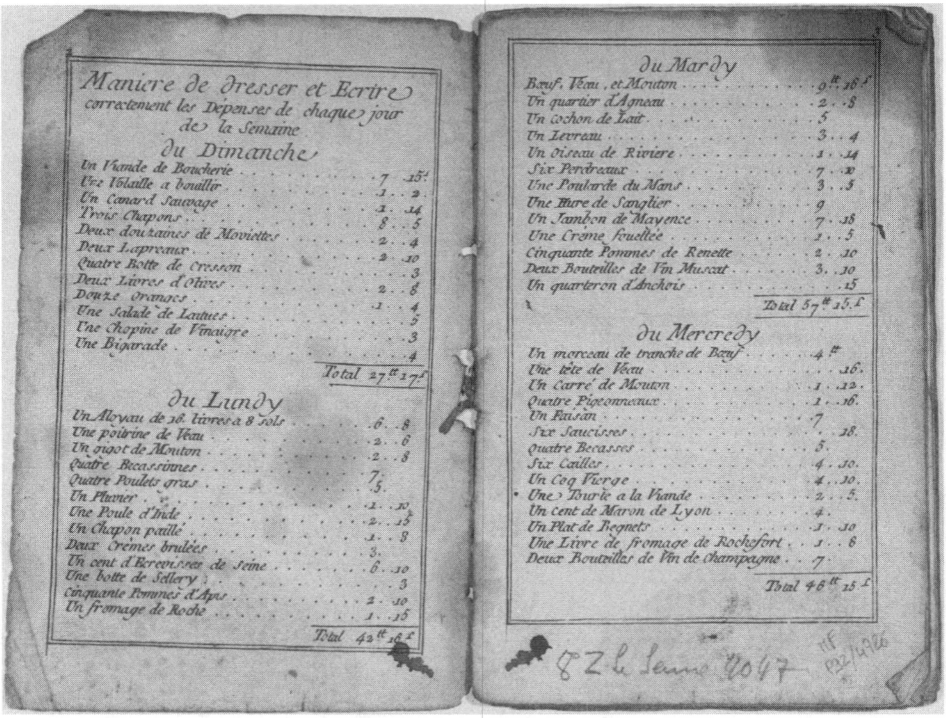

Maniere de dresser et Ecrire correctement les Dépenses de chaque jour de la Semaine

du Dimanche

Un Viande de Boucherie	7	15
Une Volaille a bouillir	1	2
Un Canard Sauvage	1	14
Trois Chapons	8	5
Deux douzaines de Moviettes	2	4
Deux Lapreaux	2	10
Quatre Botte de Cresson		3
Deux Livres d'Olives	2	8
Douze Oranges	1	4
Une Salade de Laitues		5
Une Chopine de Vinaigre		3
Une Bigarade		4
Total	27 ##	17 s

du Lundy

Un Aloyau de 16. livres a 8 sols	6	8
Une poitrine de Veau	2	6
Un gigot de Mouton	2	8
Quatre Becassinnes	7	
Quatre Poulets gras	5	
Un Pluvier	1	10
Une Poule d'Inde	2	15
Un Chapon paillé	1	8
Deux Crèmes brulées	3	
Un cent d'Ecrevisses de Seine	6	10
Une botte de Sellery		3
Cinquante Pommes d'Apis	2	10
Un fromage de Roche	1	15
Total	42 ##	16 s

du Mardy

Bœuf, Veau, et Mouton	9 ##	16 s
Un quartier d'Agneau	2	8
Un Cochon de Lait	5	
Un Levreau	3	4
Un Oiseau de Riviere	1	14
Six Perdreaux	7	10
Une Poularde du Mans	3	5
Une Hure de Sanglier	9	
Un Jambon de Mayence	7	18
Une Crème fouettée	1	5
Cinquante Pommes de Renette	2	10
Deux Bouteilles de Vin Muscat	3	10
Un quarteron d'Anchois		15
Total	57 ##	15 s

du Mercredy

Un morceau de tranche de Bœuf	4 ##	
Une tête de Veau		16
Un Carré de Mouton	1	12
Quatre Pigeonneaux	1	16
Un Faisan	7	
Six Saucisses		18
Quatre Becasses	5	
Six Cailles	4	10
Un Coq Vierge	4	10
Une Tourte a la Viande	2	5
Un cent de Maron de Lyon	4	
Un Plat de Begnets	1	10
Une Livre de fromage de Rochefort	1	6
Deux Bouteilles de Vin de Champagne	7	
Total	46 ##	15 s

Fig. 3.5. Instructions for keeping kitchen accounts. From *Livre necessaire pour touttes sortes de personnes* (Paris: Mondhare, 1776), 2–5. Photos: Bibliothèque nationale de France.

ing that cooks had been keeping accounts long before the publication of this text. By studying the lesson's account, the reader also learned to keep running totals at the end of each day's purchases which could help to provide a sense of the rhythm of the week's expenses. The *mémoire* concludes with a summary of each day's costs and a weekly total, thus providing accounts that included both a high-level summary and the details of individual purchases.[87] Legibility appears to have been the primary goal, and a master reviewing such a report could quickly identify patterns of expenditure and examine specific transactions. This invented kitchen's expenses, amounting to over 334 livres of fine ingredients per week, compare favorably with those of very wealthy households such as that of the prince de Lambesc, for example, whose kitchen spent an average of 370 livres per week in 1779.[88]

The skills involved in the preparation of kitchen accounts stand in stark opposition to the way that historians have typically portrayed domestic servants (and *du Jeudy*

Une Longe de Veau	2ˡ. 15.
Un Oye	2. 5.
Une Poulle de Coca	8. 6.
Quatre Pigeons Cochois	20.
Six Orties	
Une Poulle d'eau	1. 11.
Une fraise de Veau	15.
Deux douzaines d'Alouettes	1. 16.
Un Lievre	2. 11.
Deux Bizarades	12.
Une Botte de Cardon d'Espagne	16.
Deux Livres de Truffes	8.

Total 20ˡ 14ˢ

du Vendredy

Trois Brochets	12ˢ
Quatre Perches	
Une Anguille	5. 10.
Deux grosse Carpes	3. 18.
Six Tanches	4. 10.
Trois Truites	3. 15.
Une Alausé	6.
Un Saumon frais	15.
Six gros Merlans	4. 10.
Quatre Lirons de Pois	2. 8.
Six Artichaux et Cirouille	2. 4.
Un cent d'Œufs	3. 15.
Une botte d'Asperges	1. 5.
Du Verjus et des Champignon	14.
Six Choux fleurs et des Epinares	16.
Six Livres de Beure	5.

Total 80ˡ 8ˢ

du Samedy

Une poignée de Melue	5ˢ
Quatre Solles et quatre Limandes	7. 10.
Six Lottes et quatre Tanches	5. 15.
Six Maceaux	4. 10.
Deux Marousses	4. 6.
Une Raye	7.
Cent Grenouilles	2. 10
Un demi cent d'Huitres vertes	3.
Un cent de Moules	2. 5
Une douzaine d'Harengs frais	1. 15
Six têtes de Choux fleurs	1. 10
Un paquet d'Epinares	9.
Aricots verds et Herbes	10
Un plat de Goujeons	1. 8
Quatre pintes de Lait	1. 4

Total 43ˡ 18ˢ

Recapitulation
de la depense pour toute la Semaine

Du Dimanche	27ˡ 17ˢ
Du Lundy	42. 16.
Du Mardy	57. 15.
Du Mecredy	48. 15.
Du Jeudy	20. 14.
Du Vendredy	80. 8.
Du Samedy	43. 18.

Total 334ˡ 3ˢ

women in general) of the eighteenth century. Servants have long been assumed to have been largely unlettered, even though literacy rates rose markedly over the course of the eighteenth century: the percentage of literate women increased from 14 to 27 percent, and literate men from 29 to 47 percent.[89] Sarah Maza, for example, has described female servants as "for the most part illiterate."[90] Daniel Roche explains that for women in domestic service, "the question [of literacy] did not even arise."[91] France was hardly unique in this regard, and general servant illiteracy seems to have been the norm, rather than the exception.[92] But even if domestic servant women in general remained illiterate, cooks in particular most certainly were not. Women and men followed the same practices in the kitchen when it came to bookkeeping.

Besides disrupting our understanding of literacy, kitchen accounts also suggest that cooks wielded a unique fluency with numbers. Unlike literacy, numeracy has been the focus of very few serious inquiries—if only because its signs are often ambiguous—but cooks' skills seem no less exceptional in this area.[93] Keith Thomas, one of the rare scholars to investigate numeracy, has suggested that eighteenth-century Englishwomen "lagged behind [their male counterparts] in numeracy, perhaps even more than in literacy."[94] Given these findings, the fact that bookkeeping was so closely associated with French cooks is again particularly surprising. Even outside the world of domestic service, cooks' literacy and numeracy were also relatively unusual. Their systematic bookkeeping far surpassed the rough accounts kept by most artisans and instead resembled that practiced by professionals.[95] Indeed, a contemporary definition of "account book" emphasizes this public and commercial (and masculine) aspect, noting that such records were used by "merchants, businessmen, bankers, and others," hardly the crowd one might associate with servant cooks.[96]

Reading and calculating were such well-entrenched aspects of cooking that most practicing cooks rarely even bothered to indicate them when seeking employment. In advertisements specifying the occupation as "cook" (*cuisinier* or *cuisinière*), just 7 percent mention reading, writing, or calculating. In the event that employers requested literacy, they often did so for very specific reasons, such as the need for a bilingual cook. For example, in 1779, a wigmaker named Maury sought "a German cook, who only makes German food, but who knows French to do his accounting."[97] In contrast, only advertisements for more marginal types tended to promise literacy and numeracy. Servants who claimed to know only how to do a little cooking (*un peu de cuisine*) were four times more likely to mention writing or arithmetic, with nearly a third of their advertisements promising or demanding the ability to write or calculate.[98] In essence, the kind of servant who claimed numeracy was likely not much of a cook at all. These marginal applicants desperately sought to impress upon readers some sort of useful qualification, a shotgun approach that resulted in some very colorful descriptions. "A man of thirty-two, good hunter, capable of destroying all sorts of wild beasts, who knows how to read, write, count, and who knows agriculture and the wood business, [who] would like to find a position matching his talents," presented himself in 1783, for example.[99] Literacy and numeracy were simply assumed to be part of the cook's job.[100]

The Risks of Accounting

In recent decades, scholars have come to view bookkeeping as a rhetorical and gendered practice. First, they argue that by displaying a symmetric and perfectly balanced relationship between credits and debits, bookkeeping demonstrates probity.[101] Second, some historians have suggested that bookkeeping was an essentially private, masculine endeavor, which excluded women from both the physical space of its practice and the rhetorical space of its discourse.[102] In this traditional narrative, husbands secreted themselves into their private studies in order to keep the calculation of their finances hidden from their wives. Because domestic accounting records recapitulated the household's financial dealings, they needed to be kept secret. Well into the eighteenth century, family finances remained "the private preserve of men," in the words of one scholar.[103]

Cooks' accounting practices contradict this narrative and reveal that, whether delegated or arrogated, this weighty responsibility had passed from masters to servants. In eighteenth-century France, the role of masters had been reduced to only the periodic inspection of accounts to verify their accuracy. These reviews ordinarily occurred monthly or weekly, but in some households, they could happen more frequently. One mistress went so far as to order her cook to provide a detailed account of the day's expenses before she went to bed each night.[104] After reviewing their cooks' records, masters and mistresses typically signed the *mémoire* or *livre de compte* to indicate their approval. Each month, the comtesse de Brienne and her cook Peron, for example, each countersigned the kitchen accounts.[105] Marie-Anne Boucher d'Orlay noted that she had "approved the above writing" before signing her cook's accounts.[106] The prince de Lambesc wrote "settled and verified" or "seen good" before attaching his name to the documents, while the maréchale de Mirepoix wrote only her name.[107] In a few of these cases, a senior servant actually reimbursed the cooks in question, but the account books themselves continued to command the masters' direct attention. In one household, the process of account verification was extraordinarily formal, the cook's records being audited and notarized each month.[108]

In most cases, the cook's books passed muster, and the employer was satisfied that all accounts were in good order. The cook would then receive money sufficient to pay outstanding debts, as Bernard de Bonnard mentions.[109] Though many eighteenth-century commercial transactions went unpaid for months, kitchen debts were generally settled promptly.[110] Perhaps a potential shortage of veal was more pressing than a lack of new clocks, or perhaps food suppliers were simply more vigilant about collecting their debts. Even so, the delay between purchase and reimbursement varied considerably. In some households, the wait could be as brief as a few days. In others, it might be weeks. In nearly all cases, debts were settled by the cook who had initially made the purchases. In a few exceptional cases, the head cook paid merchants for purchases made by his assistant. In very wealthy households, the cook's debts might occasionally be repaid by an intermediate servant, typically the maître d'hôtel, *intendant*, or *secrétaire*. Calonne's cook Olivier, for example received his funds from another servant. Regardless of the payer, the cook would exchange some form of receipt recording the sum received and the date, either entered into the *livre de compte* or noted on a separate document. At least one household used preprinted receipts to indicate payment for goods and services received. Using these novel devices, the comte de Kerry's servants needed only to enter the place, date, and sum. Once a cook had submitted a receipt indicating her kitchen had been reimbursed, she could close the previous month's *mémoire* and begin the next.[111]

The amount of money that passed directly through cooks' hands clearly differentiated them from other servants, none of whom regularly handled finances as cooks did. The prince de Lambesc's cook dispensed around 25,000 livres annually during the 1770s, a period when the average laborer might only earn 300 livres per year.[112] Controller-General Calonne's kitchen expenses regularly exceeded 8,000 livres per month throughout 1780s, and during the meeting of the Assembly of Notables, they topped 32,000 livres one month.[113] To be sure, extraordinarily wealthy households might employ an *intendant* or *secrétaire* to help manage finances, but in households all the way down the income scale, cooks handled a significant proportion of household expenses. Moreover, whatever the overall expenditures of the household, cooks invariably oversaw a *relatively* large budget, since food costs typically accounted for at least half to two-thirds of all domestic expenses.[114]

The Thief

Although structured to provide the greatest possible transparency about expenditures, cooks' accounting nonetheless stoked fears that cooks were thieves. Any servant who actually did steal from her master faced the possibility of grievous penalties. Although in the distant past punished by amputation, *vol domestique*, or domestic theft, had been elevated to a capital crime since the thirteenth century.[115] Well into the eighteenth century, servants still occasionally received a death sentence. In 1780, for example, one Marie Launay was hanged for having stolen a gold watch and some silver table service from her master.[116] Although in Launay's case, the objects were of high value and the evidence solid—she was caught red-handed while trying to pawn the stolen items—the actual amount stolen by a servant was theoretically irrelevant. The rationale for meting out such harsh punishment was the uniquely intimate nature of domestic theft: it violated both the master's trust and the sanctity of the household. But rather than reassure contemporaries that servants might be dissuaded from stealing, the death penalty only amplified the dangers faced by masters, at least in the popular imagination. A servant inclined to steal had a potentially far greater incentive to

turn murderer, since even if caught killing her master, she faced no greater punishment, and in so doing she might escape scot-free by eliminating a key witness
against her.[117]

When associated with cooks, domestic theft assumed very specific forms,
uniquely suited to the opportunities (real and imaginary) offered by the kitchen.
One typical concern centered on the potential theft of food. Royal proclama-
tions forbidding the resale of leftover food noted that if allowed, such a practice
"would permit cooks to steal from their masters and mistresses or to take and
divide the portion of food intended to feed the [other] servants."[118] And indeed
evidence suggests that cooks were more than willing to engage in such practices.
In the 1780s, for example, the cook Pierre Lamireau gleefully profited from the
absence of his master by inviting his wife (who worked as a servant in another
household) to his kitchen for a meal. "[My master] has left, that's the reason why
you can come to the house tomorrow, my dear," he wrote her. "Come as early as
you can—we'll lunch together on whatever pleases you. As for provisions, I'll
have coffee ready to go or fresh eggs, if you like them better, but don't forget to
come."[119] According to Sarah Maza, "cooks felt entitled to these kickbacks," which
might also include skimming items like animal skins and fats for the cook's own
profit.[120]

Masters occasionally accused cooks of pilfering common household objects to
which they had exclusive access. Following the death of his wife in January 1786,
one Delamothe accused his cook, Nanette Bailleux, of stealing household linens
valued at 1,100 to 1,200 livres, a significant sum equivalent to several years' wages.
Bailleux immediately resigned her position, and she won a court judgment of
30 livres against her master for ruining her good name. With only a trivial sum
at stake in the judgment, Delamothe nonetheless appealed the sentence, declaring that his own honor was in fact on the line. From the testimony in the case,
it is abundantly clear that Delamothe never had any hard evidence implicat-
ing his cook. Instead, he embarked on a strategy of arguing that his cook had
had opportunity for theft and was a person of poor moral character. Delamothe
charged that Bailleux had access to the keys to the linen pantry, and he argued
that the close relationship between Bailleux and his late wife indicated that the
cook wielded a great deal of responsibility outside of the kitchen, a claim that
Bailleux vigorously denied. He thus cast his cook as a conniving liar who at best
misconstrued her relationship with her former mistress and at worst exploited
a terminally ill woman. Even more telling, Delamothe embarked on a systematic character assassination, warning anyone who would listen about his thieving
cook. In a *mémoire* contesting the original sentence, he protested about his "neg-

ligent servants who compiled lies to seduce the first judges."[121] Finally, he labeled Bailleux a "hussy" and a "slut."[122] By invoking the usual dangers of material and sexual desire, Delamothe sought to garner public support for his effort to restore his own honor, wounded at least as much by his cook's previous legal victory as by her alleged theft.[123]

The type of theft most often associated with cooks, however, was far more sophisticated than a few filched meals or napkins. Instead, cooks were accused of practicing a subtle and continuous embezzlement made possible by their skill with numbers and writing. Dumesnil's painting *La Cuisinière* portrays a cook engaged in the seemingly innocuous act of writing, but below the image we find a few lines of verse that suggest anything but innocence:

> Of her purchases Nicole to her mistress
> writes the account, and far from forgetting anything,
> completes it with such subtlety,
> that she knows how to insert her own [profit] within it.
> Without any scruples
> about skimming profits,
> she knows how to shoe the mule
> as well as a maître d'hôtel.[124]

Contemporary dictionaries define the odd idiom *ferrer la mule* (shoe the mule) as "to profit from the purchases made on behalf of another."[125] The phrase was of ancient origin—it is said to derive from Suetonius's *Lives of the Caesars* (second century C.E.)—but by the eighteenth century, it had become particularly associated with cooks, even though any number of other individuals could theoretically falsify accounts.[126] The allegedly common practice of cooks padding accounts also generated another euphemism, *peigner le singe* (comb the monkey, i.e., shear the master), which sadly did not attain the same degree of popularity.[127]

The image of the cook as spectacular beneficiary of ill-gotten gains was a phenomenon decidedly unique to the eighteenth century, and it found its earliest (and perhaps most complete) expression in twelve pages of verse published in 1724 as *La Maltôte des cuisinières*, which roughly translates as "The Cooks' (Illicit) Tax."[128] The work's subtitle is "the manner of shoeing the mule well," and the characters in the text discuss how techniques to guarantee that "the kitchen can be governed with profit." Assuming the form of a dialogue between an experienced cook and her naïve disciple, the former instructs the latter in the various dark arts of culinary fraud. The two cooks, identified in the work only as "La

Vieille" (The Old One) and "La Jeune" (The Young One), discuss a dizzying array of stratagems designed to line their pockets: skimming profits at the grocer and other purveyors; selling fats, ashes, candles, and really anything else at hand in the kitchen and thus easily purloined; and inflating prices paid for various items, to name just a few. "La Vieille" boasts that she earns dividends and interest from the nearly 3,000 livres she has invested with the Ferme générale, the company of private investors that collected France's salt, tobacco, and other indirect taxes.[129] And of course this explicit association of the "cooks' tax" with the real tax collector cultivated the notion that taxpayers were being soaked both from above and from below.

Although perhaps unrivaled in its detail, *La Maltôte des cuisinières* was by no means alone in its characterization of cooks as relentless cheats, and similar portrayals of cooks appeared in a wide range of media. The engraving *La Cuisinière* depicts a cook actually engaged in the act of defrauding her master, and Pierre-Germain Parisau's 1783 play *La Dinde du Mans* ("The Turkey of Le Mans") treated audiences to the sight of a careless cook confronted by her master over her suspect accounting:

> M. Grapeau: Money. Always money! You would think we were the Farmers-General. (*He reads*). "Butter, eggs, beans, charcoal, beans, embers, matches, beans, water, salt, beans." That's a lot of beans.
> Cook: A liter every day.

When pressed about her dodgy books, the cook angrily defends her accounting: "Well, look! Didn't Madame have dinner here? Didn't your clerks stop by?"[130]

The verse accompanying *La Cuisinière* not only claimed that the cook defrauded her master; it also suggested that her criminal skills rivaled those of a maître d'hôtel, a senior and exclusively male position. Similarly, in *La Maltôte des cuisinières*, the young cook praises the older cook's skill at embezzlement, which enables her to cheat "better than a maître d'hôtel."[131] As both suggest, male and female cooks alike theoretically possessed the ability to defraud their masters, though contemporaries found the prospect of a woman using her skills to embezzle particularly disturbing, perhaps reflecting the contemporary notion that mathematics effectively "unmade" women.[132] Audiger's conduct manual *La Maison reglée* (The Orderly Household) (1692) recommended that male cooks "keep good records of everything taken into their hands," while women ought "to be even more sensible and of good conscience in the accounts where she reports her expenses."[133] *La Maltôte des cuisinières*, *La Cuisinière*, and *La Dinde du Mans* all depict women, and indeed male cooks are rarely if ever portrayed as "shoeing the mule." Nonetheless, although perhaps less popular in the public imagination, male cooks found themselves accused of fraud that similarly exploited their skills and position within the household.

In 1762, Queval, ex-cook of the comtesse de Varneville, found himself embroiled in a lawsuit with his former mistress. He charged that she had irreparably damaged his reputation by wrongfully accusing him of theft, while the comtesse countered with a torrent of insinuation and innuendo intended to discredit her erstwhile cook. Queval, despite his station as a domestic servant, demanded nothing less than that

> the comtesse de Varneville be made to recognize him as a man of honor and probity and to do so officially before a notary. Second that she pay him damages and interests to repair on the one hand the wrong caused him by defaming him through odious calumny and on the other hand the undignified treatment she meted out along with the cruelty with which she chased him from her house. Third, that she be held to pay him his wages and return to him his belongings.[134]

Given the unpleasant consequences associated with *vol domestique*, Queval's concern about being wrongly labeled a thief was certainly understandable. And even if unsubstantiated, the accusation of theft alone could seriously impair a cook's chances of securing work. But what makes Queval's case especially instructive is less the dispute than the nature of the alleged theft.

Precipitating Queval's dismissal was not the loss of food, silver, or linens, but rather the disappearance of four stock certificates. Varneville asserted that she had secretly entrusted the certificates to Queval's care, informing no one else. What business, we might ask, did a servant cook have handling stock certificates? The countess claimed that the cook had in fact actually brokered the deal involving their purchase: according to his lawyer's brief, Varneville "had bought [the stocks] through the negotiation of Queval her cook."[135] Although the cook had served the comtesse de Varneville (and her parents before her) for thirty-three years, this long period of service was not invoked as an explanation for entrusting the certificates to him, and instead Varneville cited it as a sign of his moral decrepitude. Echoing the dangers illustrated by the old cook in *La Maltôte des cuisinières*, Varneville claimed that old cooks were at least as likely to steal as new ones. In her argument, cooks became thieves on the job, and she thus indicted not just Queval but his entire occupation. Issues of culpability aside, what is perhaps most striking about this case is its nonchalant attitude toward the possibility of a mere servant cook being so deeply involved in his mistress's very expensive and completely secret financial transactions. Queval's involvement is depicted as normal.

In her own brief, the comtesse de Varneville acknowledged that precious little evidence proved Queval's guilt other than the alleged disappearance of the stock certificates. Thus the case largely came down to the cook's word against his mistress's. She could only ask rhetorically, "was she obliged to keep in her service a man whose fidelity was suspect?" In the absence of evidence, her strategy for indicting Queval's reputation drew on popular prejudice against cooks. As with the story of the cook with three husbands, Queval's unseemly wealth served as a sign of his guilt. In addition to a lifetime pension of 150 livres, for example, Queval was known to have assets of twelve to fifteen thousand livres. According to the *Mémoire pour la comtesse de Varneville*, "this is a considerable fortune for a man of his station."[136] Moreover, after leaving Varneville's service, Queval was found to have a great deal of money in his possession, which again she labeled inappropriate for a cook. The Varneville case thus reveals a deep uneasiness about cooks' financial dealings. Although Queval had once wielded great financial responsibility, such activities were viewed more as a necessary evil than as a sign of trust:

> Every duty in society is reciprocal. Servants, these men like us, must not be the plaything of our caprice. Their reputation must not be sacrificed lightly. Who would deny it? But servants owe respect and recognition to their masters, to their benefactors. They are culpable when they insult them and when they slander them. The comtesse de Varneville's cause is that of all masters.

In the end, the Varneville case came down to a matter of honor, where de Varneville's word carried more weight than that of a servant cook. As her *Mémoire* argued: "The testimony of a woman of the comtesse de Varneville's station should not be suspected easily."[137]

The cases of Queval and Bailleux reveal that the concerns surrounding cooks' theft usually had less to do with material loss, murder, and capital punishment than with subtler fears about how fundamentally embedded cooks were into the private financial dealings of the household, often wielding tremendous responsibility. They also suggest that cooking was somehow a corrupting occupation, if only through the singular opportunities it presented. Perhaps the most alarming aspect of cooks' theft was its motivation: anticipating the blistering language deployed in causes célèbres, *La Maltôte des cuisinières* suggests that thieving cooks acted not only out of greed or economic necessity but also to satisfy deep anger and the naked desire for vengeance. From the opening advice "La Vieille" gives "La Jeune"—"Vengez-vous!" (Avenge yourself!)—to the plaint "C'est une destinée et bien triste et bien rude / Que de se voir reduite à vivre en servitude!" (It's a rather sad and harsh fate / To be reduced to a servile state), *La Maltôte des cuisinières* evinces the resentment of a category of workers not only able to steal from their masters but also painfully wanting to do so. No amount of pilfering could slake these cooks' thirst for material gain: "La Vieille" urges "La Jeune" to look alert and defraud her master as much as she can: "Ne vous endormez point, ferrez la mule au double" (Never let up, shoe the mule twice as much).[138]

Shoeing the mule was inherently predicated on the abuse of financial responsibility, and it was this tension between the cook's weighty responsibilities and her suspect morals that sparked such intense interest in kitchen bookkeeping. Despite their easy access to the myriad valuable objects of the kitchen, cooks were believed to commit far more complicated crimes enabled by their literacy and numeracy. The frequent and detailed representations of such activities suggest how much this inversion of the power relationship between master and servant perturbed contemporaries. The question was never whether cooks could read, write, and calculate, but whether they might do these things too well.

FOUR

Theorizing the Kitchen

Cooks must not consider the use of books beneath them.

Menon, *Nouveau traité de la cuisine* (1739)

From the seventeenth through the early eighteenth centuries, the *Dictionnaire de l'Académie française* defined *la cuisine* mainly as the "location of the house where meats are prepared and cooked," in other words, as "kitchen." Under this primary definition the 1694 and 1716 editions of the dictionary included the phrase *faire la cuisine*, which it explained as "to prepare [food] to eat." In the middle of the eighteenth century, however, the dictionary's definition of *la cuisine* began to shift in an unexpected direction, with the 1740 text declaring, "Also signifies the art of preparing meats and of cooking." This revision was significant for two reasons. First, *la cuisine* itself now directly signified cooking without any qualification. It was no longer necessary for *la cuisine* to be "done" or "made" (*fait*) to be considered cooking, which indicates that cuisine was no longer simply one act among many but a distinct process in its own right. Second, by labeling *la cuisine* an art, the dictionary signaled that cooking involved some degree of order, since according to it, arts required both "rules" and "method." The examples provided under this secondary definition illustrate the profound change in *la cuisine*'s meaning: "He learns cooking. He knows cooking well." Cooking had gone from something one did to something one knew.

What had transpired in the decades before 1740 for cooking to stray from the purely mechanical to the intellectual? The transformation of *la cuisine* from place and action to knowledge resulted from a passionate campaign conducted by cooks to theorize their work. From the 1730s on, cooks claimed to be practicing an entirely new style of cooking, which they dubbed *la cuisine moderne* or *la nouvelle cuisine* ("modern" or "new cuisine"). They made an exceedingly wide range of claims regarding the purported benefits of the new style. It required "less equipment, less trouble, and does not cost as much," the 1750 *Dictionnaire des alimens* (Dictionary of Food) claimed. "It is simpler, cleaner, more delicate, more scientific, we say, and even more varied."[1] Choosing from this broad array of attributes, some cooks focused on *la cuisine moderne*'s science by invoking the language of chemistry, the latest and most fashionable branch of scientific knowledge. Others argued for a style of cooking that was at the same time more economical and healthful. Some claimed to be able to refine the human spirit through the precise modification of diet. Whatever the approach, all shared the goal of the complete reconfiguration of cooking as an occupation that involved not just the hands but the mind.[2]

One thing *la cuisine moderne* did not do was introduce a radically different set of new recipes. As the meticulous work of food historians has shown, the cookbooks produced around *la cuisine moderne* borrowed heavily—to put it charitably—from the seventeenth-century predecessors they claimed to reject, and they would continue to appropriate recipes from the competitors that emerged during the eighteenth century.[3] Yet by focusing on food, rather than the people behind it, historians have overlooked *la cuisine moderne*'s most important contribution: the promise of an entirely new kind of cook, situated at the vanguard of French culture, who had seized control over the production of taste from elites.[4] Instead of receiving taste from above, cooks began to claim to create taste from below. They relied on the medium of print both to codify and to transmit the new theory that enabled this transformation. No longer strictly mechanical, cooking would henceforth involve the application of cooks' own theoretical knowledge to produce proper meals. Cooks fully recognized the social implications of their claims, and they campaigned for cooking to assume its rightful place in France's cultural patrimony along with the arts and sciences. Thus this "entirely new language" of *la nouvelle cuisine*, in the words of Mercier, offered nothing less than an inversion of cultural authority, with cooks asserting control over the origins of taste.

Given the dire conditions of the kitchen and the constraints of domestic service, it might at first seem highly unlikely that cooks would undertake such an ambitious task. Claims to produce cleaner and more healthful food ran counter to the widespread perception of the kitchen (not to mention the person of the cook) as a source of infection. Likewise, domestic servants lacked the institutional support that could facilitate the creation and transmission of the knowledge they proposed to produce, leaving them to rely on the publication and circulation of cookbooks. Despite these challenges, *la cuisine moderne* offered a sharp rejoinder to the criticism leveled at cooks, and cooks used cookbooks to offer a means circumventing the seemingly insurmountable barriers confronting them. Cooks were prepared to fashion their own organizing practices even if institutions were not available to them. Just as they had in arenas like the labor market, cooks harnessed the possibilities offered by the emerging world of literacy and cheap print to assert their expertise.

The Invention of the Cookbook

The earliest printed French cookbooks date to the origins of print itself, but between Gutenberg and *la cuisine moderne* the cookbook underwent significant changes. From a quantitative perspective, cookbook publication grew, albeit fitfully, from a tiny handful of fifteenth- and sixteenth-century titles to an immense eighteenth-century corpus that included dozens of competing works circulating in hundreds of thousands of copies. Taillevant's *Le Viandier de Paris* (The Victualer of Paris) first appeared in print in 1486, running through six editions by the end of the fifteenth century and a further nineteen by 1615. Bartolomeo Platina's *De honesta voluptate and valetudine* (1475) arrived in French translation as *Platine en françoys* (Platina in French) in 1505. An amalgam of a few competing texts, *Le Grand Cuisinier* (The Great Cook) followed in the 1540s, with twenty editions printed by 1620. After *Le Grand Cuisinier*, however, the cookbook market effectively evaporated. Between 1545 and 1620, French publishers confined themselves to reissuing existing cookbooks, and no new titles appeared in France. After 1620, cookbook publication in France ceased altogether, a collapse probably linked to the disruption of the Thirty Years' War (1618–1648).[5] Lending some credence to this claim, at least one author would later blame his cookbook's publication delay on the Fronde, the civil insurrections that roiled France after the termination of the war.[6]

This landscape changed dramatically in 1651 with the publication of François de la Varenne's *Le Cuisinier françois* (The French Cook), which through its innovative form and overwhelming popularity carved out a new market for cookbooks.[7] One historian goes as far as to argue that "no cookbook that is really a cookbook, properly speaking, was published in Europe" before La Varenne.[8] As the title indicates, *Le Cuisinier françois* also explicitly highlighted "French" cooking, an unprecedented approach. La Varenne's cookbook enjoyed enormous circulation, running through no fewer than forty-six editions between 1651 and 1700.[9] Moreover, it inspired a host of imitators abroad, including an English translation, *The French Cook* (1653), as well as translations of other, different cookbooks that nonetheless sought to trade on the ascendant popularity of the "French cook": *Der Französicher Koch* (1665) appeared in German; *Il cuoco francese* (1682) in Italian.[10] At home, *Le Cuisinier françois* encouraged a number of cooks to publish their own competing texts. Nicolas de Bonnefons released his *Les Délices de la campagne* (1654), Pierre de Lune his *Le Nouveau Cuisinier* (1662), L.S.R. his *L'Art de bien traiter* (1674), and François Massialot his *Le Cuisinier roial et bourgeois* (1691). Where effectively only three titles had emerged over the first two centuries of print, six new works materialized in the space of forty years, accounting for 90,000 copies.[11]

The seventeenth-century surge of cookbook publishing coincided with major changes in food. Based on his extensive analysis of early modern French cookbooks Jean-Louis Flandrin asserts: "The seventeenth century invented good taste."[12] Flandrin and other food historians point to a "culinary revolution" in the second half of the seventeenth century, which included the separation of the sweet from the savory, the decline in usage of exotic spices in favor of native herbs, and the widespread use of butter.[13] But to the extent that we can link these dramatic changes to cookbook publication, the results are not terribly impressive. By the late seventeenth century, the publication of cookbooks had again fallen into a moribund state, with few if any new cookbooks published in the four decades following Massialot's 1691 *Le Cuisinier roial et bourgeois*. If the early seventeenth-century publishing drought had stemmed from the Thirty Years' War, it is less clear what killed cookbooks at the end of the century, though the increasingly ossified culture of Louis XIV's court clearly provided little in the way of stimulation.

After a forty-year drought, cookbook publication again exploded again in the 1730s. Cooks produced as many new titles during the 1730s as they had in the previous thirty years, and the pace only continued to accelerate through the 1750s.[14] From the perspective of one critic, the torrential rate of cookbook publication was positively overwhelming: the *Encyclopédie*'s article "Cuisine" lamented the appearance "without end [of] new treatises under the names of *Cuisinier françois, Cuisinier royal, Cuisinier moderne, Dons de Comus, École des officiers de bouche,* and many others, which perpetually change method."[15] In addition to the surge in new titles, the number of copies in circulation skyrocketed. Over a quarter of a million copies of cookbooks were printed during eighteenth century, three times as many as during the seventeenth.[16] The chorus of new titles was further amplified by a rapid rate of reedition, both legitimate and counterfeit. For example, no fewer than forty-one editions of *La Cuisinière bourgeoise*, accounting for 50,000 copies, were published between 1746 and 1781, and a further eighty-one editions appeared subsequently, continuing to do so well into the nineteenth century.[17]

In addition to their vastly greater numbers, the cookbooks of the eighteenth century also differed qualitatively from their predecessors. While in most historical contexts, assigning labels like "seventeenth-century" and "eighteenth-century" would appear arbitrary, in the case of cookbooks, we are confronted with significantly different media separated by a distinct gap in production. Sixteenth- and seventeenth-century cookbooks had typically appeared in large octavo (about 7 by 10 inches) and even larger quarto formats, but the cookbooks of the eighteenth century had shrunk to fit the world of cheap and portable print. Sized at around 4.5 by 7 inches, these duodecimo books cost only around 3 livres for a single-volume work, about the price of a dozen eggs.[18] One three-volume work sold for only 7 livres 10 sols.[19] Sized and priced for a broader market, these cookbooks adopted an internal format that likewise diverged radically from earlier cookbooks. *Les Dons de Comus*, for example, offers one of the earliest and most comprehensive examples of a cookbook ordered according to nature, and it is this ordering that is perhaps most familiar to today's readers. Its distinctly recognizable form has led one scholar to describe *Les Dons de Comus* as "the first complete and methodical cookbook" aimed at a broad audience.[20]

With the single exception of a farcical piece produced by a noble, every cookbook published in France was written by a servant.[21] François de la Varenne, Pierre de Lune, and Vincent La Chapelle all indicated their servant positions and the identities of their masters in the title pages of their cookbooks.[22] François Massialot served the dukes of Chartres, Orléans, Aumont, and Louvois.[23] François Marin, author of both *Les Dons de Comus* (1739) and *La Suite des dons de Comus* (1742), worked for the maréchal de Soubise. The *cuisinier* pseudonymously identified as "Briand" in the 1750 *Dictionnaire des alimens* is reticent about the identity of his master—stating only that he was *chef de cuisine* to "M. le prince de ****"—but he nonetheless indicates that he served as a cook. It is generally agreed that Menon was a cook, but oddly little is known about this most prolific of eighteenth-century cookbook authors.[24] In rare cases, an author might avail himself of outside literary assistance in the preparation of a cookbook. The bulk of the preface of *Les Dons de Comus*, for example, has typically been attributed to two Jesuits, Pierre Brumoy and Guillaume-Hyacinthe Bougeant.[25] Contemporary readers easily discerned the difference between this section and the rest of the text, and one noted that the preface was quite simply too "full of erudition" for a work on cooking.[26] Yet however jarring this erudition might have seemed at first, a similar literary, historical, and scientific approach was quickly emulated by servant cooks in their own, competing cookbooks.

Cooks imagined the existence of a large readership of literate servants to consume their cookbooks. Menon targeted "officers of the kitchen who love their art and are jealous of its progress."[27] In another cookbook the same author sug-

COLORADO COLLEGE LIBRARY
COLORADO SPRINGS, COLORADO

gested the difference between the way a maître d'hôtel would use his volume as compared to an ordinary cook. He claimed that he wrote his earliest cookbook for his own use "knowing by experience that however skilled a cook might be, his memory does not always furnish the dishes he knows how to make at the moment he needs them." Menon entreated other cooks to participate in the project of *la cuisine moderne* by engaging with its print culture: "Cooks must not consider the use of books beneath them. It is well known that a man who only bases his work on a book could only be a bad cook if he has no foundation of knowledge in his trade [*métier*]. But when he is skilled, he is in a condition to judge a work."[28]

Cooks thus were meant to use cookbooks to learn to judge yet more cookbooks. Linked together by print, these cooks provided de facto certification and authentication of culinary knowledge. The exception proving the rule was one late eighteenth-century author who sought to differentiate his treatise on cooking from all others by declaring that it was in fact *not* intended for cooks but rather for their masters.[29]

Cooks were keenly aware of one another's printed works, and each new cookbook typically commented on its imagined position in the world of existing cookbooks, described by one author as the "Library of Cooks."[30] François Marin, for example, suggested that his own work superseded Menon's *Nouveau traité de la cuisine* (New Treatise on Cooking), which had appeared just a few months earlier.[31] The author of *Le Cuisinier gascon* (The Gascon Cook) neatly positioned his own work: "The author of *Les Dons de Comus* is knowledgeable; the *Pâtissier anglois* is witty. I pride myself only on taste."[32] A critic observed, "Everyone knows the new book titled *Les Dons de Comus*."[33] There always appeared to be room for another treatise: one cookbook noted that "it is to the public's advantage that several [cooks] work at this art."[34] The author of *La Cuisine et office de santé propre à ceux qui vivent avec œconomie et régime* (Healthful Cooking for Those Who Practice Economy and Regimen) recommended readers of "middling tables" to consult his other volume, *La Cuisinière bourgeoise* (The Bourgeois Cook); those of "great tables," his *Les Soupers de la Cour* (Court Suppers).[35] Even as cookbooks saturated the market during the 1750s, cookbook authors argued that more work remained to be done: "What! it might be said, another work on cuisine? For several years the public has been inundated with a flood of writings on this topic. I agree, but it is precisely this multiplicity of works that gives birth to this one."[36] In 1782, more than forty years after the advent of *la cuisine moderne*, one text none too modestly informed cooks of "the necessity of renouncing their old theory."[37]

Alain Girard has characterized eighteenth-century cookbooks as "a means for transmitting [cooks'] experience, the complement of an apprenticeship of word-of-mouth and demonstration."[38] Cookbook authors imagined that the rising tide of their works and their growing technical expertise would educate a new generation of cooks. According to Menon, both theory and practice "are learned nearly equally in books."[39] This theory, moreover, had the potential to revolutionize cooking. One cookbook promised, "Cooks spend their lives working without principles. Once enlightened they will be able to rationalize their art, make it understood, and in no case will they take a wrong turn."[40] Cookbooks were not shy about their imagined role in cooks' training: "Luminaries will guide [the reader] in his attempts. He will even profit from his mistakes."[41] At the same time, cookbooks swore to bring their authors tangible benefits: Girard suggests that elite cooks created "brand images" for themselves by publishing cookbooks. These cooks also sought to foster a professional community, encouraging others, especially young cooks, to study their precepts.[42] The result, Stephen Mennell writes, was "increasing technical cohesion and social prestige" among the leading cooks, who now shared "a common repertoire of methods and even of recipes."[43]

In order to justify the ambitious objectives of *la cuisine moderne*, cookbooks engaged in two parallel and complementary rhetorical strategies: one historical, the other theoretical. The first narrative suggested that cooks had effected a profound breach with the past, and it situated *la cuisine moderne* at the core of French civilization. The second argument asserted that cooking had abandoned the particular and secret knowledge associated with the taste preferences of elite individuals. Instead, cooks now claimed that generalized, open theory governed their practices. In both cases, cooks sought to demonstrate their analytical credentials. By illustrating their mastery over historical knowledge, and in particular of classical civilization, cooks claimed an intellectual pedigree. And by arguing that abstract principles undergirded their work, they assumed the mantle of analytical reason.

From Ancient to Modern

One of the defining characteristics of *la cuisine moderne* was quite simply that it claimed to be "modern," or in the case of *la nouvelle cuisine*, "new." Both of these labels, "modern" and "new," carried extraordinary weight during the eighteenth century and embodied an unprecedented way of understanding the material world. Until the seventeenth century, the "modern" had been defined only against antiquity and thus encompassed everything that had followed the fall of Rome. But in the space of just a few decades, it came to refer exclusively only to the present and to the immediate past. According to the 1694 *Dictionnaire de l'Académie française,* "modern" meant "new, recent, that which is the latest." Along with this temporal foreshortening, "modern" also began to signify not only the very newest but also the best. This semantic shift owed much to the late seventeenth-century debate that pitted ancient against modern literature.[44] As a result of the fierce dispute that erupted between partisans of antiquity and modernity, "modern" shed its neutral or even negative connotations and instead came to signal a triumphant narrative of progress. By the mid eighteenth century, the word "modern" was everywhere, and occupations as diverse as architecture, medicine, and cooking embraced modernity to demonstrate their cultural relevance.[45] Across this wide range of human activity, to be modern was to overcome the weaknesses and excess of the past, to which cooks and architects alike now consigned poor taste. "[T]here is between modern cooking and its predecessor almost the same difference as there is between modern and Gothic architecture," Menon asserted in his cookbook *La Science du maître d'hôtel confiseur.* "In place of these edifices loaded with ornament contrived with painful symmetry, an elegant simplicity makes all the beauty and principal merit of our desserts."[46]

Over the same period, "novelty" underwent a similar transformation. During the seventeenth century, the word elicited at best an ambivalent response, and "new" did not necessarily imply "better." Early definitions of "novelty" suggest how it could provoke a skeptical response: in the context of a "new thing," one dictionary claimed, novelty "is often understood in a bad way."[47] Cookbook authors of the period were equally dubious about the benefits of novelty. One cookbook warned its readers against the dangers of ice—and in particular the allegedly lethal practice of drinking iced champagne—by labeling it a "deadly novelty" and a "fatal invention."[48] A few seventeenth-century cookbooks made declarations of novelty, but the stagnant nature of that period's publishing stripped those claims of any real meaning. Nicolas de Bonnefons, for example, admitted that his 1654 *Les Délices de la campagne* (Delights of the Countryside) had languished for years before ever reaching the presses.[49] Likewise, after decades of reprints, La Varenne's *Le Cuisinier françois* and Pierre de Lune's *Le Nouveau cuisinier* could hardly purport to be new.

In contrast, the eighteenth century's *la cuisine moderne* was by definition always "modern" or "new," and from the 1730s on, one cook after another would claim to at last be revealing the true "new" cuisine. Vincent La Chapelle was the first to apply the term "modern" in his *The Modern Cook* (1733). He forcefully challenged the use of the word "new" in the continuing reeditions of La Varenne's aging mid-seventeenth-century cookbook:

Although *Le Cuisinier françois*, called "royal and bourgeois," is too old and of a nature impossible to follow anymore, not having been expanded or abridged for more than thirty years, this does not prevent the holder of the copyright [*privilège*] from putting at the head of his book that it is "new." Those who happen to be curious and want to take the trouble to examine it will find quite the opposite."[50]

La Chapelle suggested that cuisine had radically changed since the last great wave of cookbooks of the seventeenth century had appeared, and he asserted a horizon of obsolescence that radically upset earlier understanding of what constituted "new" cooking. Arguing that even the best cuisine from previous decades would no longer pass muster, La Chapelle claimed that "should the Table of a great Man be serv'd in the Taste that prevail'd twenty Years ago, it would not please the Guests, how strictly soever he might conform to the Rules laid down at that Time."[51] La Chapelle's unprecedented claims to modernity advanced an already impressive career. At the time of *The Modern Cook*'s publication, he had just left the service of Lord Chesterfield in London to cook for the prince of Orange and Nassau. He would later go on to serve Louis XV's mistress Madame de Pompadour.

Other cookbooks rapidly followed La Chapelle's example. The author of the cookbook *Les Dons de Comus* (1739) promised, "If novelty in a work were a sure guarantee of its success, I could certainly count on the singularity of my method."[52] The quickening pace of publication brought accelerating cycles of fashion, with each new cookbook proudly staking its claim to novelty. Even *La Cuisinière bourgeoise*—as if it were not novel enough with its feminine and bourgeois focus—in an early edition added the word "new" to its title, just to be safe.[53] The establishment of a relatively recent but demonstrably inferior past paved the way to establish the superiority of new, modern cuisine. Any style of cooking which preceded the 1730s by more than a few years now fell under the rubric of *l'ancienne cuisine* ("old cuisine"). Such was the emphasis on the new that one critic derided cooks for "proscribing without quarter the dishes that are any older than a year."[54]

The historical significance of *la cuisine moderne* did not end with merely a favorable comparison against the immediate past. Rather, cooks traced an extensive genealogy deep into ancient history, culminating with their work at the summit of millennia of cultural progress. In his 1691 *Le Cuisinier roial et bourgeois* (The Royal and Bourgeois Cook), François Massialot sketched an early outline of the triumphal historical narrative that would define later cookbooks, describing an occupation that had declined from antediluvian austerity into corruption and excess only to rebound in recent years. Later cookbooks greatly expanded on Massialot's model, generally opening with an assessment of diet in the state of nature. For example, despite its promise not to "write the history" of cooking, the 1739 *Les Dons de Comus* (The Gifts of Comus [the god of festivity]) offered no fewer than twenty pages following the evolution of cuisine from its origins of "simple necessity" to the current day's "modern Luculluses."[55] The cookbook suggested that the life of primitive man resembled "that of the peoples of America who, limited to simple necessity, did not yet think of surplus."[56] The 1750 *Dictionnaire des alimens* concurred that this imagined past was a time of "temperance and frugality," when there were "no cookbooks among [men], because they had no need for them." And why would they, when the "ordinary food of the first peoples of the world" consisted of "dairy [products], vegetables, bread cooked in embers, and boiled, grilled, or roasted meat?"[57]

This idyllic environment allegedly unraveled when people began to tire of the monotony: "the habit of always eating the same things gave rise to disgust; disgust gave birth to curiosity; curiosity to experimentation; and experimentation to sensuality."[58] Soon refined dining arrived from Asia, the cradle of sumptuous living. According to one cookbook, "Luxury and delicacy of the table were born in Asia among the Assyrians and Persians, and without a doubt the quality of the climate contributed more than a little to rendering these peoples so voluptuous." The Greeks next adopted Asian cuisine and began to refine it. The same cookbook claimed, "The Greeks, with their genius so appropriate for perfecting all the arts and for refining all pleasures, did not neglect those of the table."[59] Greek preeminence in cuisine was then in turn eclipsed by the Romans, who first learned and then improved upon the Greeks' secrets: "The Greeks' inventive genius burnished Roman opulence. The Romans, born to outdo everyone, soon overtook their masters."[60] Menon wrote "of Romans softened by Asian luxury, of delicate and sensual Romans, such as were a Lucullus, an Apicius, and others before and after Augustus."[61] Other contemporary cooks agreed that their Roman predecessors had encouraged the wildest excesses of ancient diners: in addition to bringing to "their tables, at immense cost, all that was most rare in the other parts of the world," they allegedly went so far as to decoct a beverage of pearls.[62] Some accounts reported still more astounding profligacy: according to the *Dictionnaire des alimens*, the Romans indulged in a dish known as the Trojan Boar, a sort of classical turducken involving a swine stuffed with a score of progressively smaller animals that culminated with a diminutive nightingale.[63] This notion of Roman gastronomic decadence was widely shared beyond the world of cooks:

Mercier reproached the Romans' culinary prodigality as matched in intensity only by the fanatical austerity of the Spartans, best exemplified by their grim "black sauce" prepared from the entrails of a hare.[64]

French cooks traced the narrative's progress forward through the catastrophe of Rome's fall, with the eventual inheritance of the "debris" of Roman cooking— through nothing other than a stroke of geographic luck—by the Italians. The neighboring French then took advantage of their own proximity to tap into the culinary wisdom of the ancients.[65] "The Italians sophisticated all of Europe, and they are the ones, without a doubt, who taught us how to cook," *Les Dons de Comus* asserted, a belief that was widely shared.[66] According to one encyclopedia entry for "cuisine," the French received "from the Italians, and especially those who served at the court of Catherine de Médicis, this art which it seems we have again refined, and which is sometimes so harmful to health."[67] The chevalier Louis de Jaucourt similarly blamed "the throng of corrupt Italians" who had accompanied de Médicis to France.[68] Despite fervent and widespread contemporary belief in this narrative, historians have thoroughly discredited the notion that any Italian, let alone Catherine de Médicis, imported Italian cuisine into early modern France.[69] Yet the accuracy of this purported connection is far less suggestive than the fact that eighteenth-century cooks and diners alike were convinced of French cuisine's Italian roots. The persistence of this myth suggests an overriding desire to establish historical continuity with ancient Rome and Greece. For French cuisine to assume an exceptional role, it required a suitable culinary genealogy, linking present-day cooks to antiquity via Italian intermediaries. Just as the Romans had inherited and elaborated on the talents of the Greeks, so the French could claim to have improved the cuisine brought from Italy. As the cook Menon declared, the Romans "refined the preparation of meats in their time, just as we can today."[70]

The self-proclaimed preeminence of French cuisine dated at least from the mid seventeenth century, when François de la Varenne declared France the leader "above and beyond all other nations of the world, of civility, courtesy and decorum in all kinds of conversations." As a result, "it is no less esteemed for its manner of living, genteel and delicate."[71] La Varenne situated cuisine within the context of an ascendant and radiant France, which already surpassed all other nations in manners and propriety. He offered his cookbook *Le Cuisinier françois* so that cooking might also constitute part of the culture other nations so desperately wanted to imitate. Yet in contrast to cooking, other aspects of French culture enjoyed the formal support of state-sponsored institutions, all devoted to the regulation of taste: the Académie française (1635) and later the Académie des

Inscriptions et Belles-Lettres (1663) promoted French language, literature, and history; painting and sculpture (1648), music (1669), and architecture (1671) each received in turn its own academy. By the eighteenth century, therefore, France had a rich tradition of establishing institutions devoted to precisely the sorts of aesthetic concerns that preoccupied cooks, even if cooks themselves were left to fend for themselves.

Nearly a century after La Varenne, *Les Dons de Comus* argued that France still maintained its lead: "France is the country where cooking is done best, and for a long time the capital has especially distinguished itself in this regard. It could not be reasonably contested that a certain elegance, propriety, and delicacy are found nowhere else."[72] Even according to a critic of *la cuisine moderne*, "thanks to the century's good taste, our dishes have become a school of civility and compliments."[73] In the absence of an institution, French cooks displayed their superiority through their prodigious output of cookbooks, surpassing their own Italian "masters" by publishing three times as many treatises, according to the claim of one cookbook.[74] By historicizing cooking, cooks situated it in a civilizational narrative and included themselves in France's cultural ascendancy. As a result, by the middle of the eighteenth century, the superiority of French cooks was unquestioned, at least among the French. And with *la cuisine moderne*, cooks claimed to have inaugurated a new age of progress, in which they could capitalize on their own achievements. Flush with the promise of modernity, cooks argued that they could trade the punishingly slow advancement of the premodern past for a future that marched steadily toward perfection.

From Secret to Open

Before *la cuisine moderne* could spread unimpeded throughout France and beyond, it needed to be packaged in an easily transmissible form. Portability, in the medium of the cookbook and in the persons of cooks themselves, provided one necessary element, but equally important was the severing of culinary knowledge of the kitchen from its exclusive association with elite individuals. Prior to the eighteenth century, any knowledge relating to cooking drew its authority not from the progress of civilization and the triumph of intellect but rather from the particular identities of noble masters. When they wrote their cookbooks, seventeenth-century cooks explicitly justified their prowess by referring to the social status of the masters they served. The authors of two of these early cookbooks, for example, proudly displayed their cooking credentials on their title pages: La Varenne worked for the marquis d'Uxelles while Pierre de Lune had served the duc de Rohan. Both claimed to have "found the secret" of cooking while in their masters' employ, with La Varenne pointing to his ten years' experience working in a single household, and de Lune happily announcing his success at "appeasing a difficult palate."[75] By relaying this hard-won secret knowledge to a wider audience, La Varenne and de Lune both burnished and exploited their masters' reputations for superior taste.

With their focus on secrecy, cookbooks comprised just one example of the broad range of "books of secrets" in vogue throughout Europe during the sixteenth and seventeenth centuries.[76] All such texts purported to expose secret knowledge gleaned from social elites, and they often present themselves as coming from the pens of noblemen, as shown by the titles of *Les Secrets du seigneur Alexis Piemontois* (The Secrets of Seigneur Alessio of Piedmont) and Pierre Erresalde's collection of cosmetics and remedies *Nouveaux secrets rares et curieux donnez charitablement au public par une personne de condition* (New Rare and Curious Secrets Charitably Given to the Public by a Person of Condition). The public's insatiable appetite for books of secrets sustained the publication of over a hundred editions and translations of the Alessio work alone between 1555 and 1699. This appetite, in turn was predicated on the perception of a chasm between elite and popular knowledge, "social secrecy," in the words of one historian of science.[77] As in the broader category of books of secrets, seventeenth-century cookbooks reveal a world where such social secrecy was the key to selling copies, with cooks modestly suggesting that they functioned merely as transparent transmitters of elite knowledge without playing any role in its formation. And indeed, given the importance placed on the social status of the secrets' purported original source, any interference on the part of cooks would have been understood as distorting and devaluing the knowledge that readers so eagerly sought. From the perspective of the recipient, secret cooking knowledge required few special skills or talents. Taste originated with elites, and cooks learned taste either by serving culturally sophisticated masters or from acquiring this knowledge secondhand, perhaps via cookbooks. Cooks played no active role in fashioning taste themselves and only served to make it manifest in the form of the dishes they served. In the pre-Enlightenment world of secret cookery, knowledge of the kitchen did not and in fact could not evolve without the direct influence of elite taste.

The transmission of knowledge from elites to the public was not without social risk, since it threatened to undermine elite authority by revealing knowledge forbidden to the masses. In the case of cookbooks, such disclosure could also jeopardize the carefully accumulated cultural capital of established cooks. For example, when Nicolas de Bonnefons promised in 1654 to enlighten readers regarding the preparations "our best cooks have become accustomed to give to all foods eaten in Paris," he effectively eliminated the competitive advantage enjoyed by these "best cooks" in the marketplace of cooks' services.⁷⁸ Cookbook authors openly acknowledged this risk: Pierre de Lune worried that his text's revelation of culinary secrets would seem "criminal" in the eyes of those cooks "not as advanced" as he.⁷⁹ But these cooks argued that whatever harm a few individual cooks might suffer, the publication of culinary secrets served a greater good. When François Massialot, a self-described "royal cook," offered in 1691 to instruct his readers "without hiding anything most fashionable and in usage at Court, in the other best tables," he assured his readers that he decided to "divulge the secrets of his art in order to oblige the public, the common good outweighing the individual." According to Massialot, the benefits of his disclosure far exceeded its risks; this author of one of the last of the secret cookbooks asserted that such a magnanimous gesture was "forgivable."⁸⁰

At least one seventeenth-century cook failed to share the general enthusiasm for couching cooking knowledge in terms of secrecy. In 1674, the author of *L'Art de bien traiter* (The Art of Entertaining Well), identified as "L.S.R.," sought to discredit the cookbooks associated with his fellow cooks' secret knowledge, promising his readers that they would "vow that [he] was right to reform this antique and disgusting manner of preparing things." Despite its claim to spring from elite tastes, L.S.R. found the existing style of cooking riddled with flaws. Along with disorder and excessive expense, it was moreover "without honor." L.S.R. ridiculed the old style of cooking, with its "mountains of roasts" and "bizarrely served" dishes. He brazenly mocked his predecessor François de la Varenne, whose recipes he labeled "absurdities and disgusting lessons." Challenging the public's mindless adherence to La Varenne's "doctrine," L.S.R. asked his readers: "Are you not already quaking at the thought of a soup of teals in mulled wine, of tenderloin in sweet sauce? Can you gaze without horror on this beef shank soup *au tailladin,* this *soupe de marmite*? That of a fried calf's head, does it not make you laugh, or rather weep out of compassion?"⁸¹

L.S.R. even questioned the judgment of those who craved La Varenne's secret knowledge, calling them a "foolish and ignorant populace." By definition, secret cookery had required a public ignorant of its details, and according to L.S.R., that ignorance had now come to represent a liability, anticipating the sentiment that cooks half a century later would unanimously share, when interest in secret cookbooks had evaporated. Although books of secrets continued to appear during the eighteenth century—*L'Albert moderne* (1768) is a notable example—cookbooks would no longer rely on the promise of revealing secrets for sales.⁸²

Whatever the risks posed by cooks divulging culinary secrets, the interests of elites were never in danger. Seventeenth-century cookbooks might undermine the authority of the few cooks fortunate enough to be privy to elite taste, but the authority of those elites themselves did not suffer. Even when L.S.R. derided his fellow cooks' perpetuation of secret cookery, he expressed no concern for elite masters, but rather for the ignorant and foolish masses who might be deceived by outmoded cookbooks. As long as the vector of cultural transmission ran from elites to cooks, cooks' roles as intermediaries did not particularly trouble anyone. This landscape remained relatively unchanged for decades, and the cookbook market stagnated at the beginning of the eighteenth century. When cookbooks promoting *la cuisine moderne* interrupted this lull, they abruptly adopted a profoundly different approach to the genesis of culinary knowledge. In contrast to the particularism of secret cooking, *la cuisine moderne* framed its knowledge in generalized and open systems that traced their roots, not to the caprice of individual nobles, but rather to rational systems founded on natural order. Thus, while the title of Menon's *Les Soupers de la Cour* (1755) suggests royal exclusivity, its preface instead makes clear the author's preference for openness, even noting that a few readers might recognize their own inventions among the cookbook's recipes.[83]

Culinary Systems

Although the particular details could vary dramatically from cookbook to cookbook, together they comprised the theory that undergirded *la cuisine moderne* and distinguished it from the allegedly disordered practices of earlier cooks. This distinction, in turn, marked cooking's transition from mere practice to knowledge. Embedded in each cookbook's form was a system of taste, and the arrangement of the cookbooks reveals something of the understood typology of food, as well as the cook's place within it. Cooks eagerly joined the effort to catalogue and order the kitchen, and their cookbooks proposed an imaginative variety of systems ranging from seasonal to alphabetic to natural. These cookbooks ultimately constituted part of the larger project of establishing typologies and classification that has long been associated with the Enlightenment. The celebrated classificatory projects of Linnaeus and Lavoisier imposed new nomenclature on the worlds of natural history and chemistry, and Diderot and d'Alembert's *Encyclopédie* sought nothing less than to organize and represent the sum total of human knowledge. Yet these well-known undertakings comprised only the most conspicuous manifestations of a much broader and deeper effort to systematize the material world. Far less visible, but drawing on the same principles, cooks aimed to theorize their own artisanal knowledge, and the impact of this program would extend far beyond the dining table. For cooks, however, such system-building was not a purely intellectual exercise devoid of practical significance.[84] Instead, the classification of food gave meaning to the materials and practices of cooking in an attempt to counter the kitchen's disorder, and both the creation and exercise of these systems empowered cooks. Tracing the evolution of these systems, we can observe the increasing importance of the "natural" and of cook's intervention into the relation between diner and nature.

Calendars

Mid-seventeenth-century cookbooks proposed culinary systems that were essentially temporal or cyclical, usually following the religious calendar. By dividing his *Le Cuisinier françois* into three sections, François de la Varenne enabled readers to plan meals based on the Church's restrictions on meat consumption. According to La Varenne, he had arranged his work "according to the diverse styles of meals that are made during days of meat, of fish, of Lent, and particularly the day of Good Friday."[85] His first section covered *gras* meals, which could incorporate any ingredients, including meat. Next La Varenne treated *maigre* foods, which excluded meat but retained eggs. Finally, he turned to the dishes that could be consumed during Lent, when even eggs were proscribed. The 1662 cookbook *L'Escole parfaite des officiers de bouche* (The Perfect School of Kitchen Officers) likewise divided its recipes between *gras* and *maigre*.[86] Nearly all of these early cookbooks contain some form of alphabetic index at the end, and even these indices sometimes distinguish between *gras* and *maigre* foods.[87]

Like secret knowledge, the liturgical formula was oppressively prescriptive. With all foods divided into essentially two categories, an essentially binary system riddled with conundrums resulted. Did eggs constitute meat? Were waterfowl to be considered fish? Questions like these plagued theologians and cooks alike. The financial implications of the answers were not inconsequential—in Paris, fish typically cost far more than meat—but seventeenth-century cookbooks tended to gloss over this detail. Physicians weighed in on the issue, since they were frequently consulted in order to substantiate the need for a medical dispensation.[88] Within households, the proscription of meat might be unevenly followed. Although one mistress dutifully ordered her cook to omit all meat from the meals of her servants on Catholic *maigre* days, she instructed him to make an exception for her Protestant chambermaid, "who is not of your religion."[89]

Because *gras* and *maigre* days occurred throughout the year, the distinction had little in common with seasonal variation in availability and quality of ingredients. In an attempt to provide a finer ordering of recipes, some seventeenth-century cooks began to structure their texts according to the seasons. Pierre de Lune divided his *Le Nouveau cuisinier* into four seasons, beginning with the "first season" of January, February, and March. With his move, we see the initiation of a shift toward a more natural order, but even with such seasonal divisions, cooks remained acutely sensitive to the importance of the religious holidays which invariably fell within one or the other of these calendar seasons. *L'Art de bien traiter* uses major Catholic feasts as points of demarcation to divide the year into seasons for which it provides appropriate recipes. Both it and de Lune proposed meals appropriate during the period running from Easter to the feast of St. John, for example. In spite of these overtures toward seasonal order, the influence of religion on the structure of seventeenth-century cookbooks remained overwhelming: it was not by chance that Nicolas de Bonnefons began his *Les Délices de la campagne* with nearly 100 pages devoted exclusively to bread and wine.[90]

In the eighteenth century, the religious distinction between *gras* and *maigre* faded in importance as an organizing principle of cookbooks. By the 1730s, cookbooks like *Les Dons de Comus* and *Le Cuisinier moderne* gave only lip service to the concepts of *gras* and *maigre* by promising to hew to them in their title-page descriptions. This decline did not go unnoticed, and the physician Philippe Hecquet lamented the unavailability of a *Le Cuisinier catholique* (The Catholic Cook) to compete with increasingly secular cookbooks.[91] In fact, the structure of these cookbooks had moved toward systems that were at once more complex and less overtly religious. Invoking the language of nature, seasonal divisions fully displaced liturgical rhythms and provided the only remaining evidence of the temporal cycles that had defined earlier cookbooks. *L'Art de bien traiter* had anticipated this shift, undertaking to reveal what one could "naturally serve during the different seasons of the year," but eighteenth-century cooks would take its system to its logical conclusion.[92] Menon, for example, prepended a letter code to each recipe heading in his *Manuel des officiers de bouche*, signifying its appropriateness either for spring, summer, fall, winter, or all seasons. Some recipes received more than one code, indicating more extensive seasonal availability. Menon had reduced to a simple formula the calculus of preparing meals according to the complexity of seasonal variety.

Alphabets

The declining influence of temporally organized systems was matched by the ascendance of more abstract, analytical models of cooking. In 1691, Massialot deviated from the typical temporal arrangement by writing an essentially alphabetically organized cookbook, with entries ranging if not all the way from A to Z at least from *abattis* (giblets) to *vive* (weever, a fish). Massialot's alphabetic taxonomy informed the design of a slew of imitators, with no fewer than three alphabetically organized "dictionaries" of the kitchen appearing by the middle of the eighteenth century and a broad range of cookbooks that included various alphabetizing strategies. The 1750 *Dictionnaire des alimens* promised that readers would find "under each of the letters of this dictionary the manner of preparing different dishes."[93] The 1762 *Dictionnaire domestique portatif* (Portable Domestic Dictionary) folded kitchen knowledge into a three-volume treatise encompassing agriculture and animal husbandry, including such esoteric topics as bee-keeping and silk production. To accommodate these astonishingly heterogeneous contents, the author hewed to a strict alphabetic arrangement.[94] Alphabetic order's accessibility was the key to its utility, according to the 1767 *Dictionnaire portatif de cuisine, d'office et de distillation* (Portable Dictionary of Cooking, Desserts, and Distillation): "Its usage is simple; it is that used in all dictionaries, whose alphabetic order comprises the entire method."[95] Alphabetic arrangement was hardly limited to "dictionaries" of cooking, with some cookbooks adopting the organization for the entire text, like Menon's *Cuisine et office de santé* (1758), and virtually every other cookbook providing some form of alphabetic tables to guide the reader.

Alphabetically arranged cookbooks thoroughly disrupted the order of older, cyclical cookbooks: *gras* and *maigre* ingredients appropriate to any season now appeared in an undifferentiated continuum. Unlike their dogmatic predecessors, these cookbooks encouraged cooks to approach their work as involving discrete building blocks. One cookbook described the method, "For example, under the word 'beef,' you will find the definition of this animal, its usage in the kitchen, and for the different parts of this animal, the diverse preparations for which they can be used."[96] Such an alphabetic arrangement served not only neophytes, but also experienced cooks, whose memory might not "always be lively enough to recall clearly."

This particular cookbook freely acknowledged that it had borrowed its contents from elsewhere, but it remained confident of the novel utility of alphabetic organization: "If this work resembles many others we currently have, it will have the particular merit of requiring no sort of work to search its contents."[97] One author suggested that dictionary form allowed for a more concise work, since it alleviated the need for a table of contents in a book that was "already too thick." Moreover, with a dictionary format, there was no need for a table of contents, since one was "easily able to find the [dishes] one can use."[98] Alphabetic ordering played at least a supporting role in most other later cookbooks, since even those which eschewed dictionary form often provided an alphabetical index of dishes. Menon's *Manuel des officiers de bouche*, for example, has an alphabetical index that includes "comments on every food and explanations of several terms of the art."[99]

Nature

If alphabetical ordering exploded cooking into modular components able to be endlessly recombined, a new emphasis on "nature" provided a theoretical framework for doing so. Beginning in the 1730s, cooks began to propose an organic system of interrelationships among foods based on natural order. Like culinary dictionaries, cookbooks that promoted these taxonomies were essentially nonlinear, ordering food into individual and infinitely recombinable elements. At the same time, they provided a system for understanding and exploiting the interrelationships among foods. François Marin gave considerable thought to the structure of his work and meticulously articulated his cookbook's organizational strategy to his readers:

> [A]fter a list of fat and lean soups, I describe the anatomy of heavy or butcher's meats. I indicate the different uses that one can make of them in the kitchen, and their varying degrees of goodness. This section includes the history of beef, veal, mutton, and lamb, which I do not separate from mutton. The pig, which is such a great resource, follows naturally, and comprises the subject of a special article. After this, I move on to poultry, and then to venison and game, and I follow the same methods as with butcher's meat. Ocean fish and freshwater fish, vegetables, and herbs make up separate articles, and finish the first part of my book.[100]

Marin purports to be following nature's rules in his ordering of subjects: pork "naturally" follows other butcher's meats; lamb is subsumed under mutton; "natural order dictates" that fowl come after butcher's meat; then the "orders" and "classes" of domestic and wild animals are treated; after meat, "order demands" a discussion of fish. Finally, "vegetables and roots naturally must follow after eggs."[101]

Adhering to natural order simultaneously freed cooks to work with the component parts of cuisine. In his *La Science du maître d'hôtel cuisinier*, Menon credits the "wisdom and fecundity of nature" with the variety of sensory and physiological experiences of dining. Small wonder that, like Marin, he sought to organize his cookbook along similar natural lines.[102] Menon proposed that the taxonomy adopted in his own cookbook would encourage its readers' creativity: "By reading this book it will be easy to profit from my ideas and to imagine an infinity of dishes to serve as either hors-d'oeuvres, side dishes, entrées, or *entremets*."[103] Revealing the stocks and sauces that could be used for any number of dishes and courses would teach Menon's readers "what is essential [in order] to be a good cook."[104] Menon urges diners to place themselves in the hands of a cook knowledgeable enough to exploit nature, "which guides him in his work, [and] when he knows how to consult it is ready to fulfill his desires: a judicious and wise mixture of natural flavors gives you a dish as healthful as it is agreeable."[105]

The proposition that cooks could think to create new dishes broke radically with the earlier understanding of cooks as mere vehicles for elite taste. In 1691, Massialot had suggested that cooks needed to know little more than the rote replication of elite dishes: "It is necessary to explain the manner of each preparation to them so that they can succeed without difficulty, and this is what we shall do in what follows, by hiding nothing of what its most in fashion and in use at the Court, and at other better tables."[106] By the 1750s, a completely different understanding of the cook's role as arbiter of taste held sway. Cooks now knew the "qualities" of the ingredients they employed; they would determine the preparations themselves. Worried that his new French cook was simply making up dishes, the duke of Newcastle wrote to his former cook Clouet for advice, who responded, "As regards his made-up *entrées* and *entremets*, French cuisine has never been anything else but making up."[107] Because expert knowledge of taste had passed from master to cook, difficulties could easily arise when a cook worked for a master of lesser taste who failed to appreciate his creations. As Clouet explained to his former master, "It is also extremely unfortunate for a cook when his master cannot judge for himself, so that he is all too often judged by critics who have no knowledge." When one Parisian cook openly feuded with his master in the 1780s—he preferred to revel in the compliments paid by his master's guests—he exposed how masters had ceased to be infallible judges of a cook's success.[108] Cooks now held the knowledge, not their masters.

Over the course of the eighteenth century, cooks transformed their occupation from a purely mechanical action to an activity that involved the mind and the hands. This shift relied on the intensive use of printed cookbooks to constitute a corpus of knowledge—one observer called it "an entirely new language"—that detached the quality of cooking from the status of its consumer.[109] Through the systematic application of the Enlightenment's most powerful organizing strategies, alphabetical and natural order, cooks established a new cultural authority that distanced them from their seventeenth-century predecessors, and indeed from the masters they served. Once cooking became something that could be known, cooks endeavored to ensure that the knowledge resided only with them.

FIVE

The Servant of Medicine

The science of cooking is the servant of medicine.
COQUINA MEDICINAE FAMULATRIX EST.
Menon, *La Science du maître d'hôtel cuisinier* (1749)

"Like all other arts, cooking has its rules and principles, and if practice has some advantages, then theory also has others," Menon observes in his 1755 cookbook *Les Soupers de la Cour* (The Court Suppers). "Only the union of the two can achieve perfection."[1] This neatly summarizes, not only the professional ambitions of cooks, but indeed the very notion of "profession" as it emerged over the first half of the eighteenth century.

A wide range of pursuits ranging from the fine arts to medicine and science began during this period to proclaim their dual dependence on both theory and practice, a marriage that practitioners contended would propel them beyond the achievements of their predecessors and elevate them above their peers. In a 1744 defense of surgery, François Quesnay described occupations that involved both the mind and the hands as "arts" that "honored those who cultivated them" and "radiated understanding and invention."[2] Along with surgeons like himself, Quesnay included in this category geometers, architects, sculptors, painters, chemists, and other "artists." In contrast, he derided the "sterile speculations" of philosophers, who used only their minds, while at the opposite extreme he lamented those occupations that "require only memory, eyes, and hands." Quesnay damned these last with the faintest of praise, identifying them merely as "skilled workers." In his view, only those rare occupations that managed to bridge the worlds of the mind and the hands could make the fullest use of human faculties.

Though perhaps more eloquent than most, Quesnay was hardly the first to make such an argument. In the 1730s, the cook Vincent La Chapelle had asserted that the interaction of theory and practice formed the core of modern cooking: "There are Rules in all Arts; and such as desire to become Masters of them must conform to those Rules, which however is not alone sufficient; Experience and a continual Practice being required, in order to attain Perfection."[3] Menon seized on this formula for culinary perfection when he sought to refine cooking's "rules and principles" by uniting theory and practice. In his 1749 cookbook *La Science du maître d'hôtel cuisinier*, Menon further expounded on the relationship between the practices of the past and the new theory in a passage surprisingly audacious even in the context of *la cuisine moderne*:

> It is agreed that skilled hands, sound judgment, a delicate palate, and sure and fine taste are the qualities absolutely necessary for a good cook. I daresay these no longer suffice. Whosoever possesses all of these talents in cooking will never be more than a manual laborer guided by routine alone, what in medicine is called an empiric. Servile slave of custom, an artist of this character will neither think of imagining some new dish nor change any practice that he has learned. And if he does, it will be only after several attempts and with much expense that he can hope for any success. But give him knowledge of the qualities of the foods he uses, of the juices with which he desires to make an agreeable mixture, and you will spare him time, labor, and money.[4]

Practical experience coupled with theoretical knowledge of cooking thus became the essential new standard by which to judge cooks, since it was this interaction between the infinitely malleable "rules" of cooking and its concrete practices that fueled *la cuisine moderne*'s vitality. Cooks who lacked this knowledge—however skilled they might be—would now be disdained. Only cooks practicing *la cuisine moderne* could always be "sure of the results of their operations" sparing both expense and danger.[5] The promise of certain results brought cooking into the realm of science, which according to one contemporary definition extended to include "certain and evident knowledge of things by their causes."[6] Like a scientist, a cook could guarantee the uniformity of his results, even when attempting to create a dish that had never before existed. Knowledge led to certainty and certainty to success.

The historian of medicine Thomas Broman has found in such arguments the most basic definition of professions, which in his analysis are nothing more than "occupations that claim to join theory and practice."[7] Although some scholars are reluctant to apply the word "profession" to the eighteenth century, this union of theory and practice, by any name, is precisely what cooks and surgeons, among others, set out to achieve.[8] In claiming to bridge the worlds of theory and practice, surgeons benefited from the unique confluence of prestige and status associated with empirical expertise and a liberal profession.[9] When Menon reflected that cooking was the "servant of medicine," he unmasked *la cuisine moderne's* radical transformation of the cook's social role. No longer simply bound within the private master-servant relationship, cooks would escape the limits of domestic service and pursue a public role as intermediaries between doctors and patients. Conceiving that their work could provide tangible improvements to the bodies of those whom they served, cooks proposed to reformulate the practices of cooking as informed by science and medicine.

Cooks focused their attention on dietetics, the medical field preoccupied with the relationship between diet and health. As mediators between diners and their dinners, cooks needed only to rewrite a role they already played. Armed with the latest chemical and medical science, they targeted two key physical functions: appetite and digestion. Through their manipulation and refinement of these faculties, cooks professed to be able to improve bodily health. Though they would succeed in convincing contemporaries that cooking could constitute a medical science, cooks ultimately would face considerably greater skepticism over whether they could wield this power responsibly.

Dietetics

Well before the introduction of *la cuisine moderne*, cooks engaged in practices that were widely believed both inside and outside the medical world to affect health. These beliefs were extremely long-standing: the blurred division between medical treatise and cookbook dated at least to ancient Greece.[10] But if the relationship between medicine and cooking was venerable, it was also moribund, and medical cookery had slid from prominence to become, in the words of one scholar, the "poor cousin" of other, more prestigious medical fields.[11] Dietetic works circulating in the eighteenth century included badly outdated texts, like the Salerno School's fifteenth-century aphorisms on dining.[12] Dietetic theory rarely evolved. In the late sixteenth century, the Bolognese physician Baldassare Pisanelli characterized dining as the "continuous transmutation of eating and drinking" required to sustain the human body.[13] In Pisanelli's analogy, deprived of proper foods, the body would simply consume itself, like a lamp running dry: "without oil, the entire wick burns."[14] More than a century later, French physicians proposed virtually unchanged models. In his own treatise on the medical properties of food, the faculty of Paris physician Louis Lémery, a member of the Académie royale des sciences, argued that food replenished the "continuous dissipation" of the human body's "own substance."[15] As late as 1790, Pisanelli's explanation of dining remained nearly unchanged, with the physician Jourdan Lecointe claiming that "the continual losses of the human body can only be healthfully replenished by daily offering the juices the most analogous to its perfect constitution, which by their nature are the most proper to feed and fortify it."[16]

From an early date, cooks openly borrowed this language of sustaining the body's functions. In 1652, for example, *Le Cuisinier françois* promised recipes that could "conserve and maintain the good state of health."[17] François Massialot's *Le Cuisinier roial et bourgeois* (1691) argued that though "all these dishes could contribute to the corruption of the body … they also serve to sustain it."[18] Beginning in the 1730s, however, the tenor of such claims shifted markedly, as cooks began to contest physicians' exclusive dominion over the discourse of food and heath. They rapidly appropriated the dietetic systems devised by physicians, creating their own tables and dictionaries of alimentary properties, along with sophisticated taxonomies of cuisine. Yet *la cuisine moderne* imagined more than just the recapitulation of existing medical wisdom. By redefining cooking as a largely scientific endeavor, cooks could claim to facilitate or even modify the chemical processes of the human body. Fully aware of the audacity of his proposal, Menon went to great lengths to demonstrate his deep respect for doctors. He promised that if cooks ever formed a guild, they would never dream of insubordination: nothing could "inspire sentiments of independence" from doctors. In exchange for this "legitimate submission," Menon demanded respect from medicine.[19] By asserting even such a self-effacing role, cooks hardly conceded to doctors. Instead they sought to convert themselves from opponents into collaborators. At the heart of this collaboration, cooks offered to exploit their unique access to two of the human body's most important functions: appetite and digestion.

Appetite

In eighteenth-century France, the words *appétit* and *goût* possessed both figurative and physical meanings, just their equivalents "appetite" and "taste" do in English. On the one hand, they explicitly referred to the physical functions of detecting flavor and sensing hunger, respectively. Through the organs of the tongue, throat, and even stomach, flavors could supposedly penetrate into the body. Likewise, at the appropriate moment, the body would desire to eat. *Appétit* could also express the "faculty of the soul by which it is capable of desiring" while *goût* signified a level of "discernment," "subtlety of judgment," and "sensibility."[20] According to the *Encyclopédie*'s entry "Goût," this duality of meaning was universal, existing "in all known languages."[21] During the eighteenth century, these terms were also closely linked to health, and physicians and laymen viewed them as essential indicators of the body's underlying condition. Physicians encouraged the belief in the relationship between appetite and health by arguing that a diner's taste preferences manifested the body's immediate physical needs through appetite. Arnulphe d'Aumont, for example, claimed that appetite served as a "source of signs appropriate for judging" the body's losses and needs.[22] According to Lémery, appetite "contributes to health" because it leads diners "to seek the foods [they] need."[23] To meet these needs, physicians proposed formulating cooking "by taste and by reason of health."[24]

This understanding of taste and appetite spread far beyond the realm of medical theory, ultimately landing in the hands of cooks. François Marin claimed that his bouillon recipe's simplicity ensured its superiority "for taste and for health."[25] By making the appropriate foods taste best at just the right moment, appetite would in an ideal world regulate consumption. Cooks agreed on this function and lauded its inherent design, with Menon writing "the sense of taste is a gift [nature] has made to us."[26] Commentators like Mercier acknowledged the relationship between appetite and health as a commonplace: "It is ceaselessly repeated to us in verse and in prose that appetite is the most perfect cook."[27] Appetite, according to this model, could potentially substitute for the skills of the cook, since it could make any food taste delicious.

Unfortunately, a diner's taste and appetite could malfunction, leading her to consume the wrong foods. According to the physician Nicolas Andry, "tastes vary, and it is ordinarily by taste rather than by principles that we judge the good and bad qualities of a food in the world. Each claims that what he likes the best is the most healthful, and thus arises this variety of opinions on the nature of each food."[28] Because in principle taste ought to have compelled diners to eat well, physicians struggled to account for disgust for otherwise salubrious foods. In an effort to explain such behavior, Lémery proposed that a bad experience with a poorly prepared meal might leave "traces in the brain," which recalled the offending meal "with violence." Doctors were similarly puzzled by disorders such as pica, which drove sufferers to eat substances wholly inappropriate for consumption, like charcoal, plaster, and soil.[29] But whatever the underlying causes, doctors recognized that appetite did not always function properly. In such cases they proposed to treat appetite, not merely as the manifestation of the body's needs, but rather as a symptom requiring its own treatment.

Physicians unsurprisingly insisted that such manipulations remain exclusively under their control. The Scottish physician George Cheyne (1671?–1743), the period's foremost expert on diet, suggested that "a doctor can attempt something to revive taste that has been lost as a result of sickness."[30] Lémery argued that doctors followed "more reliable rules" and thus avoided the perils of obeying a potentially fickle taste.[31] Food itself assumed medical dimensions as d'Aumont contrasted "the best-administered" foods with ones "of poor quality" or "inappropriate" for an individual diner's constitution.[32] As the abbé Collet warned cooks tending to sick people, "in trying to wake their appetite, they must not exceed the regime prescribed by the doctor."[33] Nonetheless, doctors' ability to manipulate the appetite remained sharply circumscribed by limited understanding of human physiology. Indeed, the diversity of the terminology used to describe the human body's relevant sensory organs suggests considerable uncertainty about exactly how the senses operated. To describe the tongue's structure, for example, medical texts used a broad and overlapping range of terms including *fibrilles* and *houppes nerveuses* (nervous fibrils and tufts), *pyramides, champignons,* and *mamelons* (nipples) to describe the same protrusions.[34]

Perhaps because of the uncertainty surrounding the operation of taste, doctors shied away from prescribing general diets.[35] "The variety of complexions, ages, regions, and seasons requires that [a diet] be administered diversely," Pisanelli had suggested, and most physicians heeded this advice.[36] Cooks seized this opportunity and appropriated similar medical language in their effort to control the appetite. Menon, for example, analyzed the effect of overly strong flavors on the "papilla" and the "fibers" of the tongue.[37] By capitalizing on their unique access to one of the body's sensory organs, cooks moreover proposed to influence metaphysical taste as well. Stimulating the anatomy of the tongue was tantamount to stimulating the spirit, and in *Les Dons de Comus,* Marin argued that cooks could affect both the palate and the mind at the same time:

> Bodily taste and spiritual taste depend equally on the configuration of the fibers and organs destined to produce their diverse sensations. The delicacy of these two sorts of tastes assuredly proves the delicacy of the organs that correspond to them, and consequently one can, it seems to me, ascend from bodily taste to a very delicate principle which is shared in some way with purely spiritual taste.[38]

Mercier delighted in the interest taken by cooks in the tongue's anatomy. He praised cooks practicing *la cuisine moderne,* who would "interrogate every nervous fiber and all the hidden marvels of a profound taste will appear by [their] address." Taking cooks' claims at face value, Mercier asserted that the best cooks exercised a taste "capable of seizing all the nuances of the nervous papilla."[39]

This manipulation of appetite was fraught with danger, since cooks risked disrupting the human body's natural preferences. Capers, for example, "naturally" carried a "disagreeable taste," but cooks could easily eliminate it by preparing them with salt and vinegar.[40] Because the sense of taste ordinarily steered diners away from capers, cooks' actions necessarily interfered with the body's self-regulation. This ability to deceive the palate led to accusations that cooks shortened lives through the production of deceptively appetizing dishes, leading to "estrangement from our forefathers' simple and frugal manner of living and on the multitude of dishes whose secret man has sought."[41] One medical guide suggested that the "sumptuosity" of princes' tables undermined their bodies, since here one was most likely to find the least healthful dishes. The author instead counseled "eating moderately and simply."[42] Lecointe painted a vivid image of the consequences of overeating:

> One is often at the table for three hours, and one eats out of habit—without appetite, taste, or pleasure—a multitude of foods because the nervous fibers of the palate and the stomach, still coated with the yesterday's badly digested foods, do not have the strength to savor the new ones. Dulled and drowned in a mucky saburra [a granular deposit of the stomach] of undigested raw bits, they have lost all their sensitivity and altered the quality of the gastric juices destined to dissolve our food.[43]

Physicians argued that diners confronted with such excess would invariably make poor choices at the table, with inevitably deleterious consequences. Dining at the wrong time of day or eating too much at a given meal could easily overwhelm the stomach, resulting in a buildup of dangerous compounds. According to Cheyne, "The inaccurate choice of foods is ordinarily the cause of the accumulation of salts [that are] so acrid and corrosive."[44] Lémery quoted the axiom "gluttony has killed more people than the sword."[45] Such criticism seeped into the popular consciousness, with one critic noting how *la cuisine moderne*'s sauces were accused of "being harmful to health through the excitement of the appetite."[46]

In an era when moderation was widely viewed as the key to longevity, cooks' ability to stimulate the appetite threatened to curtail lives. One guide to healthy living suggested, "If you lack a doctor, three things will compensate for it: happiness, moderate rest, and diet. Do not drink without thirst or eat when you have a full stomach. If you observe these things well, you will live for a long time."[47] The press sustained the notion that frugal living led to longevity: among the endless astonishing accounts of the lives of centenarians appearing in the *affiches*, the theme of moderation (often verging on asceticism) consistently appeared. Denis Gille, who had lived to be 98, "ate little" and "was never sick." Marie David purportedly reached 150 subsisting on nothing other than alms. An English beggar attained the age of 152. Frequent news accounts of fasting further supported the notion that food was intrinsically unhealthful. A thirteen-year-old boy survived for over a year without consuming food or drink: he lost nothing through secretions, his skin reputedly functioning like a snake's.[48] Even the occasional exception—Jean Jacquemot, who had lived to be 107, had allegedly smoked "at least twelve pipes a day" and drunk homemade gin as his "ordinary beverage" —proved the rule regarding food, since these immoderate individuals never overate.[49]

Manipulation of the appetite not only led to overeating; it also allegedly damaged the body, particularly when cooks overused or misused seasoning. Lémery maintained that seasoning had medical benefits, because it was "sometimes necessary to help in the digestion of foods and in their distribution."[50] Seasoning's value in such applications was a double-edged sword, since according to Lémery, cooks could easily use it to stimulate the appetite at inappropriate times, with invariably deleterious effects. According to Lémery, "[seasoning] excites in us extraordinary fermentations, which give our humors an extremely strong acridity and corrupt them in little time." Responding to the supposed reforms of *la cuisine moderne*, Lecointe was considerably less circumspect in his criticism of seasoning, declaring that overspiced dishes contained an "acridity that dries, burns, and chars our fibers, our stomach, our intestines, and spreads into our blood this voracious inflammation that consumes in little time even the most vigorous temperaments."[51]

Partisans of *la cuisine moderne* openly acknowledged the risk of seasoning. According to *La Suite des dons de Comus*, it was "ordinarily the stumbling block of the most skilled people, and the part of our work that demands the most attention." As the cookbook noted, spices were widely held to possess quasi-elemental properties that required an extraordinarily fine degree of judgment:

> Salt, pepper, and other spices—ingredients more precious than gold when they are employed properly, but true poisons when they are squandered—should be handled like gold itself and dispensed with economy and intelligence by a light hand. Otherwise, no matter what you try to do to salvage things, you will ruin all the fruit of a long labor and in the place of the crude salts that you have separated by elixation, you will substitute pure corrosives in your foods.[52]

Nearly fifty years later, Louis-Sébastien Mercier echoed this view nearly verbatim, declaring spices to be "ingredients more precious than gold when combined skillfully and dosed accordingly but true poison when they are overused."[53] The contradiction between the culinary and medical assessments of spices fueled the notion that cooks represented a mortal threat to society. The *Dictionnaire critique, pittoresque, et sentencieux*, for example, quipped that a ragout was a "dish that by its seasoning should wake the appetite and that harms the health as much as it pleases the taste."[54] Late in the century, one amateur reformer of the kitchen went so far as to suggest abandoning seasoning altogether, substituting delicious pork for the "poisonous seasonings that cooks have the bad habit of using in abundance."[55]

In the face of such skepticism, cooks countered with a delicate balancing act: *la cuisine moderne* would appease the appetite without fundamentally altering it. Menon claimed that readers would find in his cookbook nothing but "natural and simple dishes, commendable by their salubrity, which innocently flatter taste, rouse the appetite without irritating it, and whose benign flavor renders the organs joyous without altering health."[56] Using anatomical terminology, Menon elsewhere contended that he could assemble an array of flavors uniquely suited to each diner. For example, those with dull palates should consume "a dominant salt in proportion to the collapse of their organ's fibers and an acidic and corrosive juice, which by altering the tissue will make it felt."[57] For the delicate and sensitive diner, he would instead compose a "harmony of flavors," catering to the tongue the way a musician would try to please the ear.[58] Suggesting the extent to which this metaphor captured the imagination, Polycarpe Poncelet's distillation manual *La Chimie du goût et de l'odorat* (The Chemistry of Taste and Smell) proposed its own order of flavors analogous to the musical scale: "seven full notes comprise the fundamental base of sound music; the same number of basic flavors comprise the base of savory music."[59]

By invoking anatomy, cooks not only encroached on doctors' authority; they also effectively inverted the age-old notion that appetite was the best cook. Instead, the skilled cook could induce the most perfect appetite. But if cooks could play the palate like a musical instrument, how did their actions affect the body's own sense of what it ought to consume? Lémery responded that if "appetite is altered in some manner . . . all the body's functions are affected, and one suffers extremely dangerous illnesses."[60] By disrupting the sense of taste over the long term, cooks could theoretically drive the body into disrepair, since its daily needs would meet with the wrong replenishment.

Digestion

If appetite and the sense of taste acted as the gatekeeper to what entered diners' mouths, then digestion determined what permeated into their bodies by breaking down foods into their component parts. To explain this process, doctors had essentially always relied on cooking to furnish a model. As Daniel Roche explains, "For a long time, the stomach was thought of as sort of a pot that, boiling with internal heat, cooked the substances one had ingested."[61] Contemporaries were well aware of this explanation's hoariness—it dated at least to Hippocrates—but in the eighteenth century, it continued to resonate for physicians, who frequently labeled the stomach's digestive function *coction*, which could also mean "cooking."[62] Heated by the body and its organs, food broke down into its constituent parts, allowing nutrients to pass into the bloodstream. Thanks to this metaphor, the practices of the cook became entirely conflated with the process of digestion in both medical and popular discourse. In his *Traité des aliments*, Lémery described *coction* as the "preparation of foods" undertaken by the cook, involving seasoning, frying, roasting, or boiling.[63] He also noted that the wrong foods could interrupt the *coction* of the stomach, whose operation he proceeded to detail. Writing near the end of the century, Lecointe described *coction* primarily as cooking, but notably referred to undigested food as "raw."[64] Mercier on the other hand preferred the digestive sense of the word when he suggested that *la cuisine moderne*'s delicacy prepared foods for a "laudable *coction*" without the "crude parts" that would otherwise "fatigue the stomach."[65] One description of the usage of preserved foods noted that specialized *coction*—here cooking—would "render them more digestible."[66]

A variety of new mechanistic models of the stomach competed for supremacy in the seventeenth and early eighteenth centuries. Some scientists proposed that the stomach's heat or pressure broke down foods; others that a sort of crushing and rotting action dissolved them; a few that foods simply digested themselves.[67] One theory even maintained that armies of tiny worms facilitated digestion.[68] Amid this variety, the notion of *coction* continued to influence digestive theory. In 1710, the physician Raymond Vieussens, a member of the Académie royale des sciences and the Royal Society, declared digestion to be essentially a process of fermentation, a variant of the metaphor of cooking. According to Vieussens, the stomach "cooks [food] through the action of its own yeast." Vieussens likewise retained the language of the kitchen when describing the resulting "broth" produced in the stomach.[69]

As with appetite, digestion was the object of intense interest during the eighteenth century, and researchers across Europe conducted extensive experiments to uncover its secrets. The Swiss pharmacist Henri-Albert Gosse ate meticulously prepared meals and then regurgitated them at precise intervals, sifting through his vomit to identify the rate at which his stomach processed different foods. A

Scottish contemporary meanwhile did the same.[70] By the mid eighteenth century, the new science of chemistry had come to influence medical understanding of the digestive process. According to the *Encyclopédie*, "a sort of concordance of all the systems" now reigned, with chemistry largely dominating the discourse.[71] Anne-Charles Lorry argued that digestion involved a range of actions: dissolvents, movement and heat, protection against outside elements, and a natural pressure that extracted the useful elements from the crude.[72]

Unlike mechanistic models of the stomach, which largely preserved the notion that cooking and digestion were analogous processes, the growing influence of chemical theory threatened to sever the relationship between the two. Cooks responded by insisting that cooking itself was informed by chemistry. "*La cuisine moderne* is a form of chemistry," *Les Dons de Comus* announced in 1739.[73] *La Suite des dons de Comus*, added, "In effect this chemical analysis is the whole object of our art."[74] Such claims circulated widely, and by mid-century, few questioned them.[75] Writing in the *Encyclopédie*, Diderot agreed: "insofar as our cuisine is concerned, it cannot be disputed that it is an important branch of chemistry."[76] The *Encyclopédie*'s article on chemistry included a discussion of cooking, noting that "*Panificium* [breadmaking] is certainly in the domain of *chemistry*: cooking is a type of domestic *chemistry*."[77] The argument that cooking had entered the world of science convinced booksellers to categorize the latest cookbooks under the headings like "Arts and Sciences. Medicine. Chemistry" and "Pharmacopeia, Chemistry, and Alchemy."[78]

The fact that cooks laid claim to chemistry is all the more remarkable given the importance ascribed to the emerging science. For medical practitioners, chemistry represented the very latest and best in the physical understanding of the material world, and knowledge of chemistry was a sign of expertise. One surgeon seeking employment declared that he was "up to date on chemistry." A surgery student boasted that he had practiced chemistry for a "long time" and "worked in the laboratories of the most famous chemists."[79] Around the same time, pharmacists began to use a working knowledge of chemistry to elevate themselves above less-enlightened apothecaries, and later pharmacists themselves experienced further division when self-proclaimed "chemists" eschewed pharmacy.[80] Chemistry was regarded as the quintessential intellectual pursuit of the eighteenth century, just as physics had been to the seventeenth century.

The appellation "chemist" conveyed novel scientific authority: doctors identified themselves as "physician-chemists" in order to appear more knowledgeable. By claiming to harness chemical processes, cooks also exploited the growing popular appeal of chemistry. When a new edition of Poncelet's *La Chimie du goût et de l'odorat* appeared in 1774, a review declared the work "attractive by its subject." Apothecaries and other self-styled scientists carried out public demonstrations of chemistry in order to drum up business. One advertisement for such an event promised experiments on eggs and milk, and the apothecary Guillaume-François Rouelle, a member of the Académie royale des sciences, offered a chemistry course featuring "an analysis of vegetable, animal, and mineral substances."[81] None other than the founder of modern chemistry, Antoine Lavoisier, conducted intensive chemical investigation into the production of meat bouillon.[82] By comparing the specific gravity, fat, and evaporated mass of various cuts of beef from a single animal, Lavoisier sought to maximize the efficiency of food production.[83] If chemistry could involve cooking, then could cooking involved chemistry.

With the assertion that they practiced chemistry, cooks sought to invert the metaphor of cooking and digestion, just as they had intervened in the relationship between appetite and diet. In 1739, *Les Dons de Comus* asked its readers: "then what is the driving purpose of the cook if not to facilitate digestion by the preparation and cooking of meats? To aid the stomach's functions by exciting its faculties and often to change solid food into a sort of artificial chyle, such as we see in extracts and restoratives?"[84] Three years later, the book's sequel *La Suite des dons de Comus* reiterated this point, asking what the cook's function was,

> If it is not to detach these juices from their natural viscosity or the particles that envelop them by cooking, baths, and extracts so that they pass into the blood with less difficulty? If it is not to help the stomach's digestive faculties by mixture of the mildest or most active juices, according to need? If it is not also to thin the salts that render these juices corrosive and to correct their acids with appropriate ingredients?[85]

La Suite des dons de Comus openly hitched cooking to medicine and chemistry by citing Philippe Hecquet's treatise on digestion and claiming that digestion is a "sort of elixation."[86] Cooks argued that their work could actually reinforce the human body's otherwise degraded digestive capacities: one cookbook suggested that if they were to eat meat, human beings needed to cook, because they had "neither the beak, the claws, nor the teeth appropriate for this type of carnivorous lifestyle" and their stomachs were "not hot enough to digest" it, unlike those of wolves.[87] To cook was to be human.[88]

While initially chided as pretentious, such claims were soon adopted by other cooks.[89] In 1749, Menon argued that the ideal cook "subtilizes the crude parts of food" in order to separate the coarse from the refined. Moreover, cooking "perfects, purifies, and in some way spiritualizes juices." The dishes that resulted "must therefore carry into the blood a great abundance of purer and finer spirits."[90] In the pursuit of this perfection, cooks became obsessed with precisely extracting the perfect bouillon from a mountain of meats, often labeling it "quintessence." Originally an alchemical term—quite literally the fifth element— quintessence remained an important principle for chemists, who used the word to describe extraction and refinement. According to a guide to contemporary occupations, chemists had, "through long study and accomplished experience acquired the art of decomposing and extracting the quintessence of all sorts of minerals and vegetables."[91] Cookbooks placed quintessence at the center of their narratives: *Les Dons de Comus* asserted that quintessence was "the foundation of cuisine" and "soul of sauces."[92] As the notion of quintessence gained traction, one humorous dictionary quipped, "Refinement has been pushed so far that no one wants anything but quintessences and elixirs."[93] In response to these claims, the *Journal de Trévoux* admitted in a review of Menon's *La Science du maître d'hôtel cuisinier* that dishes prepared in the latest fashion might "undergo an anticipated digestion" and would thus "enter more easily into the blood and the vessels."[94] Mercier fully agreed that cooks had effectively seized control over the process of digestion, arguing that it "leaves no fat at all in its fluids, and its artfully mixed spices tone the stomach and facilitate its function so that foods are more or less easy to digest."[95] Thus if doctors had once described digestion as a sort of cooking, cooks now claimed that their cooking constituted a form of digestion. Cooks had effectively twisted medical discourse in their favor, arguing that they could improve diners' health through scientifically informed cooking.

Cooks' claims to exercise chemical knowledge found vindication in the ways that the tools of the kitchen increasingly overlapped with the equipment associated with chemistry and medicine. One merchant promised that at his shop one could find "everything concerning cooking, pastry making, and chemistry."[96] Likewise one Delaporte sold "chemistry vessels" along with porcelain, ceramics, glass bottles, and corks.[97] As early as 1682, Denis Papin introduced his "Machine," essentially a pressure cooker which could render "the oldest and toughest cow . . . as tender and good-tasting as the best-chosen meat."[98] A century later, however, cooks were offering their own scientific stoves. In 1781, Louis Nivert designed his own contraption based on the principles of "chemical chemistry," promising that it would "give an idea of the [medical] action of water and fire on foods" (fig. 5.1).[99] The cook cited his device's scientific pedigree, remarking that "if this device were hermetically sealed, it would be Papin's machine." A number of other "economical" or "scientific" stoves appeared during the eighteenth century. In 1761, one Vaniere advertised his "economical and portable kitchen hearth" ap-

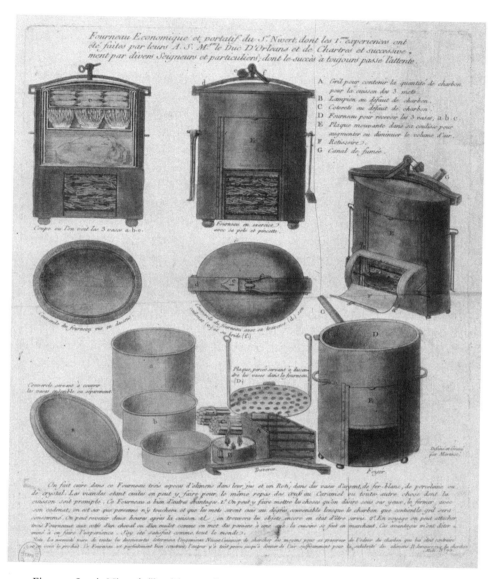

Fig. 5.1. Louis Nivert's "health stove." Louis Nivert, *Nouveau fourneaux économiques et portatifs, extrait de la Gazette de santé, du dimanche 1er octobre 1780, no. 40* (Paris: Veuve Ballard et fils, 1781). Photo: Bibliothèque nationale de France.

proved by the Académie royale des sciences and the faculty of medicine.[100] In 1790, Lecointe put his "health stove" at the center of a three-volume work on cooking and medicine.[101]

Though cooks enjoyed a measure of success in portraying their work as chemistry, they faced a far greater challenge in casting themselves as actual chemists, and they were only rarely depicted as such. Taking cooks' claims at face value, Mercier asserted that "the cook is a chemist who performs metamorphoses; he changes, he corrects nature."[102] The appellation "chemist" also applied to women. One almanac illustration (fig. 5.2) displayed a cook at work along with the accompanying verse: "Every year *nouvelle cuisine,* / Because every year tastes change; / And every day, new dishes: / So be a chemist, Justine."[103] Tellingly, this chemist-cook's kitchen was uncharacteristically spotless, with clean and orderly equipment wielded by a cook actually preparing food without any sign of promiscuity or fraud. Despite these odd cases, however, the overwhelming majority of commentators declined to endorse the notion that cooks could act as chemists. Chemistry was quite simply too dangerous to be trusted to cooks, as the title of one eighteenth-century play *Le Chimiste, ou le diable officier* (The Chemist, or the Devil Cook) suggests.[104] According to one contemporary guide to occupations, those who attempted to practice chemistry "without method and without principles . . . ruin themselves and ruin those who are stupid enough to listen to them, believe them, and lend them assistance."[105]

The Poisoner

Cooks' lofty claims to be able to regulate appetite and digestion only intensified concerns about the powerful effect of diet on health, and charges of poisoning inevitably arose. In a few rare cases, this poisoning assumed the form most familiar to today's readers: deliberate harm from the intentional addition of a toxic substance. One 1787 news account, for example, breathlessly claimed that a Paris cook had recently poisoned thirty-two people in retaliation for being fired. Although none of his alleged victims died, the accused cook had himself purportedly later consumed a lethal dose of his own poison.[106] News of the cook's suicide likely raised few eyebrows, given that convicted poisoners were burned alive and their ashes were scattered to the winds. For the most part, however, cooks were actually thought more likely to protect their masters from deliberate poisoning than to cause it. One conduct manual suggested that cooks guard the kitchen against intruders who might poison the master, warning kitchen boys to prevent anyone from approaching "either the pots or dishes, so that no one throws any-

o LA CUISINIERE. o

84.

Tous les ans nouvelle cuisine,
Car tous les ans changent les goûts;
Et tous les jours nouveaux ragoûts:
Soyez donc chimiste, Justine.

Fig. 5.2. A "chemist" prepares her *cuisine moderne. Almanach utile et agréable de la loterie de l'Ecole royale militaire, pour l'année 1760* (Paris: Prault père, 1760), pl. 84. Photo: Bibliothèque nationale de France.

thing [in them]." At the very least, the author argued, such vigilance could more-over protect the cook from being accused of making mistakes.[107] Nivert's "health stove" had safety locks and "closed with a key which you can take with you."[108]

Despite the obvious potential for high drama, a completely different kind of poisoning gripped the popular imagination, based not on deliberately slipping victims a toxic cocktail but rather on the protracted and unintentional corruption of their bodies. Unlike the calculated addition of a poison like arsenic, which was sold only as a carefully controlled substance during the eighteenth century—apothecaries who dispensed it were required to register the names, occupations, and addresses of buyers, who in turn had to be heads of households—accidental, gradual poisoning was far more difficult to control.[109] Sometimes this insidious corruption centered around the hygiene (or rather lack thereof) of the cook's practices and the cleanliness of the kitchen; in other cases it revolved around the food itself. Just as cooks were imagined to steal steadily and clandestinely from their employers, it was thought that they could injure their masters' bodies by slow and nearly imperceptible degrees.

The poisoning cook often figured in jeremiads penned by physicians and other critics. Occasionally, these cooks were portrayed as corrupting the foods they handled through their own poor hygiene and then in turn the bodies of those they served. An anecdote from the 1780s suggests the abject filthiness of the cook in the popular imagination:

> These cooks really have the blackest hands! One of them was white only on the tip of the index finger he dipped incessantly in the sauces and which he sucked. One day his master said to him, "Oh, your hands!" "Ah, monsieur! That's nothing. If only you saw my feet!" The master fled.[110]

One contemporary account noted with disdain that an older style of cooking resulted in ingredients spending "a very long time in the hands, which were not of an extreme cleanliness."[111] And if the cook's person was believed to be filthy, his cooking utensils were potentially even dirtier. One doctor urged that "molds destined to form so many sophisticated delicacies cease to be manipulated by the often disgusting hands" of cooks.[112] The cook's presumed lack of hygiene was only one aspect of a more general impropriety, which also included drunkenness. Mercier tells of one inebriated cook staggering through the production of his master's meal.[113] Women, moreover, were hardly immune to the temptations of drink, even if considered cleaner than their male counterparts—Mercier notes regarding cooks, "Female animals are in the end cleaner than males."[114] One 1785 advertisement sought a good female cook who was "sober for drink," and a historian of domestic service notes that women cooks in general reputedly had an "immoderate penchant for alcohol and sweets."[115]

An incident from the late 1780s illustrates the genuine panic incited by fears of dirty and careless cooks. One morning, a Monsieur d'Anisson summoned his cook, Pierre Lamireau, to complain about the state of his kitchen and to order Lamireau to clean the pots used to prepare the previous evening's meal. When Lamireau replied that the dishes were in a serviceable enough state, d'Anisson flew into a rage. According to Lamireau, his master "began to hurl invectives, saying that I wanted to poison him, along with similar foolishness, all driven by his madness."[116] D'Anisson's accusation of poisoning was hardly unprecedented, and it drew on a host of images depicting cooks as poisoners. These images, however, most commonly portrayed the cook's poisoning as stemming not from simple filth or negligence but rather from the ways in which cooks prepared food. For example, Bernard-François Lépicié's 1742 engraving of Chardin's *La Ratisseuse* (The Peeler) displays a cook innocently paring vegetables, while just below her an ominous snippet of verse warns readers, "When our ancestors took from nature's hands, / These vegetables, guaranteed by their simplicity / The art of making a poison of our food, / Had not yet been invented."[117] Cooks disrupted natural order through their artifice, with deleterious consequences. Such fantasies drew strength from scientific journals and medical treatises that also cultivated the image of a cook who, far from transmuting nature's bounty into healthful cuisine, produced dishes that instead corroded health. The *Journal de Trévoux* neatly declared contemporary cooking to be "an assassin art [which] hides a subtle poison beneath a pleasant sensation."[118] In each of these examples, we find the cook's "art" held accountable for producing toxins, and the poisoning was all the more dangerous inasmuch as delicious foods concealed it.

Accused of exploiting their culinary expertise to trick diners into eating dangerous foods—"pleasant poisons," in the words of one medical book—cooks allegedly transformed culinary variety into a mortal threat to bodily health.[119] Contemporaries lamented the multitude of choices facing diners, with one physician declaring, "The true poison is the great number of dishes on our tables." The same doctor placed the blame squarely at the feet of cooks, asking his readers, "Must we renounce nature's delicious pleasures because the art of the cook has transformed them into poisons?[120] The *encyclopédiste* Louis de Jaucourt savaged cooks as those who produced "poison rather than foods useful and proper for the preservation of health."[121] He attributed this danger to cooks' chemical aspirations, contrasting "our domestic chemists who work ceaselessly to poison us; and our doctors who work to cure us."[122] Even relatively benign cooks, like the one who figures in the anonymous play *Chacun son rôle: Le Médecin gourmand* (Each His Part: The Gluttonous Doctor) created irresistibly delicious food that led to overeating. Moreover, the quantity, variety, and preparations of dishes thus mattered at least as much as the quality of the foods themselves. Such concerns expressed anxiety over the cook's role as arbiter between the natural world and the human body, a role that cooks accepted and even exploited. Indeed, faced with relentless accusations, some cooks even admitted the possibility they might accidentally concoct "secret poisons."[123]

This threat of poisoning extended far beyond the master-servant relationship. Cooks were accused, for example, of endangering the health of the urban poor. One court sentence took the opportunity to blast cooks for their alleged role in the distribution and sale of illegally acquired leftovers, which "can give rise to another problem that concerns the health of this city's inhabitants, since most of the different types of meats—having been mixed together and often kept for a long time—go bad, especially during the present season, and are capable of sickening the poor people who buy them."[124] As with seducing and robbing their employers, poisoning by cooks thus had broader destabilizing social consequences, threatening not only their masters above but also the poor below. They jeopardized the health of those foolish or desperate enough to buy leftovers from them.

The Cook's Credentials

Cooks freely acknowledged the risk of poisoning. They were careful not to deny the possibility of poisoning outright. Food *did* affect health, and some cooks *had* poisoned diners, they acknowledged. One cookbook, for example, promised to exclude all "imposter dishes that under seductive enticements hide a secret poison."[125] But, as Menon artfully asked, should the entire occupation be blamed for the mistakes of a few, poorly trained cooks?[126] By acknowledging the past failures of individual cooks, *la cuisine moderne* preserved the belief that cooks could influence the human body. If cooks possessed the power to harm, then by extension they also could cure.

Cooks increasingly labeled the preparation of meats "dissection," a word that carried an unambiguously medical connotation, inasmuch as *dissequer* (to dissect) was a "surgical term" meaning "to open the body of an animal in order to study its anatomy."[127] Such terminology marked a radical departure from the traditional notion of meat carving as an essential social skill for elite men.[128] *La Suite des dons de Comus* and *Le Traité historique et pratique de la cuisine* (Historical and Practical Treatise on Cooking) each proffered "a small treatise on the dissection of meats."[129] In his *Les Soupers de la Cour*, Menon provided instructions on "the understanding and dissection of the pig."[130] A later edition of *La Cuisinière bourgeoise* asserted that it would instruct readers in "the manner of recognizing, dissecting, and serving all kinds of meats."[131] William Verral, a British disciple of the renowned French cook St. Clouet, drew a parallel between his own occupation and surgery: "a surgeon may as well attempt to make an incision with a pair of sheers *[sic]*, or open a vein with an oyster-knife, as for me to pretend to get this dinner without proper tools to do it."[132]

Cooks did persuade some diners that they could improve health. For example, a few individuals firmly believed that their cooks could cater to their bodies' needs: Bernard de Bonnard called on his servant to cook for him "in the name of [his] appetite, of health and of the especially natural pleasure of eating healthy and well-prepared things."[133] The cook Jalaguier took steps to modify meals to suit the declining health of his master—though not particularly successfully: the master lived only to thirty-two.[134] The idea that cooks could positively influence health also percolated into popular depictions. One character in the play *L'Ancienne et nouvelle cuisine* observed, "your *gigot à l'épigramme* / and your sauce Robert / cure a sick person better / than all the *Grand Albert* [a book of remedies]."[135]

Louis-Sébastien Mercier remained wholly convinced of the cook's power over health. "*La cuisine moderne* is preferable to *l'ancienne* for health as well as for taste," he asserted. "A good cook makes us live longer because he gives unction to dishes and prevents them from becoming corrosive. Nature gives us foods completely crude; the cook corrects and perfects them." Indeed, Mercier was the ultimate partisan of *la cuisine moderne*'s health claims; the new style, he wrote, was "advantageous for health, for the length of life, for the balance of humors, and therefore the balance of temperament. It is certain that we are in better health and better fed than were our fathers." He labeled the cook a "doctor-physician," albeit one who cured the "mortal illnesses" of hunger and thirst. According to Mercier, *la cuisine moderne* had already improved diet: "The interest of health is no longer separated from good taste, which has proscribed those burning juices and all those caustic dishes of *l'ancienne cuisine*."[136]

Even critics of *la cuisine moderne* viewed the shift toward medicalizing cooking as inevitable, with one skeptic predicting that "one of these days we will require *la nouvelle cuisine* to make sauces that take the place of remedies and that fortify the stomach."[137] No one challenged the belief that cooking involved chemistry, nor did anyone dispute the potential for cooks to influence the body. Instead, debate centered around whether cooks could exercise this power responsibly. Here cooks met with fierce resistance from the medical community. Lecointe vehemently argued for what amounted to a return to the seventeenth century, with cuisine "subordinated" to the master's taste and health, not the cook's own judgment.[138] From a strictly technical perspective, cooks had not proposed anything very radical, and they had mostly confined themselves to repackaging existing chemical and medical theory. Why then did they arouse such vitriolic opposition?

We can explain this distrust of cooks in part as stemming from contemporary understanding of the proper practices that surrounded science. Cooks' "disguise" of ingredients, for example, revealed a lack of scientific trustworthiness. In 1674, *L'Art de bien traiter* promised to show readers how "to prepare, disguise, and serve properly all sorts" of foods. Massialot's 1691 *Le Cuisinier roial et bourgeois* described one dining regimen as involving the disguise of dishes according to the vegetable season.[139] According to Audiger, cooks needed to know how to "disguise [foods] according to the lord's taste."[140] Disguise could assume a more literal form, too, with one cookbook providing instruction on "the art" of eliminating from slightly spoiled and "dubious" fish "the taste of fish and all bad tastes."[141] Despite the new emphasis on natural forms, cookbooks promoting *la cuisine moderne* continued to describe cooking as "disguise": the 1758 *Traité historique et pratique de la cuisine* offered instruction on disguising "all the different butcher meats that are served on the best tables."[142] Mercier wrote of a meal where dishes made with vegetables imitated "all the fish furnished by the ocean" in both flavor and appearance. Such was the transformative power of *la cuisine moderne* that Mercier furthermore claimed to have eaten other dishes "prepared with such art that I could not imagine what they could have been."[143]

According to critics of *la cuisine moderne*, the language of "disguise" undermined any pretensions to the transparent and accurate representation of nature that science demanded. What Mercier experienced as delight could just as easily induce a feeling of deception in others. As one particularly sardonic critic of cooks quipped, "The great art of *la nouvelle cuisine* is to give fish the flavor of meat, meat the flavor of fish, and to leave vegetables without any flavor at all."[144] Skilled cooks could supposedly transmute anything into a dish that was not merely edible but seemingly delectable, but these accomplishments often smacked more of quackery than of chemistry. Even Mercier recounted the tale of a cook serving his own leather breeches to his master after "boiling and macerating them in the most appetizing sauces."[145] A cookbook countered that while servant cooks possessed the ability to effect such transformations, only a public caterer (*traiteur*) would stoop to such measures: one supposedly prepared an old pair of buffalo hide gloves in a manner that the diners found "excellent."[146] Breeches and gloves sounded positively appetizing when compared to some of the raw materials reputedly utilized by unscrupulous cooks. "How many cats," Dr. Lecointe mused, "have found their tomb in the center of a pâté?"[147]

Though on the face of it preposterous, such stories must be taken seriously in one regard: they impugned cooks' capacity for moral judgment, which from the perspective of the eighteenth century also precluded the exercise of reason. Absent these qualities, cooks could not join the company of scientists, despite their success at reinventing cooking as a science. Cooks' love of disguise thus comprised just one aspect of a larger problem. These servants essentially lacked the "moral and epistemic capacity" essential to the creation and validation of scientific knowledge.[148] In this period the production of science was defined at least as much by the identities of the people behind the research as by the findings themselves. Tellingly, though scientists frequently had servants perform the experiments for them, these proxies could not themselves do science. Only the gentlemen behind the servants were recognizable as legitimate scientific practitioners. In this environment, it thus comes as little surprise that despite their scientific aspirations, servant cooks were criticized as "people who often have neither principles nor true talents" and that they judged food only by its taste, not by its scientific properties.[149] Cooks likewise failed to meet the similar standards for medical practitioners. According to one contemporary medical handbook, the best doctors possessed four qualities: intelligence, knowledge, experience, and probity. This last quality was in some measure the most important, since without it a doctor would exercise the other three "in vain." Probity alone assured the "fruit" and even the "existence" of the doctor's other qualities. Cookbooks could impart knowledge through the new theories and taxonomies of food, and cooks could gain experience in the kitchen. Even doctors acquired knowledge and experience in the same ways.[150] But how would cooks acquire intelligence and probity?

Physicians typically underpinned their diagnostic capabilities with familiarity with classical languages, a knowledge that outsiders typically lacked.[151] During the first quarter of the eighteenth century, they disparaged surgeons for requiring instruction in French rather than Latin, and they cited this ignorance as definitive proof of surgeons' inability to analyze illnesses from a theoretical perspective.[152] Unsurprisingly, when surgeons sought to move from guild to faculty in the mid eighteenth century, they lobbied for the requirement of a liberal education that would include Latin, reinforcing the notion that a command of that language was essential in order to participate fully in the intellectual culture of medicine.[153] Even for those operating decidedly outside the liberal occupations of medicine, law, and theology, Latin played something of a totemic role. The engineer Joseph Amy published his treatise on fountains and Paris's insalubrious water in both Latin and French, side by side.[154] In order to theorize and act on theory, one needed to be able to understand (and make oneself understood in) Latin.

Cooks recognized that facility with Latin signaled analytical capacity, and they larded their cookbooks with classical epigrams and literary references in a vain effort to display their intellectual credentials. When Menon made his declaration that the science of cooking is the servant of medicine, he clearly indicated the provenance of his quote, citing the commentary of Aelius Donatus on Terence's second-century-BCE comedy *Andria*. This self-conscious deployment of classical Latin (along with an earlier reference to Horace's poetry) was aimed at establishing cooks' literary and linguistic bona fides, and by extension at demonstrating a certain level of analytical expertise. But without the formal support afforded by the royal faculties that sustained physicians and surgeons, cooks' pretensions often produced anything but the desired effect. In such a seemingly inappropriate context, knowledge of Latin could be downright hilarious: Rabelais, for example, famously had his vulgar giant Gargantua learn Latin with predictably comic results. In the context of cooking, we find that contemporary dictionaries defined the epithet "kitchen Latin" as a "very nasty Latin," suggesting that in the mouths of cooks, any such intellectual pretensions degenerated into barbarism.[155]

Even more damning than cooks' lack of intellect were their myriad character defects, which adversely affected any of their efforts at science. According to Diderot, it was not just knowledge but also its dissemination that defined scientists. Unlike artists, who were "unknown, obscure, and isolated," scientists wrote about and debated their discoveries. In contrast, artists did "almost nothing for their glory."[156] Cooks, it must be admitted, arrived at the same conclusion. Menon, for example, equated dissemination with glory, writing of other authors, "I want to follow them and to glorify my art as they have glorified theirs."[157] The writing and reading of cookbooks promised moreover to clad cooking in the trappings of the liberal professions. Menon claimed that by the 1750s only bad cooks "affect[ed] to scorn the works proper to instruct them." Such cooks "would blush to be caught reading a book discussing their art." Menon urged his fellow cooks to emulate the liberal professionals who needed to read to remain current in their fields, asking them, "Does one see a doctor, lawyer, or architect blush to read books concerning his profession?"[158] Menon could hardly have been more audacious in his linking of domestic servant cooks to those perched at the occupational apex of the Third Estate.[159] For him, reading and authoring were the sine qua non of professional activity.

Unfortunately, as a medium, cookbooks could just as easily transmit bad information as good. The author of one treatise on health and dining declared that existing cookbooks like *Les Dons de Comus* and *La Cuisinière bourgeoise* were nothing more than "informal compilations that very unfaithfully gather together everything that everyone already knows." He cautioned that the information contained in these cookbooks held little worth, however "voluminous they are."[160] Even cooks acknowledged the risks of inaccuracy: one press announcement for a cookbook complained about the circulation of counterfeit copies that could potentially lead to dangerous accidents.[161] To prove its authenticity and reliability, Menon's signature adorned each legitimate copy of *La Science du maître d'hôtel, cuisinier*. According to physicians, however, it was not just cookbooks that could not be trusted; it was the cooks themselves. Dr. Lecointe offered scathing criticism of cooks' efforts to create a body of culinary knowledge, calling them "poorly digested compilations" and "scattered debris of obscure or inaccurate memoirs." Rather than facilitate the faithful transmission of knowledge, the circumstances of cooking actually conspired against it: "Good cooks communicate these things only with regret, because fear of losing their reputations or of harming their fortunes imposes on them the law of revealing only those things already known to the whole world, and of remaining silent on or disguising all the essential preparations without which one cannot succeed."[162]

Lecointe believed that under the proper conditions cooks could be controlled, and he even admitted to working "under a good cook who directed [his] first efforts."[163] Despite these exceptions, in the doctor's estimation, most cooks preferred to lie rather than to share their knowledge. Unlike scientists, who shared and validated knowledge, cooks disguised the truth to serve their own selfish aims. The majority of cooks were not "good" like Lecointe's, and they quite simply could not be trusted.

Cooks presented their work as the rational and beneficial manipulation of nature through novel combinations of ingredients and seasonings, contending that they could manipulate appetite and taste, with attendant physiological and even spiritual results. They furthermore argued that using scientific cooking methods, they could ease the process of digestion, simplifying the body's conversion of food into nutrients. In response to cooks' pretensions to medicine, doctors launched a vigorous attack on *la cuisine moderne*, labeling it a dangerous fad that threatened to destroy diners' constitutions. Yet while doctors challenged cooks' claim to function as scientists, they did not contest cooks' assertion that cooking itself was a science. Cooks thus succeeded in promoting the linkages between chemistry, cuisine, and health even as they ultimately failed to gain full recognition as legitimate practitioners of this new science.

Conclusion

Funeral elegies make people laugh, comedies make them cry, an
opera is a sonata, a poem is a history, a history is a novel.

Roland Puchot Des Alleurs, *Lettre d'un patissier anglois au
nouveau cuisinier françois* (1739)

Although cooks intended for *la cuisine moderne* to correct the deficits contemporaries imagined them to suffer, their effort to reinvent themselves often generated
precisely the opposite result. Far from being seen as imposing much needed order
on the kitchen and its practices, cooks were instead perceived as unleashing forces
they could not control. By profoundly altering the way that foods tasted, cooks
jeopardized natural order. As the Roland Puchot Des Alleurs' *Lettre d'un patissier
anglois* (Letter of an English Pastry Cook) humorously suggested, *la cuisine moderne* risked contaminating French culture as well. According to this admittedly
hyperbolic squib, cooks threatened nothing less than to turn the entire world
upside-down, undermining civilization rather than contributing to it. They were
a menace. Or at least so believed the public, which invariably considered cooks
to threaten the bodies and morals of those around them. During the eighteenth
century, a steady stream of images, texts, and performances cultivated and reinforced popular perceptions of a threatening, even terrifying cook. In paintings,
engravings, medical treatises, fictional accounts, and theatrical plays, cooks appeared as dangers, private and public, imperiling their masters and subverting
social order. Most such depictions were intended primarily to entertain, but the
relentless tide of images nonetheless encouraged the belief that cooks really could
poison, rob, and seduce their masters.

William H. Sewell has suggested that eighteenth-century representations of
women's work reveal the fantasies of "the artists and the print-buying public
about working girls," but little about the work itself.[1] One is tempted to say the
same about representations of dangerous cooks, but these fantasies in fact do tell
us something about cooks' work, at least in the way it was understood by con-

temporaries. Although most representations of cooks did indeed operate in the world of fantasy, the fears surrounding cooks had very real origins and manifestations. Representations of danger were colored both by the specific conditions of cooks' labor and by reactions to the claims they put forth about their occupation. At the same time, the fantasies embedded in these representations show the extent to which cooks and their work threatened social order.

Cooks suffered much of the same hostility directed at servants in general, who were imagined to be, in the words of Cissie Fairchilds, "lazy, lusty, dishonest, and possessed of a low-animal-like cunning."[2] Masters accordingly believed that their servants were all too ready to rob or murder them.[3] As new preferences regarding familial privacy emerged over the course of the eighteenth century, live-in servants found themselves increasingly unwelcome.[4] And yet these allegedly dangerous servants were deeply woven into the fabric of domesticity, sharing a roof with masters and serving their most basic needs. As one eighteenth-century commentator noted: "the wealth, the reputations, and the lives of masters [were] in some sense in their hands."[5] Despite this generally low opinion of domestic service, cooks were imagined as more menacing still. The dangers associated with cooks were seen, not as mere crimes of opportunity, but as either sophisticated schemes or fatal miscalculations.

Were cooks really so dangerous? In stark contrast to the dangers they were imagined to represent, studies of domestic service under the Old Regime typically conclude that servants were actually less likely to commit crimes than were members of the general population.[6] Compared with other servants, cooks appear even more innocent. Only once does a cook appear in the many pages devoted to the transgressions of domestic servants in Robert Anchel's exhaustive review of the varieties of eighteenth-century criminal behavior. This single case is decidedly underwhelming, too: the cook had fled her master after just two days on the job, taking with her some personal effects that were not her own.[7] I do not mean to suggest that cooks were always or even occasionally well behaved. However, the disparity between reported crimes and convictions and the danger cooks were imagined to represent is striking. First, there is a quantitative disjuncture. Although very few cooks were convicted as seductresses, thieves, and poisoners, they were consistently depicted as such in fictional narratives and visual imagery, and the same characterizations were frequently deployed in legal proceedings to cast doubt on cooks' moral integrity. Second, and more important, representations of danger differed qualitatively from the few documented cases of crime. Rather than pedestrian servant crimes like petty theft, cooks were instead associated with insidious seduction, covert embezzlement, and chronic poisoning.

Every aspect of cooking could potentially inspire fear: its location, its practices, the cook's body, and, of course, the food itself. Some cooks, usually women, weakened the moral framework of the households they served through dissolute behavior in and around the kitchen. Allegedly seductresses and thieves—often employing their charms as the former as a means of guaranteeing their success as the latter—such cooks perverted the order of the master-servant relationship by exercising dominion over their putative masters. Other cooks threatened bodily health by stimulating diners to overeat, and these cooks tended to be male. Either through inattention or incompetence they purportedly prepared dishes that corroded the health of their diners, effectively poisoning them. To be sure, these roles could be reversed—male cooks were sometimes accused of theft, and women could be portrayed as poisoners—and this inversion highlighted cooks' uncertain status as practitioners of an occupation that was understood as neither definitively masculine nor feminine. Unlike other contemporary workers, cooks muddled and blurred gender distinctions, which only raised further questions about the risks they posed.

Underlying all of the dangers associated with cooks was a curious tension between incompetence and expertise. On the one hand, through negligence or moral laxity, cooks could subject their masters to financial loss or poisoning. On the other hand, cooks possessed a level of expertise that potentially allowed them to inflict extraordinary harm on their masters. To defraud and embezzle required financial acumen. To deceive sophisticated and refined palates, cooks needed to effect powerful kitchen transformations. Masters found themselves losing control as cooks effortlessly gained dominion over appetites and the senses. Cooks stole away money and health imperceptibly, and by degrees masters died a slow financial and physical death. Cooks' unchecked sexuality served not the prurient interests of masters but rather servants' own desires. Most troubling of all, this assault was far from painless and usually pleasurable. Cooks fully understood the gravity of the charges leveled against them; however, in arguing that they had seized control of the kitchen and tamed its risks, they faced the irony that they appeared only more terrifying. Understanding the potential power of cooking only made cooks more dangerous, not less. At a time when skill was considered to be in the person and not the work, no amount of elevating the importance of the work could improve cooks' own individual qualities.

In addition to their perceived personal defects, cooks attempted their reforms amid particularly dire circumstances. The kitchen functioned like something of a public workshop—with all its attendant risks, sensory and otherwise—that had invaded the residence. Efforts to introduce hygiene and order to kitchen design reflected growing concerns about it. Architects had progressively distanced kitchens from the masters' space in response to the perception that their location compromised the convenience, comfort, and health of the household. Absent the oversight of the employer, however, the kitchen was essentially abandoned to slide into chaos. Rather than bringing it under control, quarantine only increased perceptions of the kitchen as remote and disorderly, and as it became ever more distant, its reputation for anarchy grew and architects inevitably intensified their efforts to shield masters from its corrupting influence. Isolated in their kitchens, in a sense neither inside nor outside the house, cooks wielded a remarkable degree of autonomy, mediating between market transactions and external filth, on the one hand, and the increasingly sheltered space of domestic comfort, on the other.

Similar feedback loops developed in response to concerns about the safety of cooks' tools and the accuracy of their account books. Despite endless worries about the danger of copper poisoning, masters never took action to ensure the proper care of kitchen utensils. Instead, cooks, whose trustworthiness was considered doubtful at best, continued to attend to the repair and maintenance of their equipment. Likewise, in the face of widespread fears of embezzlement, masters continued to trust cooks with kitchen bookkeeping. By complaining about cooks and yet failing to act, masters undermined their own authority. The bookkeeping practices that cooks employed to impose order on the kitchen—far from allaying fears about the kitchen's disarray—provoked concerns about cooks turning these skills against their masters. In the public world of print, cooks sought to distance themselves from the private contamination of domestic service by casting themselves as practitioners of a new public expertise. By marketing their services in the *affiches*, they compelled masters to negotiate with them in the essentially neutral space of the press.

Cooks' forays into the world of print went far beyond the realm of employment advertisements. In published cookbooks, they proposed nothing less than a total reinvention of cooking's role in society. By inserting it into the grand arc of civilizational progress, cooks posited cuisine as a reliable indicator of the health of the body politic, ranging from the ascetic tastes that reflected the vigor of the Roman Republic to the grotesque depravity that signaled the late Empire's decay. Tracing triumphal advancement through the seventeenth and eighteenth centuries, cooks located themselves in the vanguard of French culture, strengthening their argument to seize cultural authority from their masters. Situating *la cuisine moderne* at the head of centuries of historical development, cooks also attempted to decouple it from the vagaries of history and embark on a new era of perfection.

By crafting systems of taste that no longer derived from the identities of masters, cooks could assume a newly potent role in the master-servant relationship. The adoption of print practices associated with cookbooks would create and dissemi-nate expertise, and cooks who mastered this knowledge would inexorably drive cooking toward a state of perfection.

Finally, armed with the principles of *la cuisine moderne*, cooks attempted to establish themselves not only as engineers of taste but also as medical practitio-ners. While far from asserting any degree of equality, they positioned themselves as the worthy subordinates of doctors, carving out a new form of servitude that bound them not to their masters but to the liberal professions. Drawing on the latest in chemical and anatomical theory, cooks sought to intervene in the body's functions and to externalize them, improve them, and impart entirely novel health benefits to diners. In this effort, cooks met with mixed success. On the one hand, they largely succeeded in characterizing cooking as involving chemi-cal transformations with medically significant consequences. On the other hand, cooks encountered fierce opposition when they attempted cast themselves as re-sponsible practitioners of this science of the gullet. Although they adopted the language and knowledge of science, cooks could not make a convincing case that they could manipulate the body without harming it.

This setback does little to diminish the importance of French cooks, who played a surprising role in eighteenth-century intellectual life. They bridged the domestic and the professional, and they did so with a labor force that included both women and men, and with an expertise that made no exclusive claims to be masculine or feminine. Although far removed from scientific academies and medical faculties, cooks persuasively argued that their work brought chemical principles and operations to bear on the human body. In so doing, they elevated a corner of lowly domestic service to a highly paid occupation that contributed to the ascendancy of French culture, an enduring achievement that would persist well beyond the Old Regime. However controversial, these mechanical workers successfully transformed cooking into a science of the Enlightenment.

ABBREVIATIONS

AN Archives nationales de France
AP Archives personelles et familiales
ARS Bibliothèque de l'Arsenal
BHVP Bibliothèque historique de la ville de Paris
BNF Bibliothèque nationale de France
EST BNF Département des estampes et de la photographie
MC Minutier central des notaires de Paris
NAF BNF Manuscrits occidentaux—nouvelles acquisitions françaises

Introduction

1. Jaucourt, "Cuisine."

2. *L'Ancienne et nouvelle cuisine* (1757), BNF MSS NAF 2862, 29.

3. Macquer, *Dictionnaire raisonné universel des arts et métiers*, s.v. "Cuisine."

4. Roberti, "Ad un professore di belle lettere nel Friuli," vii. Quoted in Camporesi, *Exotic Brew*, 33.

5. Mennell, *All Manners of Food*, 96, 202; Lehmann, "Les Cuisiniers anglais face à la cuisine française," 79–80; Lehmann, "Politics in the Kitchen," 80.

6. Desjardins and Pharoux, "Le Journal de Castorland," 87.

7. Rivarol, *De l'universalité de la langue française*, 40.

8. Rosenblatt, "On the 'Misogyny' of Jean-Jacques Rousseau," 105; Colwill, "'Women's Empire' and the Sovereignty of Man."

9. For a thorough tour of the continuous evolution of the word "empire," see Pagden, *Lords of All the World*, 12–17.

10. See, e.g., Mennell, *All Manners of Food*; Wheaton, *Savoring the Past.*

11. Jean-Louis Flandrin and Philip and Mary Hyman tirelessly analyzed recipes to trace such changes. See, e.g., Flandrin, "Distinction"; id., *Arranging the Meal*; Hyman and Hyman, "Livres de cuisine"; and *Food*, ed. Flandrin, Montanari, and Sonnenfeld.

12. See, e.g., Trubek, *Haute Cuisine*; Ferguson, *Accounting for Taste*; Pinkard, *Revolution in Taste.*

13. Trubek and Ferguson note the emergence of a new style of cooking without investigating the cooks behind it. Moreover, both scholars ground their studies in the nineteenth century, when the dynamism of the previous century's cooks had already ossified into "traditional" French cooking. Spang's *Invention of the Restaurant* characterizes *la cuisine moderne* as the food of the Enlightenment and precursor to the restaurant rather than the output of servant cooks. Most recently, Pinkard has continued the trend of exclusively studying cookbooks and food, rather than the people who actually created such things—her *Revolution in Taste* even includes a lengthy appendix of contemporary recipes.

14. Baker, *Inventing the French Revolution*, 4–5.

15. Petitfrère, *Œil du maître*, focuses more narrowly on literary representations, but shares the same general interest in analyzing domestic service primarily as a relationship between master and servant. Fairchilds, *Domestic Enemies*, suggests that in the absence of a trade (*métier*), domestic service instead constituted a condition (*état*), since a servant was defined "not by the sort of work he did but instead by the fact that he lived in a household not his own in a state of dependency on its master" (3).

16. Maza, *Servants and Masters*, 291–292; Petitfrère, *Œil du maître*, 174–176. In recent years, British historians in particular have begun to question these assumptions. Hill, *Servants*, criticizes scholars for concentrating their research on the wealthiest of households, and by extension on the experiences of male servants (10). Steedman, "Service and Servitude," faults historians for essentially replicating eighteenth-century attitudes toward domestic servants through their reluctance to analyze them as workers.

17. Sewell, *Work and Revolution in France*, 24.

18. Petitfrère, *Œil du maître*, 10–12.

19. Fairchilds, *Domestic Enemies*, 236.

20. Maza, *Servants and Masters*, 328–329; Fairchilds, *Domestic Enemies*, 234–235, 240.

21. The percentage of cooks' ads placed by men by increased from 47% (1 January 1787 to 14 July 1789) to 60% (14 July 1789 to 31 December 1791).

22. *Petites affiches*, 29 January 1795.

23. Mérigot, *La Cuisinière républicaine*, 5–6.

24. Banner, "Why Women Have Not Been Great Chefs," argues, e.g., that "women have not been great chefs because the rôle has not been open to them" (212). Schiebinger, *Mind Has No Sex?* juxtaposes "domestic cooking" performed by "wife and mother" with "professional preparation of food" by "the male chef" (116). Edwards, "Patriotism à Table," contrasts "the professional cooks of private homes" and "women who cooked for their families," arguing that cookbooks targeted the former nearly without exception(246). Most recently, Davis, "Men of Taste," sets out to avoid "the problematic division between men and women's cooking" but ultimately resorts to categorizing "domestic servants, overwhelmingly female" (4) and "kitchen officers . . . primarily male" (16) as two separate groups.

25. See, e.g., Crowston, *Fabricating Women*; Hafter, *Women at Work*; Sheridan, *Louder Than Words*.

26. Hafter, *Women at Work*, 92–93, 292.

27. See, e.g., Ferguson, *Accounting for Taste*, 21. Theophano, *Eat My Words*, similarly claims that some eighteenth-century cookbook writers targeted "professional chefs" while others wrote for "a domestic audience" (172).

28. Lehmann, "Politics in the Kitchen."

29. Mennell, *All Manners of Food*, argues that Frenchness or French training was a far more powerful determinant than gender, and that in England "the gap between professional and domestic cookery was little developed" (202).

30. AN T 261/3 (1786) and BNF MSS NAF 6580, "Quelques faits se rapportant à l'histoire locale écrits par M. de St. Amans après 1750."

31. Gelfand, *Professionalizing Modern Medicine*; Ramsey, *Professional and Popular Medicine in France, 1770–1830*.

32. For a succinct characterization of the historiography of French medicine, see Jones, "Great Chain of Buying," 14–15. For a more detailed account, see Brockliss and Jones, *Medical World of Early Modern France*, 1–33. For a representative account of dynamic surgeons prevailing over backward physicians, see Wellman, *La Mettrie*, 10–33.

33. Jones, "Great Chain of Buying," 14.

34. On midwives, see Gelbart, *King's Midwife*. On dentists, see Jones, "Pulling Teeth." Brockliss and Jones, *Medical World of Early Modern France*, argues that the medical profession was anything but closed to outsiders, and that there was no formal distinction between elite and popular medicine; instead, a "penumbra" of heterogeneous competing interests orbited a "core" of incorporated physicians and surgeons (14).

35. For an overview of the genre, see Maza, *Private Lives and Public Affairs*.

ONE · *Defining the Cook*

1. Loyseau, *Traité des ordres et simples dignitez* (1610). Vardi, "Abolition of the Guilds," 707. For the influence of such models up to the French Revolution, see Sewell, "Etat, Corps, and Ordre."

2. Crowston, "Engendering the Guilds," 341. On economic organization, see Sonenscher, *Work and Wages*. For more on the social functions of the guild, see Kaplan, "Social Classification."

3. Loyseau, *Traité des ordres et simples dignitez*, 51.

4. For the low estimate, see Roche, *People of Paris*, 26. Fairchilds, *Domestic Enemies*, points to contemporary estimates and later scholarship for the higher numbers (1).

5. Davis, "Men of Taste," 35–36. Davis's work is the best and most comprehensive treatment of Paris's culinary guilds.

6. Ibid., 16.

7. Based on analysis of AN MC, Arno 1751 and Arno 1761 databases of Paris notary

records. Servants cooks are moreover likely severely underrepresented compared to guild cooks, since in these same two samples, only 744 and 695 *domestiques* appear, respectively, at a time when there were tens of thousands of servants in Paris.

8. Fairchilds, *Domestic Enemies*, 3.

9. Hafter, *Women at Work*, 291.

10. Maza, *Servants and Masters*, 291–292; Petitfrère, *Œil du maître*, 174–176.

11. Steedman, "Service and Servitude," 130. Steedman provides the best account of the ways in which eighteenth-century ideas about political economy and twentieth-century historical bias continue to color the way servants are viewed.

12. For a comprehensive account of one of the rare guilds for women workers, see Crowston, *Fabricating Women*. Under certain circumstances, women could occasionally function as masters in male guilds. For a study of such exceptions, see Hafter, "Female Masters."

13. AN 352 AP 34, Sophie Silvestre to Bernard de Bonnard (12 August 1783).

14. Claude Fleury, *Devoirs des maîtres et des domestiques*; Audiger, *La Maison reglée*; Collet, *Instructions et prières*.

15. Claude Fleury, *Devoirs des maîtres et des domestiques*, 213–214.

16. Mercier, *Tableau de Paris*, 11: 229.

17. Claude Fleury, *Devoirs des maîtres et des domestiques*, 215.

18. Ibid., 210–211.

19. See, e.g., Collet, *Instructions et prières*, 304.

20. Beginning in the mid eighteenth century, dictionaries regularly began to include "chef de cuisine" in their usage examples for "chef." See, e.g., Académie française, *Dictionnaire*, 3rd ed. (1740), s.v. "Chef."

21. Audiger, *Maison reglée*, 56.

22. Ibid., 44.

23. Claude Fleury, *Devoirs des maîtres et des domestiques*, 214.

24. AN T* 451/2 (1787).

25. AN T 261/1 (January and February 1784).

26. Audiger, *Maison reglée*, 57.

27. Although the *affiches* were primarily advertising sheets, historians who have studied them have generally neglected this commercial content, especially the notices related to employment. Censer, *French Press in the Age of Enlightenment*, e.g., focuses on the social and economic questions raised by the *affiches*. Feyel, *Annonce*, offers one possible explanation for this aversion, suggesting that the "infinite repetition" of advertisements has "discouraged analysis" (1129). Even though there is no longer a total lack of critical studies of the *affiches*, much work remains to be done. Jones, "Great Chain of Buying," seeks to focus scholars' attention on the commercial advertising that constituted the bulk of the *affiches'* content, an approach that I share, and Martin explores the *affiches'* medical advertising in depth in "Il n'y a que Maille" and *Selling Beauty*. In contrast, work that seeks to decode political culture and national identity through the pages of the *affiches* still neglects their most immediate value as artifacts of markets for a wide range of goods and services. See, e.g., Auerbach, "Encourager le commerce et répandre les lumières."

28. At first, cooks were quite literally bought and sold in these newspapers. On 18 January 1760, the *Affiches de Nantes* published the following notice: "Those wishing to purchase a negro aged about twenty, handsome, excellent subject, and good cook should contact the advertising bureau." While the *affiches* predate the arrival of employment advertisements, they do so just barely. For the most comprehensive listing of the affiches, see Sgard and Candaux, *Dictionnaire des journaux, 1600–1789.*

29. I build here on the analytical frameworks established by historians of the press. Feyel, *Annonce,* itemizes "gender, age, skills possessed or required, [and] the type of job requested or offered" (1133). Censer, *French Press in the Age of Enlightenment,* lists four general types of attributes contained in the employment: "special skills, appearance, character, and intellectual abilities" (63).

30. See, e.g., AN T 254, Pierre Lamireau to Anne Farcy.

31. See, e.g., *Petites affiches,* 6 January 1785, and 15 January 1791. A man named Gondeville, and later his wife, ran a *bureau de confiance et de sûreté pour les domestiques*—claimed to have been established for forty years—at 10, rue de Tiquetonne in Paris. A study of this agency would doubtless provide fascinating insight into another aspect of domestic service. *Petites affiches,* 10 January 1793, suggests another employment agency for servants, with an annual subscription fee. For a passing mention of such an agency, see Sabattier, *Figaro et son maître,* 23.

32. In my sample of 628 ads, 467 (74%) used the terms "age," "mature," "young," or indicated the cook's age in years.

33. *Petites affiches,* 13 January 1781 and 12 February 1795.

34. *Petites affiches,* 11 January 1781.

35. *Petites affiches,* 11 February 1779. It should be noted that French units of linear measurement ran slightly longer than their standard equivalents: one French inch equaled about 1.066 standard inches. Thus a height of five *pieds* eight *pouces* would be slightly over six feet tall in today's units.

36. *Petites affiches,* 19 January 1781.

37. *Petites affiches,* 23 January 1781.

38. *Petites affiches,* 29 January 1781.

39. *Affiches de Rouen,* 18 January 1771.

40. *Petites affiches,* 21 January 1785. *Petites affiches,* 22 January 1785.

41. *Petites affiches,* 23 January 1781.

42. *Affiches de Metz,* 20 October 1785.

43. *Petites affiches,* 4 January 1791.

44. *Petites affiches,* 13 January 1783 and 10 January 1785.

45. *Affiches de Bordeaux,* 17 May 1770.

46. *Affiches des Évêchés et Lorraine,* 4 August 1785.

47. *Affiches de Bordeaux,* 12 December 1771.

48. About 47% sought male cooks; 52% asked for female cooks.

49. See, e.g., *Petites affiches,* 6 February 1795.

50. AN 352 AP 39, Bernard de Bonnard to Sophie Silvestre (14 August 1783).

51. Mercier, *Tableau de Paris,* 5: 82.

52. Hill, *Servants,* 25.

53. *Affiches de Bordeaux*, 2 September 1773.

54. Rétif de la Bretonne, *Contemporaines communes*, 614.

55. *Affiches de Rouen*, 1 March 1771.

56. AN T* 217.

57. Audiger, *Maison reglée*, 59–60.

58. Maza, *Servants and Masters*, 277–278.

59. For the male cook's death, see AN 352 AP 4–7, 8 October 1781. Copious correspondence between Bernard and Sophie over the course of 1782 discusses the new cook. See, e.g., AN 352 AP 34, 28 June 1782 and 23 August 1782.

60. *Affiches de Metz*, 9 October 1773.

61. *Petites affiches*, 13 March 1777.

62. *Petites affiches*, 13 January, 1781.

63. In my sample, there were approximately seven times as many married cooks looking for service as masters seeking a married cook.

64. *Petites affiches*, 31 January 1785.

65. *Petites affiches*, 24 January 1789.

66. Fairchilds, *Domestic Enemies*, 81.

67. *Petites affiches*, 23 January 1775.

68. *Petites affiches*, 22 January 1781.

69. *Petites affiches*, 26 January 1783.

70. Joly de Fleury, *Mémoire pour Me. Philippe-Baptiste Michaux*, 2.

71. Ibid., 3; Joly de Fleury, *Observations sur le memoire de Barbe Lievine Pieters*, 2.

72. Of my sample of 628 advertisements, 226 (36%) specified a cook who was "known," had "good references," possessed good "morals" or "certificates" of good behavior.

73. *Affiches de Bordeaux*, 25 July 1773.

74. *Affiches de Bordeaux*, 15 January 1778.

75. *Affiches de Bordeaux*, 22 January 1778.

76. Based on a reading of a seventeenth-century conduct manual, Roche, *People of Paris*, argues that the chief requirement for servant women was that they be "good and honest" (201), but as we shall see, a woman's cooking expertise could sometimes trump her moral probity.

77. *Affiches de Bordeaux*, 16 April 1778.

78. *Affiches de Toulouse*, 8 June 1785.

79. *Petites affiches*, 29 January 1785.

80. *Petites affiches*, 11 January 1783.

81. See, e.g., *Affiches de Bordeaux*, 25 March 1773, 12 March 1778, 26 March 1778; *Petites affiches*, 16 January 1779, 28 February 1779, 24 March 1779.

82. *Affiches de Bordeaux*, 6 December 1770.

83. *Petites affiches*, 16 January 1779.

84. Censer, *French Press in the Age of Enlightenment*, 63.

85. This common phrase *peu de cuisine* appears in 17% of advertisements seeking or offering a servant who could do some cooking (105 out of 628).

86. *Affiches de Metz*, 7 August 1773.

87. *Petites affiches*, 6 February 1779.

88. *Affiches de Bordeaux*, 3 September 1778.

89. *Petites affiches*, 15 February 1779.

90. *Affiches de Bordeaux*, 7 October 1773.

91. Though commonly known simply as *La Cuisinière bourgeoise*, the cookbook was published in its first edition under the title *La Nouvelle cuisinière bourgeoise* (1746). For an account of its many editions, see Alain Girard, "Triomphe de *La Cuisinière bourgeoise*."

92. In my sample, fifty advertisements using the phrase *cuisine bourgeoise* involved women, while twenty-four involved men.

93. *Affiches de Metz*, 26 May 1785.

94. *Petites affiches*, 24 January 1789.

95. *Petites affiches*, 26 January 1785; 14 February 1785; 2 April 1781; 16 January 1783; 17 January 1791; 17 January 1789; 31 January 1789.

96. Mennell, *All Manners of Food*, 77.

97. *Petites affiches*, 16 January 1791.

98. *Affiches de Metz*, 7 August 1773. A large number of such German-speaking cooks appear, rather unsurprisingly, in Metz along the frontier.

99. *Petites affiches*, 21 January 1781.

100. *Petites affiches*, 30 April 1781.

101. *Petites affiches*, 8 January 1783.

102. *Petites affiches*, 16 January 1781.

103. *Affiches de Metz*, 9 October 1773.

104. *Affiches de Bordeaux*, 29 January 1778.

105. Sonenscher, *Work and Wages*, 70.

106. Sabattier, *Figaro et son maître*, 23–24.

107. Hecht, *Domestic Servant Class*, 152. Quoted in Hill, *Servants*, 24.

108. Sabattier, *Figaro et son maître*, 24.

109. Sgard, "Échelle des revenus," 425.

110. Sabattier, *Figaro et son maître*, 24.

111. Sgard, "Échelle des revenus," 426–427.

112. Ibid., 425.

113. See, e.g., *Affiches de Normandie*, 18 January 1771, 24 May 1771; *Affiches de Bordeaux*, 29 July 1773, 2 September 1773; *Petites affiches*, 26 January 1779, 10 January 1781; *Affiches de Metz*, 7 and 28 April 1785.

114. *Petites affiches*, 17 February 1777, 3 January 1785; *Petites affiches*, 2 April 1781; *Petites affiches*, 23 January 1775.

115. *Affiches de Bordeaux*, 13 June 1771. *Petites affiches*, 7 February 1795.

116. *Petites affiches*, 18 January 1783 and 17 January 1787. In a few extreme cases during the Revolution, cooks asked for no wage payment at all.

117. Censer, *French Press in the Age of Enlightenment*, finds that employment advertisements in the *affiches* "never discussed monetary remuneration" (63).

118. *Affiches de Toulouse*, 8 June 1785 and *Petites affiches*, 17 January 1789.

119. *Petites affiches*, 14 January 1783.

120. *Petites affiches*, 2 January 1785.

121. Mercier, *Tableau de Paris*, 10: 343–344.

122. Rétif de la Bretonne, *Contemporaines communes*, 609.

123. *Petites affiches*, 15 January 1785.

124. *Affiches de Toulouse*, 30 November 1785.

125. *Petites affiches*, 10 January 1793.

126. Voltaire, "Lettre à l'occasion de l'impôt du vingtième," 306.

127. Mercier, *Tableau de Paris*, 5: 78.

128. MC ET/XXXV/653 (10 April 1748).

129. Mennell, *All Manners of Food*, 202.

130. To the cook and the pastry cook, he suggested 300 and 200 livres, respectively. For the two kitchen boys, the one pastry boy, and the kitchen girl, he counseled 75 livres each. Audiger, *Maison reglée*, 12–13.

131. Maza, *Servants and Masters*, 279–282.

132. AN T 261/3 (1784–1786).

133. AN T 451/7 (1778–1780).

134. AN T 491/2 (1777).

135. AN T* 201/3 (1743–1750); AN T* 491/2 (1745–1761); AN T 451/7 (1778–1779); AN T 491/3 (1786–1787).

136. AN T* 491/2 (1745–1761).

137. *Affiches de Rouen*, 20 September 1771.

138. *Petites affiches* 15 January 1785.

139. Maza, *Servants and Masters*, 102.

140. *Petites affiches*, 31 January 1789.

141. *Affiches de Toulouse*, 30 November 1785.

142. AN T* 491/2 (1745–1761).

143. BNF MSS Joly de Fleury 2489–2490.

144. Mercier, *Tableau de Paris*, 12: 316.

145. See, e.g., *Essai sur la préparation des alimens*, 8.

146. La Varenne, *Cuisinier françois*, "Le Libraire au Lecteur."

147. Roche, *People of Paris*, finds that over 90% of servants in Paris were from the provinces (26).

148. Rétif de la Bretonne, *Contemporaines communes*, 607.

149. *Maltôte des cuisinieres*, 2.

150. AN T* 491/2 (1745–1761).

151. The description describes the cook as assuming the elegant "tone" rather than "airs" of Paris. *Galerie des modes et costumes français*, pl. 11.

152. Hufton, *Poor*, 95–96.

153. Braudel, *Civilization and Capitalism, 15th–18th Century: The Structures of Everyday Life*, 203.

154. Mercier, *Tableau de Paris*, 10: 343.

155. Lune, *Nouveau cuisinier*, "Au lecteur."

156. *Affiches de Rouen*, 18 January 1771.

157. *Petites affiches*, 25 March 1779.

158. *Affiches de Bordeaux*, 20 June 1771.

159. For more on French cooks moving abroad, see Wheaton, *Savoring the Past*, 160–172.

160. *Affiches de Bordeaux*, 17 May 1770.

161. *Petites affiches*, 20 April 1781.

162. *Petites affiches*, 24 January 1783.

163. *Affiches de Nantes*, 16 December 1763.

164. Mennell, *All Manners of Food*, 202.

165. Sedgwick, "Duke of Newcastle's Cook."

166. *Petites affiches*, 17 January 1789.

167. AN T 254 (7 February 1788).

168. AN 352 AP 34, Sophie Silvestre to Bernard de Bonnard (10 November 1782).

169. Mercier, *Tableau de Paris*, 10: 343.

170. Collet, *Instructions et prières*, 307.

171. AN T* 451/2; AN T 261/3.

172. La Chapelle, *Cuisinier moderne*, 3, 7–8.

173. BNF MSS Joly de Fleury 2490 (1772).

174. AN T 261/1 (April 1787).

175. AN T* 201/17.

176. Crowston, "Engendering the Guilds," 341.

177. Figures based on a comprehensive Arno search of the notarial records for 1751 and 1761, AN MC.

178. For more on the knowledge assumed by eighteenth-century cookbooks, see Sherman, "'Whole Art and Mystery of Cooking.'"

179. *Essai sur la préparation des alimens*, 8–9.

180. The process of training remains largely unknown even for occupations that had guilds, according to Crouzet, "Some Remarks on the *métiers d'art*," 271–272.

181. *Petites affiches*, 6 February 1779; *Petites affiches*, 12 January 1783.

182. Lune, *Nouveau cuisinier*, "Au lecteur."

183. *Petites affiches*, 18 March 1779; *Petites affiches*, 3 April 1781.

184. AN 352 AP 39, Bernard de Bonnard to Sophie Silvestre (10 September 1783).

185. AN T* 201/3; AN T 491/2; AN T* 470/35.

186. La Chapelle, *Cuisinier moderne*, 8.

187. Mennell, *All Manners of Food*, 77.

188. *Petites affiches*, 8 January 1783.

189. *Affiches de Bordeaux*, 10 September 1778.

190. *Petites affiches*, 17 January 1789.

191. AN T 254, Pierre Lamireau to Anne Farcy, 1786.

192. Goodman, *Republic of Letters*, 58–60, 185.

193. Mercier, *Tableau de Paris*, 11: 234–235.

194. Quoted in Sedgwick, "Duke of Newcastle's Cook," 315. Translation Sedgwick's.

195. Mercier, *Tableau de Paris*, 11: 233.

196. AN T* 265/2 (June 1787 to July 1789).

197. AN T* 491/2 (1748).
198. AN T* 201/3 (1752).
199. Mercier, *Tableau de Paris*, 10: 344.
200. AN T* 261/4 (1787).
201. *Petites affiches*, 16 January 1783; 8 January 1787; 20 January 1787.
202. Troyansky, *Old Age in the Old Regime*, 185–186, 193–202.
203. Ibid., 192–193.
204. Viollet de Wagnon, *Auteur laquais*, 120. Troyansky finds just one example of servant receiving a pension (147).
205. AN T* 479/36 (30 June 1754); AN T* 470/35 (1754–1756); AN 4 AP 297 (1785); AN T 491/2 (late 1770s).
206. *Mémoire pour la comtesse de Varneville*, 17.
207. *Affiches de Rouen*, 12 July 1771.
208. MC ET/XXIX/415 (15 December 1733); AN T* 491/2 (1745–1761); MC ET/XIV/342 (27 June 1751).
209. *Petites affiches*, 24 March 1779.
210. *Petites affiches*, 13 January 1781; 25 April 1781; 3 January 1789; 16 January 1783; 20 January 1787; 14 January 1779; 11 January 1783.
211. *Petites affiches*, 3 January 1789.
212. Mercier, *Tableau de Paris*, 10: 340.
213. *Ancienne et nouvelle cuisine* (1757), BNF NAF 2862, 27.
214. Nivert, *Nouveau fourneaux économiques et portatifs*.
215. Ramazzini, *Essai sur les maladies des artisans*, lv.
216. In addition to the deaths mentioned in household wage records, Bernard de Bonnard's cook also simply worked until his death in 1781. AN 352 AP 4–7, 8 October 1781.
217. Crowston, "Engendering the Guilds," 343.

TWO · *Corrupting Spaces*

1. Le Camus de Mézières, *Génie*, 191–194, 193, 195, 201.
2. For relevant descriptions in architectural manuals, see Leblond, "De la nouvelle manière," 185*11; Briseux, *Architecture moderne*, 56; Blondel, *De la distribution des maisons de plaisance*, 1: 83; Jombert, *Architecture moderne*, 114; Le Camus de Mézières, *Génie*, 191. For an archival description of such a kitchen, see AN T 208/2, f. 2.
3. AN T 447/3, f. 3. Leblond, "De la nouvelle manière," 185*11.
4. Briseux, *Architecture moderne*, 56; Jombert, *Architecture moderne*, 114.
5. Savot, *Architecture françoise des bastimens particuliers* (1624), 67; Blondel, *De la distribution des maisons de plaisance*, 1: 83; Le Camus de Mézières, *Génie*, 192.
6. AN T 212/1 (white); AN T 208/8, f. 140 (gray); AN T 261/4; AN T 208/8, f. 140; AN T 261/4, f. 10.
7. The ancien régime's great innovation in kitchen heating was the seventeenth-century *fourneau*, or stove. Sylvie Girard, *Histoire des objets de cuisine et de gourmandise*, 225. The stove made its first dictionary appearance in 1694, but Carbonnier, *Mai-*

sons parisiennes des lumières, suggests that it became common after 1750 (326). Revel, *Culture and Cuisine,* likewise locates its arrival in the eighteenth century (190).

8. AN T 261/1, AN T 254, and AN T 208/3 (1787). Le Camus de Mézières, *Génie,* 193.

9. Worktables appear in several kitchens in Blondel, *Architecture françoise,* e.g., *distribution* XVI, pl. 2, and *distribution* XXX, pl. 1. "In the middle of the room there will be a long table of beech wood." Guadet, *Élements et théorie,* stresses the importance of having a table as large as possible (118–119). Sinks are mentioned in a number of architectural treatises, e.g., Le Camus de Mézières, *Génie,* 193.

10. The only potentially unfamiliar element would have been the stove, or *potager,* a seventeenth-century innovation that became common in the eighteenth century. For a brief history of the innovation of the stove, see Sylvie Girard, *Histoire des objets de cuisine et de gourmandise,* 225.

11. Mignot, "De la cuisine à la salle à manger," 21, 27. Le Muet was also arguably the inventor of the modern dining room. For an account of the novelty of the dining room and its significance, see Collins, "Problem of the Enlightenment Salon," 157–167.

12. Mignot, "De la cuisine à la salle à manger," 20–21.

13. Savot, *Architecture françoise des bastimens particuliers* (1624), 66, 68. The *salle de commun* was typically located adjacent to the kitchen for convenience.

14. Bullet, *Architecture pratique,* 62–63.

15. Mignot, "De la cuisine à la salle à manger," 16–18. I am numbering the floors according to American convention. In French usage, the *appartement* was moved from the *rez-de-chaussée* to the *premier étage.*

16. Guadet, *Élements et théorie,* however, suggests that the basement kitchen was an English import (115).

17. Mignot, "De la cuisine à la salle à manger," 30. Mignot identifies the period 1640–1660 as the height of the popularity of the "Roman" kitchen. Architectural historians typically identify Blondel as overly enthralled by the ancients, though here he clearly displays a preference for "modern" forms.

18. Savot, *Architecture françoise des bastimens particuliers* (1673), 42, quoted in Mignot, "De la cuisine à la salle à manger," 21. Mignot attributes these remarks to Savot and implies that they are contemporaneous with Le Muet, *Manière de bien bastir pour touttes* [sic] *sortes de personnes* (1623), but since they do not appear in earlier editions, it is far more likely that they are by François Blondel, who edited the 1673 edition of Savot.

19. This preference for Roman design proved cyclical and was revived in the early nineteenth century in Dubut, *Architecture civile.* Dubut placed all kitchens in the *corps de logis;* most were on the ground floor without even a mezzanine to insulate them from the apartments above. For a comprehensive account of the debate between ancient and modern styles, see DeJean, *Ancients Against Moderns.*

20. I borrow the translation "space planning" from Benhamou, "Parallel Walls, Parallel Worlds," 2n7.

21. The best recent study of the transformation of Parisian residential space is

Carbonnier, *Maisons parisiennes des lumières*. Coquery, *Hôtel aristocratique*, has explored the central role of these new residential spaces in urban commerce. For a treatment of Parisian residences in English, see Gallet, *Paris Domestic Architecture of the 18th Century*. The most influential study of the sociological function of the period's residential design remains Elias, *Court Society*.

22. Blondel, "Distribution." Although described in detail in the *Encyclopédie*, the architectural sense of *la distribution* did not appear in the *Dictionnaire de l'Académie française* until 1835.

23. Goodman, *Republic of Letters*, 84–89.

24. Blondel, *Architecture françoise*, 21.

25. Ibid., 21–22. According to a handwritten liner note (likely by the marquis de Paulmy), Blondel was "one of the greatest theorists we have in France of his art." See BNF Arsenal copy (4° ScA 4144). Concurring with this assessment of Blondel's talents, Eleb-Vidal and Debarre-Blanchard call him a "great theorist" (*Architectures de la vie privée*, 40). Blondel's remarkable achievements included the contribution of over four hundred articles to the *Encyclopédie* (Benhamou, "Parallel Walls, Parallel Worlds," 1).

26. Blondel, "Distribution."

27. The eighteenth-century architectural lexicon included five classical orders: Doric, Tuscan, Ionic, Corinthian, and composite, or Roman. See, e.g., "Ordre" in the *Encyclopédie*.

28. Alembert, "Moderne."

29. Leblond, "De la nouvelle manière," 185*3, 185*4.

30. Briseux, *Architecture moderne*, 56.

31. Jombert, *Architecture moderne*, 113.

32. Architects also frequently referred to *convenance*, which is often translated as "convenience" or "decorum." See Benhamou, "Parallel Walls, Parallel Worlds," 1. For a recent study of how the emerging idea of comfort structured eighteenth-century furnishings and residential space (though with no discussion of the kitchen), see DeJean, *Age of Comfort*.

33. Leblond, "De la nouvelle manière," 185*1, 185*3.

34. Jombert, *Architecture moderne*, 113.

35. Blondel, *Architecture françoise*, 269.

36. Gallet, *Paris Domestic Architecture of the 18th Century*, 65.

37. Leblond, "De la nouvelle manière," 185*3.

38. Briseux, *Architecture moderne*, 56.

39. Collet, *Instructions et prières*, 306. The *office* prepared fruits and sweets; it could be incorporated into the kitchen or have its own distinct space.

40. *Relation de ce qui s'est fait et passé au sujet d'une Cuisinière qui avoit trois maris vivans*.

41. Corbin, *Foul and the Fragrant*, 166.

42. Savot, *Architecture françoise des bastimens particuliers* (1673), 42. François Blondel likely added this complaint to Savot's 1624 work.

43. Leblond, "De la nouvelle manière," 185*3.

44. Blondel, *De la distribution des maisons de plaisance*, 1: 38.

45. Architectural illustrations scrupulously depicted the kitchen's never-ending smoke. The "Veue et perspective de l'Hostel de Bautru, du dessien de Mr. le Veau" in Marot, *Architecture françoise*, 96, shows black clouds rising from the kitchen wing's chimney and none from any of the others.

46. Jombert, *Architecture moderne*, 113.

47. Leblond, "De la nouvelle manière," 185*3.

48. Poncelet, *Chimie du goût et de l'odorat*, xiv.

49. *Essai sur la préparation des alimens*, 32.

50. Le Camus de Mézières, *Génie*, 193.

51. Mercier, *Tableau de Paris*, 1: 213.

52. *Étrennes aux vivans*, 2.

53. Leblond, "De la nouvelle manière," 185*10; Le Camus de Mézières, *Génie*, 201. Leblond urged the use of separate dining areas for servants "to feed the servants and prevent them from interfering in the kitchen by gathering there."

54. Maza, *Servants and Masters*, 143.

55. Leblond, "De la nouvelle manière," 185*1–185*2.

56. See, e.g., Blondel, "Distribution."

57. Blondel, *De la distribution des maisons de plaisance*, 1: 79.

58. Le Camus de Mézières, *Génie*, 202.

59. Bastide, *The Little House*, 98.

60. Ibid., 99–100. DeJean describes other examples of such "flying" tables in *Age of Comfort*, 134–135.

61. Gallet, *Paris Domestic Architecture of the 18th Century*, 114.

62. Blondel, *De la distribution des maisons de plaisance*, 1: 82.

63. Leblond, "De la nouvelle manière," 185*3.

64. Blondel, "Distribution."

65. For a detailed examination of this division of space, see Benhamou, "Parallel Walls, Parallel Worlds."

66. Blondel, *De la distribution des maisons de plaisance*, 2: 123.

67. Leblond, "De la nouvelle manière," 185*3. Jombert, *Architecture moderne*, 114, also seeks to cover food for the outdoor journey from kitchen to dining room.

68. Leblond, "De la nouvelle manière," 185*12. Subordinate kitchen staff in contrast did not need to sleep nearby, e.g., a kitchen assistant could sleep just about anywhere, even "under the eaves." Le Camus de Mézières, *Génie*, 212.

69. Blondel, *De la distribution des maisons de plaisance*, 1: 81.

70. Blondel, *Architecture françoise, distribution* XII, pl. 1.

71. Leblond, "De la nouvelle manière," 185*12; Briseux, *Architecture moderne*, 56.

72. AN O 1/1680 (1757).

73. AN 352 AP 34, 23 August 1782.

74. Le Camus de Mézières, *Génie*, 212.

75. Blondel, *De la distribution des maisons de plaisance*, 1: 81.

76. Claude Fleury, *Devoirs des maîtres et des domestiques*, 211; Collet, *Instructions et prières*, 305.

77. Claude Fleury, *Devoirs des maîtres et des domestiques*, 220–221.

78. Cited in Petitfrère, *Œil du maître*, 164.

79. Lesage, *Histoire de Gil Blas de Santillane*, 2: 84–85.

80. *Mercure de France*, April 1735.

81. Maza, *Servants and Masters*, 143.

82. This fantasy excluded male cooks, however, whom images typically depicted as monstrously obese individuals wielding large knives.

83. The original of Boucher's *La Cuisinière* has since returned to France and is today displayed at the Musée Cognacq-Jay in Paris.

84. *Mercure de France*, June 1737 and June 1738.

85. Schroder, "Genre Prints," 83.

86. *La Belle Villageoise* (Paris: Huquier, ca. 1735). Musée du Louvre, Cabinet des dessins, Collection Edmond de Rothschild 19009 LR. Kíthira, one of the Ionian Islands, is the mythical home of Aphrodite. For notice of the two images as pendants, see *Mercure de France*, June 1737.

87. Louis Surugue, after *Le Hachis d'oignons,* a painting by Gerrit Dou (1613–1675), now in the Royal Collection in London. BNF EST MD 43 fol R 4643.

88. Surugue after a painting by Jacob van Schuppen, *La Cuisinière.* BNF EST ED 96 Fol. The engraving is undated, but Surugue was active at the engraving's address during the mid eighteenth century. Portalis and Béraldi, *Graveurs du dix-huitième siècle,* 3: 575–578.

89. *L'Ancienne et nouvelle cuisine* (1757). BNF MSS NAF 2862.

90. Rétif de la Bretonne, *Contemporaines communes*, 608–609.

91. AN 352 AP 34, 28 June 1782.

92. *Relation de ce qui s'est fait et passé au sujet d'une Cuisinière qui avoit trois maris vivans.*

93. Maza, *Private Lives and Public Affairs.*

94. Joly de Fleury, *Observations sur le mémoire de Barbe Lievine Pieters*, 6–7.

95. Ibid., 3. Marie Forcade's brief also refered to the cook's "indecent complacency."

96. Ibid., 2–3.

97. Yet cooks apparently did occasionally dine with their masters. An ad seeking a cook in *Affiches de Bordeaux*, 2 September 1773, said that "she would eat at the masters' table." At the same time, other advertisements suggest the importance of maintaining a strict division between servants and masters, with one young man seeking a position in a household where he would be "neither servant nor regarded as one." *Petites affiches*, 6 February 1779.

98. Joly de Fleury, *Observations sur le mémoire de Barbe Lievine Pieters*, 6, 8.

99. Farge, "Work-Related Diseases," 93–94.

100. Ramazzini, *Essai sur les maladies des artisans*, lv, 504–509.

101. See, e.g., *Gazette de santé*, 19 January 1775, 26 January 1775, 9 March 1775, 23 March 1775.

102. Nivert, *Nouveau fourneaux économiques et portatifs.*

103. Lecointe, *Cuisine de santé*, 1: 36.

104. Mercier, *Tableau de Paris*, 5: 255.

105. Among seventeenth-century architects, Le Muet alone discusses kitchens in the context of health. In his section "Quant à la santé des appartemens," he recommends that builders situate subterranean kitchens with half of their height above ground level. Le Muet, *Manière de bien bastir pour toutes sortes de personnes* (1623), 4.

106. Leblond, "De la nouvelle manière," 185*3.

107. Jombert, *Architecture moderne*, 114.

108. See, e.g., the warnings against water where "the sun no longer shines upon it." Such waters would always "spoil the soonest" and give rise to "turbid and darkish" vapors. Hippocrates, *On Airs, Waters, and Places*.

109. Leblond, "De la nouvelle manière," 185*2; Le Camus de Mézières, *Génie*, 191.

110. Leblond, "De la nouvelle manière," 185*11; Briseux, *Architecture moderne*, 56.

111. Leblond, "De la nouvelle manière," 185*3.

112. Le Camus de Mézières, *Génie*, 191.

113. Blondel, *De la distribution des maisons de plaisance*, 1: 83.

114. AN O 1/1680 (1757).

115. AN T 208/1. The new casement window would have twenty panes.

116. Leblond, "De la nouvelle manière," 185*11–185*12. Leblond suggested that the water arrive "through pipes coming from reservoirs or otherwise through the proximity of a well placed in one of its corners."

117. Jombert, *Architecture moderne*, 114.

118. Le Camus de Mézières, *Génie*, 193.

119. Roche, "Le Temps de l'eau rare," 384–385.

120. Amy, *Nouvelles fontaines domestiques*, 4. According to Amy, such devices had been in use for "nearly two centuries." Joly de Fleury's household records indicate repairs to his sand-filtered fountain, BNF MSS Joly de Fleury 2490, 111. Two such fountains are listed (in poor condition and without sand) in the notary record of the sale of a kitchen's tools, MC ET/CV/1274 (19 April 1761). They also often appear in contemporary images of the kitchen.

121. Amy, *Nouvelles fontaines domestiques*, 8.

122. Le Camus de Mézières, *Génie*, 202.

123. Leblond, "De la nouvelle manière," 185*3.

124. Jombert, *Architecture moderne*, 113–114.

125. AN T 208/1; AN T 447 (1769).

126. Leblond, "De la nouvelle manière," 185*2.

127. Jombert, *Architecture moderne*, 115.

128. Ronesse, *Vues sur la propreté des rues de Paris*, 15.

129. Leblond, "De la nouvelle manière," 185*3.

130. AN T 208/6.

131. Briseux, *Architecture moderne*, 56–57.

132. Blondel, *De la distribution des maisons de plaisance*, 1: 82.

133. Jombert, *Architecture moderne*, 115.

134. Le Camus de Mézières, *Génie*, 193.

135. Ibid., 191–195, 199, 201. Le Camus de Mézières repeatedly recommends these same iron table legs, suggesting them for each of the kitchen's dependent rooms. See Ibid., 197–200.

136. Benhamou, "Parallel Walls, Parallel Worlds," 1, sees Jacques-François Blondel and Antoine Desgodets as making the first major departures from classical orders in the first half of the eighteenth century. Le Camus de Mézières, however, pioneered the novel use of orders as a means of controlling servant space.

137. Jaucourt, "Ordre."

138. Le Camus de Mézières, *Génie*, 191.

139. Ibid., 22. The details of the order were no less masculine. "The base of the column is simple and beautiful; the capital answers in kind. The entire entablature is masculine, and however denuded of ornament, its composition pleases and satisfies the eye. A simple beauty designating force and solidity characterizes this order." Ibid., 31.

140. Ibid., 22–23.

141. Middleton, "Introduction," 31, 54.

THREE · *Pots and Pens*

1. On the production and attribution of such images of artisans and their tools, see Weigert, "Sur les Larmessin et les costumes grotesques."

2. See Bibliothèque de l'Arsenal, *Livres en bouche*, 92–93.

3. Pierre-Louis Dumesnil the Younger (1698–1781), *La Cuisinière*, engraved by Claude-Augustin Duflos around 1762. Duflos' engraving was announced for sale in Paris by the biweekly newspaper *L'Avantcoureur* (17 May 1762).

4. AN T* 451/2 (1787).

5. The Académie française's 1694 *Dictionnaire* defines *Batterie de cuisine* as kitchen utensils *de cuivre battu* (of beaten copper), but the 1718 edition inserted the word *ordinairement* (ordinarily) before *de cuivre battu*, suggesting the increasing acceptance of cooking vessels made of other metals.

6. In December 1789, some new tables were installed in the Mirepoix kitchen. AN T 208/3. On writing desks in the vicinity of the kitchen, see Goodman, *Becoming a Woman in the Age of Letters*, 203.

7. Étienne Jeaurat (1699–1789), *L'Éplucheuse de salade* (1752), engraved by Jacques-Firmin Beauvarlet (1731–1797). BNF EST MD 43 fol. R 4646.

8. Blondel, *Architecture françoise, distribution* XVI, pl. 2 and *distribution* XXX, pl. 1; Le Camus de Mézières, *Génie*, 193.

9. AN T 491/3 (August 1785).

10. AN T 208/3 (22 April 1780).

11. AN T 208/1 (29 December 1777), AN T 208/3 (22 April 1780), AN T 208/3 (10 December 1788).

12. AN T 208/3 (22 April 1780). One pot was "lost at M. Valois's residence"; two spoons were listed as "broken," while an oven was described as "bad."

13. AN T 208/3 (22 April 1780).

14. AN T* 451/2. (October 1787).

15. "État des effets appartenat à Madame La Marechal Duchesse De Mirepoix laissés à la garde du Sr. Lacroix chef d'office dans l'hotel rue d'Artois le 29 X.bre 1777," AN T 208/1 (20 December 1777).

16. Pardailhé-Galabrun, *Birth of Intimacy*, 85.

17. MC ET/CV/1274 (19 April 1761).

18. Pardailhé-Galabrun, *Birth of Intimacy*, 85; Muchembled, *Invention de l'homme moderne*, 428.

19. Roche, *History of Everyday Things*, 240; AN T 446/B (1792). Roche notes that in rural households, kitchen tools often doubled as dining utensils well into the nineteenth century.

20. AN T* 261/4 (February 1787).

21. See, e.g., "Chaudronnier," in *Encyclopédie,* ed. Diderot and d'Alembert, esp. plates I and II.

22. AN T 208/1 (1777); BNF Joly de Fleury 2490, 262; AN T 208/1 (1777); AN T* 265/2 (15 March 1789).

23. *Petites affiches,* 17 May 1751 and 8 February 1773.

24. Académie française, *Dictionnaire,* 1st ed. (1694), s.v. "Ustensile." The same definition appeared through the end of the eighteenth century.

25. Mercier, *Tableau de Paris,* 5: 344.

26. *Petites affiches,* 1 February 1773 and 8 February 1773.

27. Mercier, *Tableau de Paris,* 5: 341.

28. *Petites affiches,* 29 March 1753, 8 February 1773.

29. *Affiches de Nantes,* 16 May 1760.

30. *Petites affiches,* 1 January 1767

31. *Petites affiches,* 29 October 1767, 2 April 1770, 24 May 1751, 9 August 1751, and 8 January 1753.

32. "Etat général des Meubles appartenant à Madame La Maréchale Duchesse De Mirépoix en son hotel Chaussée Dantin" (1784) and "Etat Géneral des meubles à Madame La Marechale de Mirepoix Fait en son hôtel Rue de Varenne en Janvier 1788" (1788). AN T 208/1.

33. MC ET/XCIII/21 (8 January 1751); MC ET/XC/407 (30 July 1761); AN T 451/7 (3 October 1783); AN T* 451/2 (19 October 1787). One livre equaled twenty sols.

34. AN T 208/3 (1780). Evidence in cookbooks of this sort of equipment rental of the period is reported in Wheaton, *Savoring the Past,* 104.

35. T* 261/5 (September 1786).

36. For a brief overview of risks associated with verdigris and its associated industry, see Benhamou, "Verdigris Industry."

37. The Académie française's 1694 *Dictionnaire* gives the example "le verdet est un poison" (verdigris is a poison) s.v. "Verdet."

38. "Avis au public sur l'usage des nouvelles fontaines domestiques et de santé," in Amy, *Nouvelles Fontaines domestiques,* 3.

39. An example of such a legal memoir can be found in *Arrest du conseil d'état du Roi.* For fouling teeth, see Amy, *Nouvelles Fontaines domestiques,* 34.

40. "Chaudronnier," in *Encyclopédie,* ed. Diderot and d'Alembert, pl. 1.

41. *Mercure de France,* January 1760.

42. "Si on doit rejetter entiérement l'usage des vaisseaux de cuivre dans la prépa-ration des alimens," in Amy, *Nouvelles Fontaines domestiques,* passim; "Cuivre" and "Lardoire" in *Encyclopédie,* ed. Diderot and d'Alembert; Lecointe, *La Cuisine de santé,* 1: 131.

43. "Si on doit rejetter entiérement l'usage des vaisseaux de cuivre dans la pré-paration des alimens," in Amy, *Nouvelles Fontaines domestiques,*31. BHVP N.F. 35380 (1754).

44. BHVP N.F. 35380 (1754).

45. Pardailhé-Galabrun, *Birth of Intimacy,* 85.

46. See, e.g., "Casserolle," "Chauderon," "Chaudière," "Lardoire," "Marmite," "Poële," "Poissonière," and "Tourtière" in *Encyclopédie,* ed. Diderot and d'Alembert.

47. MC ET CV/1274 (19 April 1761).

48. Mercier, *Jezennemours,* 2: 36.

49. BNF Collection Joly de Fleury 2490, f. 252.

50. Pennell, "-'Pots and Pans History,'" 212.

51. "Si on doit rejetter entiérement l'usage des vaisseaux de cuivre dans la prépara-tion des alimens," in Amy, *Nouvelles Fontaines domestiques,* 36.

52. Amy, *Nouvelles fontaines domestiques,* 34.

53. Lecointe, *Cuisine de santé,* 1: 131.

54. Mercier, *Tableau de Paris,* 5: 7–8.

55. "Si on doit rejetter entiérement l'usage des vaisseaux de cuivre dans la prépa-ration des alimens," in Amy, *Nouvelles Fontaines domestiques,* 54.

56. AN T 451/7 (7 January 1780); AN T* 451/2 (October 1787).

57. AN T 208/3 (February–March 1788); AN T 208/3 "Etat de la Batterie de la Cui-sine de Madame La Maréchale de Mirepoix. Année 1788" (10 December 1788).

58. AN T* 261/2 (1784); AN T* 261/3 (1786); AN T* 261/4 (1787).

59. AN T* 217 (18 October 1770).

60. See, e.g., AN T 208/3; AN T 212/1; AN T 451/7.

61. Joly de Fleury 2490, 213, 226. For example, a 6 April 1770 transaction involved the rental of a *batterie,* along with the purchase of a new iron-handled copper pan.

62. AN T 451/7 (7 January 1780). See also AN T 208/3 (1788) and AN T* 261/4 (February 1787).

63. Parisau, *Dinde du Mans,* 13.

64. Audiger, *Maison reglée,* 56, 133–134; Collet, *Instructions et prières,* 309.

65. Wheaton, *Savoring the Past,* 104. This conclusion likely stems from overreli-ance on literary descriptions of kitchen staff such as conduct manuals, which usually limit themselves to the largest and wealthiest households.

66. Furthermore, the maître d'hôtel was usually a former cook.

67. A few scholars have used kitchen records to document the purchase of food and other goods and services. Smets, "À la table d'un seigneur languedocien en 1766," analyzes a single cook's accounts as indicators of food consumption to reconstruct

the daily table of a provincial noble. Coquery, *Hôtel aristocratique,* 44–47, focuses less on the cook's bookkeeping than on his receipts, treated as markers of a web of exchange centered on the *hôtel.* Both writers take cooks' doing the bookkeeping for granted. Coquery found such kitchen records more numerous than the merchant receipts that form the basis of her own research.

68. Theophano, *Eat My Words,* 165, suggests that the kitchen acted as a setting for women to read and write, but bases this assertion on the far less extensive evidence of largely recent manuscript cookbooks.

69. See, e.g., AN T 208/3 and AN T 491/2.

70. See, e.g., AN T* 260/6; AN T* 261/1–2; AN T* 265/2, AN T* 451/2; and AN T* 470/35.

71. AN T 208/3 (7 February 1788).

72. AN T 491/2. Wine (along with meals) frequently constituted a portion of servants' wages.

73. T* 261/5 (1784–1787). For examples of individual wood and charcoal receipts, see AN T 261/1 (December 1783 and January 1784).

74. AN T 491/2 (1779).

75. BN Joly de Fleury 2490, 242, 253. His cook reported expenses of 893 livres 15 sols on Easter and 981 livres 19 sols on Pentecost.

76. AN T 261/1 (March 1787).

77. AN T* 261/1 (1783–1784).

78. AN T 208/3 (1788).

79. AN T 491/2 (1775). See also, e.g., AN T 491/3 (1782–1787).

80. AN T* 451/2 (1787).

81. The liturgical calendar divided days into *gras* and *maigre,* or fat and lean, to indicate when meat was allowed or prohibited.

82. AN T* 265/2 (1789).

83. AN T* 261/2 (June 1784).

84. AN T 254, Pierre Lamireau to Anne Farcy.

85. *Livre nécessaire à touttes sortes de personnes.*

86. Indeed, Monsieur Debongout dispatched delicacies including boar, pheasant, wild duck, salmon, oysters, asparagus, and artichokes, to name a few. Ibid., 8.

87. Ibid., 5.

88. AN T 491/2 (1779).

89. Furet, *Reading and Writing,* 26.

90. Maza, *Servants and Masters,* 52. Such illiteracy among servants was hardly confined to France. For the case of servant illiteracy England, see Hill, *Servants,* 226–227.

91. Roche, *People of Paris,* 201.

92. Low literacy among servants was a transnational phenomenon. In England, illiteracy among all domestic servants ranged from 59% to 66%, and among women the rate was likely much higher. Cressy, "Literacy in Context," 317.

93. Cohen, *Calculating People,* 11.

94. Thomas, "Numeracy in Early Modern England," 113.

95. For an example of the kinds of rough bookkeeping techniques practiced by artisans, see Crowston, *Fabricating Women*, 164–165.

96. Diderot and d'Alembert, "Comptes (livres de)." The "others" included people like seamstresses, who did their own crude bookkeeping, according to Crowston, *Fabricating Women*, 164–166.

97. *Petites affiches de Paris*, 3 February 1779.

98. Out of 105 *affiches* advertisements mentioning knowledge of "un peu de cuisine," 31 (29.5%) mentioned the ability to read or write. Of 201 advertisements for the position of *cuisinier* or *cuisinière* only 14 (7%) mentioned these skills. I base this analysis on a sample of 628 employment advertisements taken from the *affiches* of Bordeaux, Metz, Nantes, Rouen, Paris, and Toulouse.

99. *Petites affiches de Paris*, 20 January 1783.

100. One man actually called himself a jack-of-all-trades (*Maître Jacques*) in his advertisement, claiming he could "read, write, clean floors, cook and do a bit of desserts." *Petites affiches*, 12 January 1791.

101. Aho, "Rhetoric and the Invention of Double-Entry Bookkeeping," 22. Aho's interpretation has heavily influenced later studies of accounting. See, e.g., Thompson, "Is Accounting Rhetorical?"; Poovey, *History of the Modern Fact*.

102. See, e.g., Wigley, "Untitled," 348.

103. Cohen, *Calculating People*, 142. Cohen finds mistresses beginning to manage household finances only at the very end of the eighteenth century.

104. AN T* 451/2 (1787).

105. AN 4 AP 304 (1787–1789).

106. AN T* 217.

107. AN T 491/2 (6 August 1776) "arreté et verifié"; AN T 491/3 (September 1785) "vu bon"; AN T 208/3 (7 March 1788).

108. AN T* 470/35 (1754).

109. AN 352 AP 39, Bernard de Bonnard to Sophie Silvestre (6 February 1783).

110. See, e.g., Lewis, "Producers, Suppliers, and Consumers," 287; Sargentson, "Manufacture and Marketing," 123.

111. AN T 451/7 (1792); AN T* 261/4 (February 1787); AN T 451/7 (1779).

112. AN T 491/2 (1776, 1779).

113. AN T* 261/5.

114. Roche, *History of Everyday Things*, 225.

115. In contrast to domestic theft, ordinary theft typically resulted in the lighter sentence of branding and a spell in the king's galleys. On 24 April 1762, for example, one Antoine Colinet was sentenced to the stocks, whipping, branding, and five years of service in the king's galleys—all for stealing a duck. Though at the time of his crime Colinet worked as a cook, he had not stolen the duck from his master, the marquis de Montesson, thus explaining the court's relative leniency. *Arrest de la cour du Parlement, qui condamne Antoine Colinet.*

116. *Arrest de la cour de parlement, qui condamne Marie Launay.*

117. Richard, *Du Louage de services domestiques en droit français*, 44–46. Richard's work remains a definitive resource on servants, crime, and the law.

118. *Sentence de police, qui fait deffenses à tous cuisiniers*, 2.

119. AN T 254, Pierre Lamireau to Anne Farcy.

120. Maza, *Servants and Masters*, 102.

121. Delamothe, *Mémoire à consulter*, 31, 34.

122. Joly de Fleury, *Précis pour la femme Bailleux*, 3.

123. For an excellent analysis of the strategy of appealing to public opinion, see Maza, *Private Lives and Public Affairs*, 12–14.

124. Dumesnil, *La Cuisinière*.

125. Académie française, *Dictionnaire*, 1st ed. (1694), s.v. "Mule." This entry remained constant through the dictionary's fifth edition in 1798.

126. According to Édouard Fournier, the phrase derives originally from section 23 of Suetonius's account of the emperor Vespasian in *De vita caesarum*. Fournier, *Les caquets de l'accouchée*, 15n1. Suetonius there relates the tale of a muleteer who supposedly used the excuse of shoeing the mules to delay the emperor. Braudel, *Civilization and Capitalism, 15th–18th Century: The Wheels of Commerce*, 28, uses it in connection with cooks.

127. *La Maltôte des cuisinieres*, 2.

128. Noting that the word was used to describe "all sorts of new [government] impositions" (*toute sorte de nouvelles impositions*), the first edition of the Académie française's *Dictionnaire* (1694), s.vv. "Maletoste," "Maletostiers," defined *maltôte* as an "undue tax" (*imposition indeuë*) and a *maltôtier* as "Celuy qui exige des droits qui ne sont point deus, ou qui ont esté imposez sans autorité legitime" (He who claims rights not due, or that were imposed without legitimate authority). Subsequent dictionaries differed little.

129. *Maltôte des cuisinieres*, 4, 11.

130. Parisau, *Dinde du Mans*, 13–14.

131. *Maltôte des cuisinieres*, 7.

132. Cohen, *Calculating People*, 142.

133. Audiger, *Maison reglée*, 56, 133–134.

134. *Mémoire pour la comtesse de Varneville*, 8.

135. Ibid., 2.

136. Ibid., 13.

137. Ibid., 18–19.

138. *Maltôte des cuisinieres*, 2, 8, 11.

FOUR · *Theorizing the Kitchen*

1. *Dictionnaire des alimens*, xiii.

2. Spary, "Making a Science of Taste," argues that no "science of taste" appeared before the nineteenth century.

3. Jean-Louis Flandrin and Philip and Mary Hyman have done the most work here. See Flandrin, Hyman, and Hyman, "Cuisine dans la littérature de colportage"; Flandrin, "Distinction"; id., "From Dietetics to Gastronomy"; Hyman and Hyman, "Livres de cuisine."

4. Recent scholarship has focused on the ascendancy of French cuisine, tracing its origins to the eighteenth century. See, e.g., Trubek, *Haute Cuisine*; Ferguson, *Accounting for Taste*; Pinkard, *Revolution in Taste*.

5. Hyman and Hyman, "Livres de cuisine," 57, 62.

6. Bonnefons, *Délices de la campagne*, "Préface au lecteur."

7. Alain Girard, "Triomphe de *La Cuisinière bourgeoise*," 505–506.

8. Revel, *Culture and Cuisine*, 120.

9. Hyman and Hyman, "Livres de cuisine," 66. Other historians offer considerably lower figures but are likely not including counterfeit editions. Girard finds only thirteen, while Ferguson identifies eighteen. Alain Girard, "Triomphe de *La Cuisinière bourgeoise*"; Ferguson, *Accounting for Taste*, 36.

10. Hyman and Hyman, "Livres de cuisine."

11. Alain Girard, "Triomphe de *La Cuisinière bourgeoise*," 500–503. For the best overview of early French cookbooks, see Bibliothèque de l'Arsenal, *Livres en bouche*.

12. Flandrin, "Distinction," 307.

13. Flandrin, Hyman, and Hyman, "Cuisine dans la littérature de colportage."

14. Alain Girard, "Triomphe de *La Cuisinière bourgeoise*," 503.

15. Jaucourt, "Cuisine."

16. Alain Girard, "Triomphe de *La Cuisinière bourgeoise*," 500–503.

17. Hyman and Hyman, "Livres de cuisine," 71.

18. *Étrennes aux vivans*, 4.

19. Marin, *Dons de Comus, nouvelle édition*.

20. Guégan, *Cuisinier français*, lxxiv.

21. The prince de Dombes was allegedly a practicing amateur cook. Bourbon, *Cuisinier gascon*.

22. La Varenne, *Cuisinier françois*; Lune, *Nouveau Cuisinier*; La Chapelle, *Cuisinier moderne*.

23. Revel, *Culture and Cuisine*, 155.

24. Fairchilds, *Domestic Enemies*, 19. Owen, "Philosophy in the Kitchen," 78, says of Menon: "This is a servant speaking." Menon's anonymity is attributed to the "low status of cooks" by Mennell, *All Manners of Food*, 143, but given the prominent display of other cookbook authors' credentials, this is not especially convincing.

25. The preface of Marin's next cookbook, *La Suite des dons de Comus*, has likewise been attributed to another author, in this case to Anne-Gabriel Meusnier de Querlon. See Mennell, *Lettre d'un patissier anglois*, xx, xxii.

26. Gastelier, *Lettres sur les affaires du temps*, 341.

27. Menon, *Soupers de la Cour*, v.

28. Menon, *Nouveau traité de la cuisine*, iii–vii. Menon also noted that masters who wished to "get involved in the affairs of their houses" could use his cookbook.

29. *Essai sur la préparation des alimens*, "Avertissement."

30. Marin, *Les Dons de Comus, nouvelle édition*, xlvii.

31. Marin, *Les Dons de Comus*, xxxiii.

32. Bourbon, *Cuisinier gascon*, "Avis au lecteur."

33. Des Alleurs, *Lettre d'un patissier anglois*, "Avertissement."

34. *Traité historique et pratique de la cuisine*, ii.

35. Menon, *Cuisine et office de santé*, 11–12.

36. Menon, *Manuel des officiers de bouche*, 3.

37. *Essai sur la préparation des alimens*, 8.

38. Alain Girard, "Triomphe de *La Cuisinière bourgeoise*," 510.

39. Menon, *Soupers de la Cour*, vi.

40. *Essai sur la préparation des alimens*, 10.

41. Menon, *Science du maître d'hôtel cuisinier*, xxvi.

42. Alain Girard, "Triomphe de *La Cuisinière bourgeoise*," 510.

43. Mennell, *All Manners of Food*, 67.

44. For a comprehensive account of this literary debate, the Quarrel of the Ancients and Moderns, see DeJean, *Ancients Against Moderns*.

45. Spang, *Invention of the Restaurant*, 46–47, argues that the widespread use of "modern" diluted its significance, but for cooks it remained an essential rhetorical strategy to assert expertise.

46. Menon, *Science du maître d'hôtel confiseur*, iii.

47. Académie française, *Dictionnaire*, 1st ed. (1694), s.v. "Nouveauté." A quarter of a century later the dictionary eliminated this aspect of the definition of "novelty," suggesting a less negative connotation.

48. *Art de bien traiter*, table of contents and 32–34.

49. Bonnefons, *Délices de la campagne*, "Préface au lecteur," blames the Fronde for the delay in its publication.

50. La Chapelle, *Cuisinier moderne*, 2. This originally appeared in English as *The Modern Cook*.

51. Ibid., i.

52. Marin, *Dons de Comus*, xxx.

53. Menon, *Nouvelle cuisinière bourgeoise*.

54. Des Alleurs, *Lettre d'un patissier anglois*, 7.

55. Marin, *Dons de Comus*, iv, xvii.

56. Ibid., iii–iv.

57. *Dictionnaire des alimens*, vi.

58. Ibid., v.

59. Marin, *Les Dons de Comus*, iv–v.

60. Ibid., viii–ix.

61. Menon, *La Science du maître d'hôtel cuisinier*, xiv.

62. Massialot, *Le Cuisinier roïal et bourgeois*, Préface.

63. *Dictionnaire des alimens*, ix.

64. Mercier, *Tableau de Paris*, 12: 315. For a description of black sauce, see Marin, *Les Dons de Comus*, vi.

65. Jaucourt, "Cuisine."

66. Marin, *Les Dons de Comus*, xvii.

67. Macquer, *Dictionnaire raisonné universel des arts et métiers*, 592.

68. Jaucourt, "Cuisine."

69. Revel, *Culture and Cuisine*, 119–120; Wheaton, *Savoring the Past*, 43–44; Mennell, *All Manners of Food*, 69–70; Hyman and Hyman, "Livres de cuisine," 60–61.

70. Menon, *Science du maître d'hôtel cuisinier*, xiv.

71. La Varenne, *Cuisinier françois*, "Le Libraire au Lecteur."

72. *Traité historique et pratique de la cuisine*, ii–iii.

73. Des Alleurs, *Lettre d'un patissier anglois*, 9.

74. Marin, *Dons de Comus, nouvelle édition*, xlvii.

75. Both La Varenne and Lune gave their masters credit in their books' opening dedications. La Varenne, *Cuisinier françois*; Lune, *Nouveau cuisinier*.

76. The promise of revealed secrecy was a "commonplace claim" in seventeenth-century English cookbooks as well, according to Sherman, "'Whole Art and Mystery,'" 116. For a comprehensive account of books of secrets, see Eamon, *Science and the Secrets of Nature*.

77. Eamon, *Science and the Secrets of Nature*, 11, 140.

78. Bonnefons, *Délices de la campagne*, 371.

79. Lune, *Nouveau cuisinier*, "Au lecteur."

80. Massialot, *Cuisinier roial et bourgeois*, "Preface," 88.

81. *Art de bien traiter*, 1–2, 4–6.

82. *L'Albert moderne* was intended to update the venerable books of secrets *Secrets d'Albert le Grand* and the *Petit Albert*.

83. Menon, *Soupers de la Cour*, ix–x.

84. Pratt, "System-Building," 425, suggests that the process of ordering itself was the goal of eighteenth-century classifiers; according to him, the eighteenth-century obsession with system-building "had no other object" than the articulation of natural order.

85. La Varenne, *Cuisinier françois*, "Amy Lecteur."

86. *Escole parfaite des officiers de bouche*.

87. Examples include the indexes used by La Varenne and Bonnefons.

88. See, e.g., Hecquet, *Traité des dispenses du carême*.

89. AN T*451/2 (October 1787).

90. Bonnefons, *Délices de la campagne*, 1–93.

91. Hecquet, *Traité des dispenses du carême*, 1: 444. Or perhaps even better, a *Le Cuisinier janséniste*, given that Hecquet was of "Jansenist persuasion" and served for five years as the physician at the Jansenist convent Port-Royal. Goldstein, "'Moral Contagion,'" 186.

92. *Art de bien traiter*, 2.

93. *Dictionnaire des alimens*, xxviii.

94. Not all dictionaries of cuisine were equally well alphabetized. The *Dictionnaire portatif de cuisine, d'office et de distillation* (1767) frequently misordered entries, e.g., placing *porc* between *poitrine* and *poivrade*. Menon's *Cuisine et office de santé* (1758) has *huîtres* after *vive*.

95. *Dictionnaire portatif de cuisine, d'office et de distillation*, vi.

96. Ibid., v–vi.

97. Such plagiarism was hardly atypical. Even the *Cuisinier moderne* borrowed liberally from Massialot's *Cuisinier roïal et bourgeois*. For more on this borrowing, see Mennell, *All Manners of Food*, 77.

98. *Dictionnaire des alimens*, xxviii.

99. Menon, *Manuel des officiers de bouche*, 576–618.

100. Marin, *Dons de Comus*, xxix.

101. Although portions of this cookbook's preface have been attributed to authors other than Marin, the language of a rationalized nature extends far beyond the book's preface, pervading the entire text of *Les Dons de Comus*. Butcher's meat and fowl comprised the first and second orders of domestic animals respectively. Large game (which included boar as well as deer) formed the first class of wild animals, while small game constituted the second. Marin, *Dons de Comus*, 59, 77. Other cookbook authors frequently discussed lamb and mutton separately and likewise divided veal from beef; e.g., in Menon's *La Cuisinière bourgeoise*, he ordered meats as beef, mutton, veal, pork, and lamb.

102. Menon, *Science du maître d'hôtel cuisinier*, iv.

103. *Traité historique et pratique de la cuisine*, v.

104. Ibid., v–vi.

105. Menon, *Science du maître d'hôtel cuisinier*, xi.

106. Massialot, *Cuisinier roial et bourgeois*, 88.

107. Sedgwick, "Duke of Newcastle's Cook," 312. The translation is Sedgwick's.

108. Pierre Lamireau to Annette Farcy, AN T/254 (1780s).

109. Mercier, *Tableau de Paris*, 5: 78.

FIVE · *The Servant of Medicine*

1. Menon, *Soupers de la Cour*, vi.

2. Quesnay, *Recherches critiques*, 23–24.

3. La Chapelle, *Modern Cook*, i.

4. Menon, *Science du maître d'hôtel cuisinier*, xxv–xxvi.

5. Menon, *Cuisine et office de santé*, 7–8.

6. Académie française, *Dictionnaire*, 1st ed. (1694), s.v. "Science": "Connoissance certaine & évidente des choses par leurs causes."

7. Broman, "Rethinking Professionalization," 836. Much ink has been spilled by scholars, particularly sociologists, in search of the nature of professions. For a representative sample of the debate, see Larson, *Rise of Professionalism*; Freidson, *Professional Powers*; Abbott, *System of Professions*.

8. Some historians are uncomfortable applying the words "profession" and "professionalization" to the eighteenth century, but what is beyond dispute is a variety of occupations newly claimed to combine theory and practice. Brockliss and Jones, *Medical World of Early Modern France*, 32–33, take the position that terms like "professionalization" introduce more problems than they resolve. For a nuanced defense of

it, see Ramsey, *Professional and Popular Medicine in France, 1770–1830*, 3–4. Gelfand, *Professionalizing Modern Medicine*, 3, oddly argues against the use of calling surgery a "profession" in its "modern sense" but goes on largely to promote the concept.

9. Gelfand, *Professionalizing Modern Medicine*, 79.

10. "From ancient times until well in the eighteenth century, the art of cooking was an essential part of medicine" (Schiebinger, *Mind Has No Sex?* 112). Revel, *Culture and Cuisine*, 118, holds that the connection was not particularly new, and that there had nearly always been some degree of overlap between medicine and dining, citing the conflation of cookbooks and medical treatises in ancient Greece.

11. Schiebinger, *Mind Has No Sex?* 113.

12. Roche, *History of Everyday Things*, 247, identifies 240 editions between 1474 and 1846.

13. Pisanelli, *Traité de la nature des viandes et du boire*.

14. Ibid., "Préface."

15. Lémery, *Traité des aliments*, "Préface." Lémery acknowledged that "Pisanelli . . . kept nearly the same ordering, and it is from him that I have borrowed it."

16. Lecointe, *Cuisine de santé*, 1: 28–29.

17. La Varenne, *Cuisinier françois*, "Le Libraire au Lecteur."

18. Massialot, *Cuisinier roial et bourgeois*.

19. Menon, *Science du maître d'hôtel cuisinier*, xxix–xxx.

20. Académie française, *Dictionnaire*, 1st ed. (1694), s.v. "Goust."

21. Jaucourt, "Goût."

22. Aumont, "Faim."

23. Lémery, *Traité des aliments*, "Préface."

24. Lecointe, *Pâtisserie de santé*, 1: 23.

25. Marin, *Dons de Comus*, 152.

26. Menon, *Cuisine et office de santé*, 8.

27. Mercier, *Tableau de Paris*, 11: 230.

28. Andry, *Traité des alimens de caresme*, "Avertissement."

29. Lémery, *Traité des aliments*, "Préface." Lémery blamed the "retention of menstrual humors" for the majority of such cases.

30. Cheyne, *Art de conserver la santé*, 86.

31. Andry, *Traité des alimens de caresme*, "Avertissement."

32. Aumont, "Faim."

33. Collet, *Instructions et prières*, 309.

34. Lémery, *Traité des aliments*, "Préface"; Lecointe, *Cuisine de santé*, 1: 17; Jaucourt, "Goût."

35. One notable exception was the diet recommended for men of letters by Tissot, *De la santé des gens de lettres*, 25–26, 151–176.

36. Pisanelli, *Traité de la nature des viandes et du boire*, "Préface."

37. Menon, *Science du maître d'hôtel cuisinier*, viii–ix.

38. Marin, *Dons de Comus*, xxvi–xxvii.

39. Mercier, *Tableau de Paris*, 12: 316–318.

40. Menon, *Cuisine et office de santé*, 81.

41. Massialot, *Cuisinier roial et bourgeois*, "Préface."

42. Ramazzini, *Art de conserver la santé des princes et des personnes du premier rang*, 47, 87.

43. Lecointe, *Cuisine de santé*, 1: 17.

44. Cheyne, *Art de conserver la santé*, 54–56.

45. Lémery, *Traité des aliments*, "Préface."

46. Des Alleurs, *Lettre d'un patissier anglois*, 15.

47. *Étrennes aux vivans*, 3.

48. *Annonces, affiches, avis divers*, 25 February 1761, 27 May 1761, 8 July 1761, 1 July 1761; *Affiches de Nantes*, 26 June 1761. Several weeks later, *Annonces, affiches, avis divers* claimed to reveal the fasting boy's polar opposite: "This man ate (but for money) an entire sheep or pig, sometimes two bushels of cherries with their stones. With his teeth he broke, crushed, and chewed glass or earthenware bases and even rather hard stones. He devoured live animals like birds, mice, caterpillars, etc. One day he was presented a writing desk covered with iron plates. He ended by tearing it to pieces and swallowing it entirely with the pens, penknife, ink, and sand. Seven eyewitnesses testified to this fact in front of the Wittenberg Senate." After adopting a more moderate diet at the age of sixty, however, this man lived to be seventy-nine. *Annonces, affiches, avis divers*, 29 July 1761.

49. *Annonces, affiches, avis divers*, 27 May 1761. Unfortunately, the report provides no indication of his diet, unless it consisted of gin and tobacco.

50. Lémery, *Traité des aliments*, "Préface." Here Lémery followed Hippocrates to the letter. See Jaucourt, "Seasoning."

51. Lecointe, *Cuisine de santé*, 1: 18.

52. Marin, *Suite des dons de Comus*, xxi–xxii.

53. Mercier, *Tableau de Paris*, 12: 314.

54. Caraccioli, *Dictionnaire critique, pittoresque et sentencieux*, s.v. "Ragout."

55. Cointeraux, *Cuisine renversée*.

56. Menon, *Cuisine et office de santé*, 9.

57. Menon, *Science du maître d'hôtel cuisinier*, ix.

58. Ibid., vi–viii.

59. Poncelet, *Chimie du goût et de l'odorat*, xix.

60. Lémery, *Traité des aliments*, "Préface."

61. Roche, *History of Everyday Things*, 247.

62. Venel, "Digestion." The word derives from the Latin *coctio*, which has the same dual sense.

63. Lémery, *Traité des aliments*, "Préface."

64. Lecointe, *Cuisine de santé*, 1: 17, 32–33, 39.

65. Mercier, *Tableau de Paris*, 12: 312.

66. Macquer, *Dictionnaire raisonné universel des arts et métiers*, 593.

67. Hecquet, *De la digestion des alimens*, 11.

68. Venel, "Digestion."

69. Vieussens, "De la nature et des proprietez du levain de l'estomach," 140.

70. Senebier, "Considérations," cx, cxiv–cxviii.

71. Venel, "Digestion."

72. Lorry, *Essai sur les alimens*, 144.

73. Marin, *Dons de Comus*, xx.

74. Marin, *Suite des dons de Comus*, xx–xi.

75. Schiebinger, *Mind Has No Sex?* 115, describes a rather different situation in England, where, she argues, chemistry had actually *disappeared* from cookbooks by the 1750s. French cookbooks, in contrast did not begin to embrace chemistry until the 1730s and continued to do so through the eighteenth century.

76. Diderot, "Encyclopedia."

77. Venel, "Chymie ou chimie."

78. *Catalogue des livres de feu M. Crosat*, 50; *Catalogue des livres de M. B.****, 59–60. Even today the Bibliothèque nationale de France categorizes gastronomy along with astronomy, chemistry, engineering, and medicine.

79. *Petites affiches*, 4 January 1787 and 30 January 1791.

80. Simon, *Chemistry, Pharmacy and Revolution in France, 1777–1809*.

81. *Petites affiches*, 21 January 1787, 8 November 1751, and 2 January 1755. *Affiches de Province*, 1 June 1774.

82. This, Méric, and Cazor, "Lavoisier and Meat Stock."

83. Lavoisier, "Mémoire sur le degré de force que doit avoir le bouillon." For the curious, the shank yielded the heaviest bouillon, while flank steak produced the thinnest.

84. Marin, *Dons de Comus*, xxiii–xxiv.

85. Marin, *Suite des dons de Comus*, xviii.

86. Ibid., xviii–xix.

87. Ibid., viii.

88. This enduring argument continues to inspire. See, e.g., Wrangham, *Catching Fire*.

89. Des Alleurs, *Lettre d'un patissier anglois*.

90. Menon, *Science du maître d'hôtel cuisinier*, xxii.

91. *Almanach du dauphin*.

92. Marin, *Dons de Comus*, xxxii.

93. Caraccioli, *Dictionnaire critique, pittoresque et sentencieux*, 323.

94. "La science du maître d'hôtel cuisinier," 1991.

95. Mercier, *Tableau de Paris*, 11: 231.

96. *Petites affiches*, 13 December 1773.

97. BNF MSS Joly de Fleury 2490, 187 (1772).

98. Papin, *Maniere d'amolir les os*, "Préface." The *Encyclopédie* dubbed his device a *digesteur*.

99. Nivert, *Nouveau fourneaux économiques et portatifs*. Nivert also advertised his device in the provinces. See *Affiches de Dauphine*, 10 November 1780.

100. *Annonces, affiches, avis divers*, 18 February 1761.

101. Lecointe, *Cuisine de santé*.

102. Mercier, *Tableau de Paris*, 12: 317–318.

103. *Almanach utile et agréable. . . pour l'année 1760*, pl. 84.

104. BNF Arsenal Rondel MS 220.

105. *Almanach du dauphin,* s.v. "Chimistes."

106. *Affiches de Toulouse,* 4 April 1787.

107. Audiger, *Maison reglée,* 58.

108. Nivert, *Nouveau fourneaux économiques et portatifs.* See fig. 5.1.

109. Sentences for poisoning invariably refer to these restrictions and urge their adherence. See, e.g., *Arrest. . . qui condamne Marie Letessier; Arrest. . . contre le nommé Pierre Guet.*

110. Mercier, *Tableau de Paris,* 11: 233.

111. *Essai sur la préparation des alimens,* 5.

112. Lecointe, *Pâtisserie de santé,* 1: 8.

113. Mercier, *Tableau de Paris,* 11: 233.

114. Ibid., 10: 340.

115. *Affiches de Toulouse,* 8 June 1785. Petitfrère, *L'Œil du maître,* 163.

116. AN T 254, Pierre Lamireau to Anne Farcy.

117. Bernard-François Lépicié after Jean-Baptiste Chardin, *La Ratisseuse,* BNF EST MD 43 fol R 4644.

118. "La science du maître d'hôtel cuisinier," 1992.

119. Cheyne, *Art de conserver la santé,* 85.

120. Lecointe, *Cuisine de santé,* 1: 14, 16.

121. Jaucourt, "Cuisine."

122. Jaucourt, "Seasoning."

123. Menon, *Cuisine et office de santé,* 10.

124. *Sentence de police, qui fait deffenses à tous cuisiniers,* 2–3.

125. Menon, *Cuisine et office de santé,* 10.

126. Menon, *Science du maître d'hôtel cuisinier,* x–xi.

127. Académie française, *Dictionnaire,* 3rd ed. (1740), s.v. "Dissequer." This definition remained unchanged from 1694 through 1798.

128. Bibliothèque de l'Arsenal, *Livres en bouche,* 157. Specialized carving manuals during the seventeenth century instructed readers in how to cut up various animals and fruits at the table. See, e.g., *De sectione mensaria* and Vontet, *Art de trancher,* both thought to date from around 1650 (ibid., 162–163). During the eighteenth century, dedicated carving manuals began to disappear, but cookbooks during the late seventeenth century had already begun to include their own sections on carving meats. See, e.g., *Escole parfaite des officiers de bouche.* Meusnier, *Nouveau traité de la civilité* (1725) stresses the importance of knowing how "to cut meats properly and with method and to recognize the best parts in order to serve them correctly" (105).

129. Marin, *Suite des dons de Comus,* 1; *Traité historique et pratique de la cuisine,* ix.

130. Menon, *Soupers de la Cour,* 2: 1–2.

131. *Mercure de France,* May 1764, 106.

132. Verral, *Complete System of Cookery,* v–vi.

133. AN 352 AP 39, Bernard de Bonnard to Sophie Silvestre, Cherbourg (10 September 1783).

134. Smets, "À la table d'un seigneur languedocien en 1766," 32.
135. *L'Ancienne et nouvelle cuisine* (1757), BNF MSS NAF 2862, 28–29.
136. Mercier, *Tableau de Paris*, 11: 234, 12: 311, 315, 318.
137. Des Alleurs, *Lettre d'un patissier anglois*, 15–16.
138. Lecointe, *Cuisine de santé*, 1: 140.
139. Massialot, *Cuisinier roial et bourgeois*, 12.
140. Audiger, *Maison reglée*, 55.
141. *Essai sur la préparation des alimens*, 32–33.
142. *Traité historique et pratique de la cuisine*, vi.
143. Mercier, *Tableau de Paris*, 5: 81.
144. Des Alleurs, *Lettre d'un patissier anglois*, 7.
145. Mercier, *Tableau de Paris*, 5: 82–83.
146. Marin, *Dons de Comus, nouvelle édition*, 167–168.
147. Lecointe, *Cuisine de santé*, 1: 25.
148. Shapin, *Social History of Truth*, 397. Shapin's chapter 8, "Invisible Technicians: Masters, Servants, and the Making of Experimental Knowledge," explores the broad limitations of servants as knowledge producers. On servants' lack of epistemological capacity, see esp. 91–93.
149. Lecointe, *Cuisine de santé*, 1: 14.
150. Mahon, *Avis aux grands et aux riches*, 25, 33–34.
151. Ibid., 19.
152. Wellman, *La Mettrie*, 21, 23.
153. Gelfand, *Professionalizing Modern Medicine*, 67, 77.
154. Amy, *Nouvelles fontaines domestiques*.
155. Académie française, *Dictionnaire*, 1st ed. (1694), s.v. "Latin": "On dit, *Du Latin de cuisine*, pour dire, De fort meschant Latin." With the dictionary's second (1718) and subsequent editions, this phrase migrated to the entry for "Cuisine" suggesting that *latin de cuisine* said more about kitchens than it did about Latin.
156. Diderot, "Encyclopedia."
157. *Traité historique et pratique de la cuisine*, i.
158. Menon, *Soupers de la Cour*, v–vi.
159. Albeit without the same explicit attempt to advance the status of cooking, the term "profession" is used to describe the occupation as early as 1674, in *L'Art de bien traiter*, 4, whose author likely cooked for court nobles according to Revel, *Culture and Cuisine*, 154–155.
160. *Essai sur la préparation des alimens*, 7.
161. *Petites affiches*, 3 October 1770.
162. Lecointe, *Cuisine de santé*, 1: 22.
163. Ibid., 8.

Conclusion

1. Sewell, "Visions of Labor," 260.
2. Fairchilds, *Domestic Enemies*, 229.

3. Maza, *Servants and Masters*, 112.

4. In addition to Maza's and Fairchilds's works on domestic service, see Flandrin, *Families in Former Times*.

5. Collet, *Instructions et prières*, iii.

6. Fairchilds, *Domestic Enemies*, 72; Maza, *Servants and Masters*, 113. Roche, *People of Paris*, 26, finds that the percentage of servants in the general population roughly corresponded with the percentage hauled before the courts.

7. Anchel, *Crimes et châtiments*, 33.

Archival Sources

Full references for documents cited from the archives listed here are given in the notes to the text.

Archives nationales, Paris

Série AP. Archives personelles et familiales. This series consists of personal and family archives dating from the Old Regime. It includes private records such as kitchen registers and household accounting documents. It also contains personal correspondence discussing cooks' employment.

Série O^1. Maison du Roi. This series consists of papers from the king's household until the Revolution. It also includes correspondence and other records related to lodging, building maintenance, and the king's acquisitions.

Série T. Papiers privés tombés dans le domaine public. This series consists of papers seized from condemned individuals and *émigrés* from Paris and its environs during the Revolution. It includes vast quantities of materials related to everyday life in these households during the last decades of the Old Regime, such as expense accounts, receipts, inventories, wage registers, construction records, and personal correspondence. Many of these documents were written by cooks.

Minutier central des notaires de Paris. This comprehensive archive of Parisian notary records includes marriage contracts, inventories, sales records, and financial instruments. In addition to numerous traditional finding aids, two complete years of eighteenth-century records have been digitally indexed as Arno 1751 and 1761.

Bibliothèque nationale de France, Paris

Bibliothèque de l'Arsenal. This collection includes a large repository of documents related to contemporary theater, including published and manuscript plays.

Collection Joly de Fleury. This manuscript collection contains administrative documents and personal papers belonging to Omer Joly de Fleury (1715–1810), *président à mortier* of the parlement of Paris. It includes detailed accounts related to his household expenses.

Département des estampes et de la photographie. This department of the Bibliothèque nationale claims to be the world's largest image repository. It includes a broad range of early modern prints and engravings relating to cooks and kitchens. The majority of this book's images come from this department.

Manuscrits fonds français et des Nouvelles acquisitions françaises. These wide-ranging manuscript collections include kitchen and medical recipes, unpublished plays about cooks, and household registers.

Musée du Louvre, Cabinet des dessins:

Collection Edmond de Rothschild. A rich array of drawings and engravings, including popular eighteenth-century engravings of genre paintings, among them paintings of cooks and scenes from everyday life.

Printed Primary Sources

Académie française. *Le Dictionnaire de l'Académie françoise.* 1st ed. 2 vols. Paris: Jean-Baptiste Coignard, 1694.

———. *Le Nouveau dictionnaire de l'Académie françoise, dédié au Roy.* 2nd ed. 2 vols. Paris: Jean-Baptiste Coignard, 1718.

———. *Le Dictionnaire de l'Académie françoise.* 3rd ed. 2 vols. Paris: Jean-Baptiste Coignard, 1740.

———. *Le Dictionnaire de l'Académie française.* 6th ed. 2 vols. Paris: Firmin Didot frères, 1835.

L'Albert moderne, ou nouveaux sécrets éprouvés, et licites, recueillis d'après les découvertes les plus récentes. Paris: La veuve Duchesne, 1768. The Bibliothèque nationale identifies the author as Pons-Augustin Alletz.

Alembert, Jean le Rond d'. "Moderne." In *Encyclopédie, ou Dictionnaire raisonné des sciences, des arts et des métiers, par une Société de Gens de lettres,* edited by Denis Diderot and Jean le Rond d'Alembert. Paris: Briasson, 1751–1772.

Almanach du dauphin ou tableau du vrai mérite des artistes célèbres et d'indication générale des principaux marchands, négociants, artistes, et fabricants des six corps arts et metiers de la ville et fauxbourgs de Paris et autres villes du royaume. Paris: Demas, 1776.

Almanach utile et agréable de la loterie de l'Ecole royale militaire, pour l'année 1760. Paris: Prault père, 1760.

Amy, Joseph. *Nouvelles Fontaines domestiques approuvées par l'Académie royale des sciences.* Paris: J.-B. Coignard; A. Boudet, 1750.

Andry, Nicolas. *Traité des alimens de caresme.* Paris: Jean-Baptiste Coignard, 1713.

Architecture vivante: La cuisinière. [Paris]: Martinet, n.d.

Arrest de la cour de Parlement, portant condamnation d'amende honorable, et d'être brûlé vif, contre le nommé Pierre Guet, pour crime de poison. Paris: Pierre Simon, 1734.

Arrest de la cour de parlement, qui condamne Marie Launay, fille cuisiniere, à être pendue et étranglée, jusqu'à ce que mort s'ensuive, par l'exécuteur de la haute-justice, à une potence qui, pour cet effet, sra plantée dans la place de greve, pour vol domestique d'une montre d'or et de couverts d'argent, dont elle a été trouvée saisie au moment où elle se disposoit à les mettre en gage au Mont-de-Piété. Paris: P.-G. Simon, 1780.

Arrest de la cour de Parlement, qui condamne Marie Letessier à être brûlée vive, pour crime de poison. Paris: Pierre Simon, 1732.

Arrest de la cour du Parlement, qui condamne Antoine Colinet, ci-devant cuisinier, au carcan, au fouet, à la marque et aux galeres, pour avoir volé un canard. Paris: P.-G. Simon, 1762.

Arrest du conseil d'état du Roi, Qui ordonne que celui du 15 mai 1753, par lequel il a été permis à Jean-François Bavard et Thérèse Premery son épouse, de faire fabriquer, vendre et débiter, tant à Paris que par-tout ailleurs, des marmites, casseroles, poissonières et autres ustensiles de cuisine de fer forgé, blanchi (étamé) en dedans et en dehors, avec queues, anses et pieds desdits ustensiles en fer noir et non blanchi, sera exécuté selon sa forme et teneur, sans que pour raison de ce ils puissent être inquiétés ni troublés par qui ce soit: Et pour l'avoir fait, condamne les Jurés-gardes de la Communauté des maîtres et marchands Chauderonniers de Paris, en tous les dommages et intérêts en résultans, et au coût du présent arrêt, le tout liquidé à trois cens livres. Paris: Imprimerie royale, 1754.

L'Art de bien traiter, divisé en trois parties. Ouvrage nouveau, curieux, et fort galant, utile à toutes personnes, et conditions. Exactement recherché, & mis en lumiere, par L.S.R. Paris: Jean du Puis, 1674. The Bibliothèque nationale identifies the author as Rolland, "Officier de bouche de la princesse de Carignan."

Audiger. *La Maison reglée, et l'art de diriger la maison d'un grand seigneur & autres, tant à la ville qu'à la campagne, & le devoir de tous les officiers, & autres domestiques en general. Avec la veritable methode de faire toutes sortes d'essences, d'eaux & de liqueurs, fortes & rafraîchissantes, à la mode d'Italie.* Paris: Lambert Roulland pour Nicolas Le Gras, 1692.

Aumont, Arnulphe d'. "Faim." In *Encyclopédie, ou Dictionnaire raisonné des sciences, des arts et des métiers, par une Société de Gens de lettres*, edited by Jean le Rond d'Alembert and Denis Diderot. Paris: Briasson, 1751–1772.

Bastide, Jean-François de. *La Petite Maison.* 1753. Paris: Gallimard, 1993. Translated by Rodolphe el-Khoury as *The Little House: An Architectural Seduction* (New York: Princeton Architectural Press, 1996).

Blondel, Jacques-François. *Architecture françoise, ou recueil des plans, elevations, coupes, et profils des eglises, maisons royales, palais, hôtels et edifices les plus considerables de Paris, ainsi que des châteaux et maisons de plaisance situés aux environs de cette ville, ou en d'autres endroits de la France, bâtis par les plus célèbres architectes, et mesurés exactement sur les lieux.* Paris: Charles-Antoine Jombert, 1752.

———. *De la distribution des maisons de plaisance et de la décoration des édifices en général.* 2 vols. Paris: Charles-Antoine Jombert, 1737.

———. "Distribution." In *Encyclopédie, ou Dictionnaire raisonné des sciences, des arts et des métiers, par une Société de Gens de lettres*, edited by Denis Diderot and Jean le Rond d'Alembert. Paris: Briasson, 1751–1772.

Bonnefons, Nicolas de. *Les Délices de la campagne, suitte* [sic] *du Jardinier François, ou est enseigné a preparer pour l'usage de la vie tout ce qui croist sur la terre, et dans les eaux.* Paris: Pierre Des-Hayes, 1654.

Bourbon, Louis-Auguste-de. *Le Cuisinier gascon.* Amsterdam, 1740.

Briseux, Charles-Étienne. *L'Architecture moderne ou l'art de bien bâtir pour toutes sortes de personnes tant pour les maisons de particuliers que pour les palais.* Paris: Claude Jombert, 1728.

Bullet, Pierre. *L'Architecture pratique, qui comprend le détail du toisé et du devis des ouvrages de massonnerie, charpenterie, menuiserie, serrurerie, plomberie, vitrerie, ardoise, tuille, pavé de grais et impression. Avec une explication de la coutume sur le titre es servitudes et rapports qui regardent les basitmens. Ouvrage tres-necessaire aux architectes, aux experts, et à tous ceux qui veulent bastir.* Paris: Estienne Michallet, 1691.

Caraccioli, Louis-Antoine de. *Dictionnaire critique, pittoresque et sentencieux, propre à faire connoître les usages du siècle ainsi que ses bizarreries, par l'auteur de "la Conversation avec soi-même."* Lyon: Benoît Duplain, 1768.

Catalogue des livres de feu M. Crosat, baron de Thiers, brigadier des armées du roi, lieutenant général pour sa majesté de la province de Champagne au département de Reims, et commandant en ladite province. Paris: Saillant & Nyon, 1771.

Catalogue des livres de M. B.***. Paris: J. B. G. Musier fils, 1769.

Chacun son rôle: Le Médecin gourmand. Comédie-proverbe. Paris: Pihan Delaforest, n.d.

Cheyne, George. *L'Art de conserver la santé des personnes valétudinaires et de leur prolonger la vie, traduite du latin de M. Cheyne, avec des remarques intéressantes.* Paris: Laurent-Charles D'Houry, fils, 1755.

Cointeraux, François. *La Cuisine renversée, ou le Nouveau ménage par la famille du professeur d'architecture rurale, par la famille Cointeraux.* Lyon: Ballance & Barret, 1796.

Collet, Pierre. *Instructions et prières à l'usage des domestiques.* Paris: Debure l'aîné, Herissant, Herissant, Tilliard, 1758.

De sectione mensaria. N.p., n.d.

Delamothe, Petit. *Mémoire à consulter pour Me Petit Delamothe, avocat, accusé, contre sa cuisinière, demanderesse en réparation d'honneur.* Paris: Veuve Hérissant, n.d.

Des Alleurs, Roland Puchot, comte. *Lettre d'un patissier anglois au nouveau cuisinier françois. Avec un extrait du Craftsman.* N.p., 1739.

Desjardins, Simon, and Pierre Pharoux. "Le Journal de Castorland."Massachusetts Historical Society, n.d. Edited and translated by John A. Gallucci as *Castorland Journal: An Account of the Exploration and Settlement of Northern New York State by French Émigrés in the Years 1793 to 1797* (Ithaca, NY: Cornell University Press, 2010).

Dictionnaire des alimens, vins et liqueurs, leurs qualités, leurs effets, relativement aux différens âges, et aux différens tempéramens; avec la maniere de les apprêter, ancienne et moderne, suivant la méthode des plus habiles chefs d'office et chefs de cuisine, de la cour, et de la ville. Ouvrage très-utile dans toutes les familles. 3 vols. Paris: Gissey, 1750. The Bibliothèque nationale identifies the authors as François-Alexandre Aubert de La Chesnaye Des Bois and Briand, a cook.

Dictionnaire portatif de cuisine, d'office et de distillation, contenant la maniere de préparer toutes sortes de viandes, de volailles, de gibier, de poissons, de légumes, de fruits, etc. La façon de faire toutes sortes de gelées, de pâtes, de pastilles, de gâteaux, de tourtes, de pâtés, vermichel, macaronis, etc. Et de composer toutes sortes de liqueurs, de ratafias, de syrops, de glaces, d'essences, etc. Paris: Vincent, 1767.

Diderot, Denis. "Encyclopedia." In *The Encyclopedia of Diderot & d'Alembert Collaborative Translation Project,* translated by Philip Stewart. Ann Arbor: Scholarly Publishing Office of the University of Michigan Library, 2002. http://hdl.handle .net/2027/spo.did2222.0000.004 (accessed 11 February 2011).

Diderot, Denis, and Jean le Rond d'Alembert, eds. *Encyclopédie, ou Dictionnaire raisonné des sciences, des arts et des métiers, par une Société de Gens de lettres.* Paris: Briasson, 1751–1772.

Dubut, L.-A. *Architecture civile. Maisons de ville et de campagne de toutes formes et de tous genres, projetées pour être construites sur des terreins de différentes grandeurs; ouvrage utile à tous Constructeurs et Entrepreneurs, et à toutes Personnes qui, ayant quelque connaissance en construction, veulent elles-mêmes diriger leur Bâtimens.* Paris: J.-M. Eberhart, 1803.

Erresalde, Pierre. *Nouveaux secrets rares et curieux, donnés charitablement au public par une personne de condition. Contenant divers remedes eprouvez utils et profitables pour toutes sortes de maladies et divers secrets pour la conservation de la beauté des dames: avec une nouvelle maniere pour faire toutes sortes de confitures, tant seiches que liquides.* Paris: Jean-Baptiste Loyson, 1660.

L'Escole parfaite des officiers de bouche: contenant le vray maistre-d'hostel, le grand escuyer-tranchant, le sommelier royal, le confiturier royal, le cuisinier royal, et le patissier royal. Paris: La veuve Pierre David, 1662.

Essai sur la préparation des alimens dont le but est la santé, l'économie et la perfection de la théorie. A l'usage des maîtresses de maison qui ne dédaignent pas de descendre jusqu'au détail de leur ménage, soit à la ville, soit à la campagne. Paris, London: Onfroy, 1782.

Étrennes aux vivans, ou l'art de vivre agréablement sans nuire à sa santé. Paris: Guill. Leclerc, 1786.

Fleury, Claude. *Les Devoirs des maîtres et des domestiques.* Paris: Pierre Aubouin, Pierre Emery, and Charles Clouzier, 1688.

Fleury, Joly de. *Mémoire pour Me. Philippe-Baptiste Michaux, Avocat en Parlement, Ecuyer, Conseiller du Roi, Contrôleur Général des Ponts et Chaussées de France, au nom et comme Tuteur de Barbe Lievinne Piecteurs, fille mineure de Gabriel Piecteurs, et Barbe Jejars sa femme, Appelant. Contre Dominique Dulac, Bourgeois de Cieutat, et Demoiselle Marie Forcade son épouse, seule et unique heritiere sous bénéfice d'inventaire du feu Sieur Jean Forcade, Bourgeois de Paris, intimés.* Paris: Paulusdu-Mesnil, 1755.

———. *Observations sur le memoire de Barbe Lievine Pieters, Appellante.* Paris: Knapen, 1755.

————. *Précis pour la femme Bailleux, ci-devant cuisinière du sieur Petit, intimée, con-tre le sieur Petit de la Mothe, receveur des rentes à la ville, appellant.* Paris: N.-H. Nyon, 1787.

Galerie des modes et costumes français. 2 vols. Paris: Esnauts & Rapilly, 1779–1781.

Gastelier, Jacques-Elie. *Lettres sur les affaires du temps.* Paris: Champion Slatkine, 1993.

Hecquet, Philippe. *De la digestion des alimens, pour montrer qu'elle ne se fait pas par le moyen d'un levain, mais par celui de la trituration ou du broyement.* Paris: François Fournier, 1710.

————. *Traité des dispenses du carême.* 2 vols. Paris: Fréderic Léonard, 1710.

Jaucourt, Louis, chevalier de. "Cuisine." In *The Encyclopedia of Diderot & d'Alembert Collaborative Translation Project,* translated by Sean Takats. Ann Arbor: Scholarly Publishing Office of the University of Michigan Library, 2005. http://hdl.handle .net/2027/spo.did2222.0000.075 (accessed 11 February 2011).

————. "Goût." In *Encyclopédie, ou Dictionnaire raisonné des sciences, des arts et des métiers, par une Société de Gens de lettres,* edited by Denis Diderot and Jean le Rond d'Alembert. Paris: Briasson, 1751–1772.

————. "Ordre." In *Encyclopédie, ou Dictionnaire raisonné des sciences, des arts et des métiers, par une Société de Gens de lettres,* edited by Denis Diderot and Jean le Rond d'Alembert. Paris: Briasson, 1751–1772.

————. "Seasoning." In *The Encyclopedia of Diderot & d'Alembert Collaborative Translation Project,* translated by Sean Takats. Ann Arbor: Scholarly Publishing Office of the University of Michigan Library, 2005. http://hdl.handle.net/2027/spo .did2222.0000.498 (accessed 11 February 2011).

Jombert, Charles-Antoine. *L'Architecture moderne, ou l'art de bien bâtir pour toutes sortes de personnes.* Paris: Chez l'Auteur, Libraire du Génie et de l'Artillerie, rue Dauphine, à l'Image Notre-Dame, 1764.

La Chapelle, Vincent. *Le Cuisinier moderne, qui apprend à donner toutes sortes de re-pas, en gras et en maigre, d'une manière plus délicate que ce qui en été écrit jusqu'à présent.* The Hague, 1742.

————. *The Modern Cook: Containing Instructions for Preparing and Ordering Publick Entertainments for the Tables of Princes, Ambassadors, Noblemen, and Magistrates. As also the least Expensive Methods of providing for private Families, in a very elegant Manner. New Receipts for Dressing of Meat, Fowl, and Fish, and making Ragoûts, Fricassées, and Pastry of all Sorts, in a Method never before publish'd. Adorn'd with Copper-Plates, Exhibiting the Order of Placing the different Dishes, etc. on the Table, in the most polite Way.* London: Thomas Osbourne, 1736.

La Varenne, François-Pierre de. *Le Cuisinier françois, enseignant la maniere de bien apprester, et assaisonner toutes sortes de viandes, grasses et maigres, legumes, Patis-series, etc. Reveu, corrigé, et augmenté d'un traitté de confitures seiches et liquides, et autres delicatesses de bouche. Ensemble d'une table alphabetique des matieres qui sont traittées dans tout le livre.* Paris: Pierre David, 1652.

Lavoisier, Antoine-Laurent-de. "Mémoire sur le degré de force que doit avoir le bouil-lon sur sa pesanteur spécifique et sur la quantité de matiere gélatineuse solide qu'il contient." In *Oeuvres de Lavoisier*, edited by Jean-Baptiste Dumas, Édouard Grimaux, and Ferdinand Fouqué, 3: 563–578. Paris: Imprimerie impériale, 1893.

Le Camus de Mézières, Nicolas. *Le Génie de l'architecture, ou L'analogie de cet art avec nos sensations.* Paris: L'auteur; Benoît Morin, 1780. Translated by David Britt as *The Genius of Architecture; or, The Analogy of That Art with Our Sensations* (Santa Monica, CA: Getty Center for the History of Art and the Humanities, 1992).

Le Muet, Pierre. *Manière de bien bastir pour touttes* [sic] *sortes de personnes, par Pierre Le Muet, architecte ordinaire du Roy, & conducteur des desseins des fortifications en la province de Picardie.* Paris: Melchior Tavernier, 1623.

————. *Manière de bien bastir pour toutes sortes de personnes, par Pierre Le Muet, . . . reveue, augmentée et enrichie, en cette 2e édition, de plusieurs figures de beaux bastiments et édifices, de l'invention et conduite dudit sieur Le Muet et autres.* Paris: François Langlois, 1647.

Leblond, Sebastian. "De la nouvelle manière de distribuer les plans." In *Le Vignole, Cours d'architecture qui comprend les ordres de Vignole, avec des commentaires, les figures et descriptions de ses plus beaux bâtimens, et de ceux de Michel-Ange . . . ,* edited by A.-C. Daviler. Paris: Jean Mariette, 1710.

Lecointe, Jourdan. *La Cuisine de santé, ou moyens faciles et économiques de préparer toutes nos Productions Alimentaires de la maniere la plus délicate et la plus sanitaire d'après les nouvelles découvertes de la cuisine Françoise et Italienne.* 3 vols. Paris: Briand, 1790.

————. *La Pâtisserie de santé, ou moyens faciles et économiques de préparer tous les genres de pâtisseries de la manière la plus délicate et la plus salutaire.* 2 vols. Paris: Briand, 1792.

Lémery, Louis. *Traité des aliments, où l'on trouve . . . la différence et le choix qu'on doit faire de chacun d'eux en particulier.* Paris: J.-B. Cusson and P. Witte, 1702.

Lesage, Alain-René. *Histoire de Gil Blas de Santillane.* 1715–1735. 2 vols. Paris: Garnier, 1920.

Le Livre nécessaire à touttes [sic] *sortes de personnes, fait en faveur du public, contenant la manière de dresser des mémoires pour la dépense de chaque jour . . . et pour différents marchands et ouvriers, des lettres de compliments . . . , des models de lettres de change . . .* Paris: Mondhare, 1776.

Lorry, Anne-Charles. *Essai sur les alimens, pour servir de commentaire aux livres diététiques d'Hippocrate.* Paris: Vincent, 1757.

Loyseau, Charles. *Traité des ordres et simples dignitez.* 1610. In *Les Oeuvres de maistre Charles Loyseau, avocat en parlement. Contenant les cinq livres du droit des offices, les traitez des seigneuries, des ordres et simples dignitez, du déguerissement et délaissement par hypotheque, de la garantie des rentes, et des abus des justices de village.* Lyon: La Compagnie des Libraires, 1701.

Lune, Pierre de. *Le Nouveau Cuisinier, ou il est traitté de la veritable methode pour apprester toutes sortes de viandes, gibier, volatiles, poissons, tant de mer que d'eau douce: suivant les quatre saisons de l'année. Ensemble la maniere de faire toutes sortes de patisseries, tant froides que chaudes, en perfection.* Paris: Pierre David, 1660.

Macquer, Philippe. *Dictionnaire raisonné universel des arts et métiers.* Paris: P. Fr. Didot jeune, 1773.

Mahon, Paul-Augustin-Olivier. *Avis aux grands et aux riches, sur la manière dont ils doivent se conduire dans leurs maladies. Par M*** Docteur en Médecine.* Paris: Ph.-D. Pierres, 1772.

La Maltôte des cuisinieres, ou la maniere de bien ferrer la mule. Dialogue entre une vieille Cuisiniere et une jeune Servante. Riom: G. Valleyre, 1724.

Marin, François. *Les Dons de Comus, ou les délices de la table. Ouvrage non-seulement utile aux Officiers de Bouche pour ce qui concerne leur art, mais principalement à l'usage des personnes qui sont curieuses de sçavoir donner à manger, et d'être servies délicatement, tant en gras qu'en maigre, suivant les saisons, et dans le goût le plus nouveau.* Paris: Prault fils, 1739.

———. *La Suite des dons de Comus, ou l'art de la cuisine, réduit en pratique.* Paris: La veuve Pissot, 1742.

———. *Les Dons de Comus, ou l'art de la cuisine, réduit en pratique, nouvelle édition, revue, corrigée et augmentée par l'auteur.* 3 vols. Paris: La veuve Pissot, 1758.

Marot, Jean. *L'Architecture françoise, ou recueil des plans, elevations, coupes et profils des eglises, palais, hôtels et maisons particulieres de Paris, et des Chasteaux et maisons de campagne ou de plaisance des environs, et de plusieurs autres endroits de France, bâtis nouvellement par les plus habils architectes, et levés et mesurés exactement sur les lieux.* Paris: Jean Mariette, 1727.

Massialot, François. *Le Cuisinier roial et bourgeois, qui apprend à ordonner toute sorte de repas, et la meilleure manière des ragoûts les plus à la mode et les plus exquis. Ouvrage très-utile dans les familles, et singulièrement nécessaire à tous maîtres d'hôtels, et ecuïers de cuisine.* Paris: Charles de Sercy, 1691.

Mémoire pour la comtesse de Varneville, intimée; contre Jean-Baptiste Queval, ci-devant son cuisinier. Paris: Didot, 1765.

Menon. *La Cuisine et office de santé propre à ceux qui vivent avec œconomie et régime.* Paris: Le Clerc, 1758.

———. *Le Manuel des officiers de bouche, ou le precis de tous les apprêts qu'on l'on peut faire des alimens pour servir toutes les tables, depuis celles des grands seigneurs jusqu'à celles des bourgeois, suivant l'ordre des saisons et des services: ouvrage très-utile aux maîtres pour ordonner des repas, et aux artistes pour les exécuter.* Paris: Le Clerc, 1759.

———. *Nouveau traité de la cuisine, avec de nouveaux desseins de tables et vingt-quatre menus, où l'on apprend ce que l'on doit servir suivant chaque saison, en gras, en maigre, et en pâtisserie, et très-utiles à toutes les personnes qui s'en mêlent, tant pour ordonner, que pour exécuter toutes sortes de nouveaux ragoûts, et des plus à la mode.* Paris: Michel-Etienne David, 1739.

———. *La Nouvelle cuisinière bourgeoise, suivie de l'office à l'usase [sic] de tous ceux qui se mêlent des dépenses de maison.* Paris: Guillyn, 1746.

———. *La Science du maître d'hôtel confiseur, a l'usage des officiers, avec des observations sur la connoissance et les proprietés des fruits. Enrichie de desseins en décorations et parterres pour les desserts.* Paris: Paulus-du-Mesnil, 1750.

————. *La Science du maître d'hôtel cuisinier, avec des observations sur la connoissance et proprietés des alimens.* Paris: Paulus-du-Mesnil, 1749.

————. *Les Soupers de la Cour, ou l'art de travailler toutes sortes d'aliments, pour servir les meilleures tables, suivant les quatre saisons.* 2 vols. Paris: Guillyn, 1755.

Mercier, Louis-Sébastien. *Jezennemours, roman dramatique.* 2 vols. Amsterdam, 1776.

————. *Tableau de Paris.* 12 vols. Amsterdam, 1788.

Mérigot. *La Cuisinière républicaine, qui enseigne la manière simple d'accomoder les Pommes de terre; avec quelques avis sur les soins nécessaires pour les conserver.* Paris: Mérigot le jeune, 1795.

Meusnier, Jean. *Nouveau traité de la civilité qui se pratique en France parmi les honnêtes-gens.* The Hague: Adrien Moetjens, 1731.

Nivert, Louis. *Nouveau fourneaux économiques et portatifs, extrait de la Gazette de santé, du dimanche 1er octobre 1780, no. 40.* Paris: Veuve Ballard et fils, 1781.

Papin. *La Maniere d'amolir les os, et de faire cuire toute sortes de viandes en fort peu de temps, et à peu de frais. Avec un description de la machine dont il se faut servir pour cét effet, ses proprietez et ses usages, confirmez par plusieurs experiences.* Paris: Estienne Michallet, 1682.

Parisau, Pierre-Germain. *La Dinde du Mans.* Paris: Cailleau, 1783.

Piemontese, Alessio. *Les Secrets du seigneur Alexis Piemontois.* Rouen: Thomas Mallard, 1588. Originally published as *I secreti del reverendo donno Alessio Piemontese* (Venice, 1555).

Pisanelli, Baldassare. *Traité de la nature des viandes et du l oire, avec leurs vertus, vices, remèdes et histoires naturelles, utile et délectables à qu conque désire vivre en santé.* originally published as *Trattato della natura de' cibi e del bere* (Venice, 1584). Translated by Antoine de Povillon. St. Omer: Charles Boscart, 1620.

Poncelet, Polycarpe. *Chimie du goût et de l'odorat, ou Principes pour composer facilement, & à peu de frais, les liqueurs à boire, & les eaux de senteurs . . .* Paris: P.-G. Le Mercier, 1755. New ed. 2 vols. Paris: Pissot, 1774.

Quesnay, François. *Recherches critiques et historiques sur l'origine, sur les divers états et sur les progrès de la chirurgie en France.* 2 vols. Paris: Charles Osmont, 1744.

Ramazzini, Bernardino. *L'Art de conserver la santé des princes et des personnes du premier rang.* Leiden: Jean Arn. Langerak, 1724.

————. *Essai sur les maladies des artisans.* Translated by Armand-François Fourcroy. Paris: Moutard, 1777.

Relation de ce qui s'est fait et passé au sujet d'une Cuisinière qui avoit trois maris vivans. Paris: Claude Hérissant, 1775.

Rétif de la Bretonne, Nicolas-Edme. *Les Contemporaines communes, ou les avantures des belles marchandes, ouvrières, etc., de l'âge present.* Leipzig: Büschel, 1789.

Rivarol, Antoine de. *De l'universalité de la langue française, discours qui a remporté le prix de l'Académie de Berlin.* Paris: Bailly, 1784.

Roberti, Giambattista. "Ad un professore di belle lettere nel Friuli." In *Raccolta di varie operette dell' Abate Conte Giambatista Roberti*, vol. 4. Bologna: Lelio dalla Volpe, 1785.

Ronesse, J.-H. *Vues sur la propreté des rues de Paris.* Paris, 1782.

Savot, Louis. *L'Architecture françoise des bastimens particuliers, composée par Me. Louis Savot. . . .* Paris: Sébastien Cramoisy, 1624.

———. *L'Architecture françoise des bastimens particuliers, composée par Me. Louis Savot . . . avec des figures et des nottes* [sic] *de M. Blondel. . . .* Paris: F. Clouzier l'aîné, 1673.

"La Science du maître d'hôtel cuisinier avec des observations sur la connoissance et les propriétés des alimens. A Paris, au Palais, chez Paulus Dumesnil, imprimeur Libraire Grand Salle au Pilier des Consultations, au Lion d'or 1749." *Journal de Trévoux, ou mémoires pour servir à l'histoire des sciences et des arts* 49 (1749): 1987–1996. A review of Menon's *La Science du maître d'hôtel cuisinier.*

Senebier, Jean. "Considérations." In *Experiences sur la digestion de l'homme et de différentes especes d'animaux, par l'abbé Spallanzani. . . . Avec des considérations sur sa méthode de faire des expériences, et les conséquences pratiques qu'on peut tirer en médecine de ses découvertes.* Geneva: Barthelemi Chirol, 1784.

Sentence de police, qui fait deffenses à tous cuisiniers, cuisinieres et autres de vendre et débiter en regrat aucuns restes de viandes cuites; et condamne en l'amende plusieurs particulieres pour y avoir contrevenu. Paris: P.-J. Mariette, Imprimeur de la Police, 1744.

Tissot, Samuel-Auguste-André-David. *De la santé des gens de lettres.* Paris: François Didot, 1768.

Traité historique et pratique de la cuisine. Ou le cuisinier instruit, de la connoissance des animaux, tant volatiles, que terrestres, aquatiques et amphibies; de la façon, de préparer les divers alimens, et de les servir. Suivi d'un petit abregé. Sur la maniere de faire les Confitures liquides et autres Desserts de toute espéce. Ouvrage très-utile, non-seulement pour les Maîtres d'Hôtel et Officiers de Cuisine; mais encore pour toutes les Communautés Religieuses, les grandes Familles, et tous ceux qui veulent donner à manger honnêtement. 2 vols. Paris: C.-J.-B. Bauche, 1758.

Venel, Gabriel-François. "Chymie ou chimie." In *Encyclopédie, ou Dictionnaire raisonné des sciences, des arts et des métiers, par une Société de Gens de lettres,* edited by Denis Diderot and Jean le Rond d'Alembert. Paris: Briasson, 1751–1772.

———. "Digestion." In *Encyclopédie, ou Dictionnaire raisonné des sciences, des arts et des métiers, par une Société de Gens de lettres,* edited by Denis Diderot and Jean le Rond d'Alembert. Paris: Briasson, 1751–1772.

Verral, William. *A Complete System of Cookery. In which is set forth, A Variety of genuine Receipts, collected from Several Years Experience under the celebrated Mr. de St. Clouet, sometime since Cook to his Grace the Duke of Newcastle. By William Verral, Master of the White-Hart Inn in Lewes, Sussex. Together with an Introductory Preface, Shewing how every Dish is brought to Table, and in what Manner the meanest Capacity will never err in doing what his Bill of Fare contains. To which is added, a true Character of Mons. de St. Clouet.* London: William Verral, 1759.

Vieussens, Raymond. "De la nature et des proprietez du levain de l'estomach." *Journal de Trévoux, ou mémoires pour servir à l'histoire des sciences et des arts* 10 (1710): 134–151.

Viollet de Wagnon, Jacques. *L'Auteur laquais, ou réponse aux objections qui ont été faites au corps de ce nom, sur la vie de Jacques Cochois, dit Jasmin.* Avignon: Girard, 1750.

Voltaire. "Lettre à l'occasion de l'impôt du vingtième." In *Œuvres de 1749 (II)*, edited by Henri Duranton, 289–314; *The Complete Works of Voltaire*, vol. 31B. Oxford: Voltaire Foundation, 1994.

Vontet, Jacques. *L'Art de trancher la viande et toutes sortes de fruits, à la mode italienne et nouvellement à la françoise.* Lyon, n.d.

Selected Secondary Sources

Abbott, Andrew Delano. *The System of Professions: An Essay on the Division of Expert Labor.* Chicago: University of Chicago Press, 1988.

Aho, James A. "Rhetoric and the Invention of Double-Entry Bookkeeping." *Rhetorica* 3, no. 3 (1985): 21–43.

Anchel, Robert. *Crimes et châtiments au XVIIIe siècle.* Paris: Libraire académique Perrin, 1933.

Arminjon, Catherine, and Nicole Blondel. *Objets civils domestiques: vocabulaire.* Paris: Imprimerie nationale, 1984.

Auerbach, Stephen. "'Encourager le commerce et répandre les lumières': The Press, the Provinces and the Origins of the Revolution in France: 1750–1789." Ph.D. diss., Louisiana State University, 2000.

Auslander, Leora. *Taste and Power: Furnishing Modern France.* Berkeley: University of California Press, 1996.

Baker, Keith Michael. *Inventing the French Revolution: Essays on French Political Culture in the Eighteenth Century.* Cambridge: Cambridge University Press, 1990.

Banner, Lois W. "Why Women Have Not Been Great Chefs." *South Atlantic Quarterly* 72, no. 2 (1973): 193–212.

Benhamou, Reed. "Parallel Walls, Parallel Worlds: The Places of Masters and Servants in the Maisons de plaisance of Jacques-François Blondel." *Journal of Design History* 7, no. 1 (1994): 1–11.

———. "The Verdigris Industry in Eighteenth-Century Languedoc: Women's Work, Women's Art." *French Historical Studies* 16, no. 3 (1990): 560–575.

Bibliothèque de l'Arsenal. *Livres en bouche: Cinq siècles d'art culinaire français, du quatorzième au dix-huitième siècle.* Exposition at the Bibliothèque de l'Arsenal, Paris, 21 November 2001–17 February 2002. Paris: Bibliothèque nationale de France; Hermann, 2001.

Braudel, Fernand. *Civilization and Capitalism, 15th–18th Century: The Structures of Everyday Life.* Translated by Siân Reynolds. Berkeley: University of California Press, 1992.

———. *Civilization and Capitalism, 15th–18th Century: The Wheels of Commerce.* Translated by Siân Reynolds. Berkeley: University of California Press, 1992.

Brockliss, L. W. B., and Colin Jones. *The Medical World of Early Modern France.* Oxford: Clarendon Press, 1997.

Broman, Thomas. "Rethinking Professionalization: Theory, Practice, and Professional

Ideology in Eighteenth-Century German Medicine." *Journal of Modern History* 67, no. 4 (1995): 835–872.

Camporesi, Piero. *Exotic Brew: The Art of Living in the Age of Enlightenment.* Translated by Christopher Woodall. Cambridge: Polity Press, 1994.

Carbonnier, Youri. *Maisons parisiennes des lumières.* Collection Roland Mousnier 27. Paris: Presses de l'université Paris-Sorbonne, 2006.

Censer, Jack R. *The French Press in the Age of Enlightenment.* London: Routledge, 1994.

Cohen, Patricia Cline. *A Calculating People: The Spread of Numeracy in Early America.* Chicago: University of Chicago Press, 1982.

Collins, Nancy W. "The Problem of the Enlightenment Salon: European History or Post-Revolutionary Politics, 1755–1850." Ph.D. diss., University of London, 2006.

Colwill, Elizabeth. "'Women's Empire' and the Sovereignty of Man in La Decade philosophique, 1794–1807." *Eighteenth-Century Studies* 29, no. 3 (1996): 265–289.

Coquery, Natacha. *L'Hôtel aristocratique: Le Marché du luxe à Paris au XVIIIe siècle.* Paris: Publications de la Sorbonne, 1998.

Corbin, Alain. *The Foul and the Fragrant: Odor and the French Social Imagination.* Cambridge, MA: Harvard University Press, 1986.

Cressy, David. "Literacy in Context: Meaning and Measurement in Early Modern England." In *Consumption and the World of Goods,* edited by John Brewer and Roy Porter, 305–319. London: Routledge, 1993.

Crouzet, François. "Some Remarks on the *métiers d'art.*" In *Luxury Trades and Consumerism in Ancien Régime Paris: Studies in the History of the Skilled Workforce,* edited by Robert Fox and Anthony Turner, 263–286. Brookfield, VT: Ashgate, 1998.

Crowston, Clare H. "Engendering the Guilds: Seamstresses, Tailors, and the Clash of Corporate Identities in Old Regime France." *French Historical Studies* 23, no. 2 (April 2000): 339–371.

———. *Fabricating Women: The Seamstresses of Old Regime France, 1675–1791.* Durham, NC: Duke University Press, 2001.

Darnton, Robert. *The Business of Enlightenment: A Publishing History of the Encyclopédie, 1775–1800.* Cambridge, MA: Harvard University Press, 1979.

Davis, Jennifer J. "Men of Taste: Gender and Authority in the French Culinary Trades, 1730–1830." Ph.D. diss., Pennsylvania State University, 2004.

DeJean, Joan E. *The Age of Comfort.* New York: Bloomsbury USA, 2009.

———. *Ancients Against Moderns: Culture Wars and the Making of a Fin de Siècle.* Chicago: University of Chicago Press, 1997.

Eamon, William. *Science and the Secrets of Nature: Books of Secrets in Medieval and Early Modern Culture.* Princeton, NJ: Princeton University Press, 1994.

Edwards, Nancy Jocelyn. "Patriotism à Table: Cookbooks, Textbooks, and National Identity in Fin-de-Siècle France." *Proceedings of the Annual Meeting of the Western Society for French History* 24 (1997): 245–254.

Eleb-Vidal, Monique, and Anne Debarre-Blanchard. *Architectures de la vie privée: Maisons et mentalités XVIIe–XIX siècles.* Paris: Éditions Hazan, 1999.

Elias, Norbert. *The Court Society.* Translated by Edmund Jephcott. Oxford: Basil Blackwood, 1983.

Fairchilds, Cissie. *Domestic Enemies: Servants and Their Masters in Old Regime France.* Baltimore: Johns Hopkins University Press, 1984.

Farge, Arlette. "Work-Related Diseases of Artisans in Eighteenth-Century France." In *Medicine and Society in France*, edited by Elborg Forster and Orest A. Ranum, 89–103. Baltimore: Johns Hopkins University Press, 1980.

Ferguson, Priscilla Parkhurst. *Accounting for Taste: The Triumph of French Cuisine.* Chicago: University of Chicago Press, 2004.

Feyel, Gilles. *L'Annonce et la nouvelle: La Presse d'information en France sous l'Ancien Régime, 1630–1788.* Oxford: Voltaire Foundation, 2000.

Flandrin, Jean-Louis. *Arranging the Meal: A History of Table Service in France.* Translated by Julie Johnson, Sylvie Roder, and Antonio Roder. Berkeley: University of California Press, 2007.

———. "From Dietetics to Gastronomy: The Liberation of the Gourmet." In *Food: A Culinary History from Antiquity to the Present*, edited by Jean-Louis Flandrin, Massimo Montanari, and Albert Sonnenfeld, 418–432. New York: Columbia University Press, 1999.

———. "Distinction Through Taste." In *A History of Private Life: Passions of the Renaissance*, edited by Philippe Ariès and Georges Duby, 265–307. Cambridge, MA: Harvard University Press, Belknap Press, 1989.

———. *Families in Former Times: Kinship, Household and Sexuality in Early Modern France.* Translated by Richard Southern. Cambridge: Cambridge University Press, 1979.

Flandrin, Jean-Louis, Philip Hyman, and Mary Hyman. "La Cuisine dans la littérature de colportage." In *Le Cusinier françois*. Paris: Montalba, 1983.

Flandrin, Jean-Louis, Massimo Montanari, and Albert Sonnenfeld, eds. *Food: A Culinary History from Antiquity to the Present.* Translated by Clarissa Botsford. New York: Columbia University Press, 1999.

Fournier, Édouard. *Les Caquets de l'accouchée.* Paris: P. Jannet, 1855.

Freidson, Eliot. *Professional Powers: A Study of the Institutionalization of Formal Knowledge.* Chicago: University of Chicago Press, 1986.

Furet, François. *Reading and Writing: Literacy in France from Calvin to Jules Ferry.* Cambridge: Cambridge University Press, 1982.

Gallet, Michel. *Paris Domestic Architecture of the 18th Century.* London: Barrie & Jenkins, 1972.

Gay, Peter. *The Enlightenment: The Science of Freedom.* New York: Norton, 1996.

Gelbart, Nina Rattner. *The King's Midwife: A History and Mystery of Madame du Coudray.* Berkeley: University of California Press, 1998.

Gelfand, Toby. *Professionalizing Modern Medicine: Paris Surgeons and Medical Science and Institutions in the 18th Century.* Westport, CT.: Greenwood Press, 1980.

Girard, Alain. "Le Triomphe de *La Cuisinière bourgeoise*. Livres culinaires, cuisine et société en France aux XVIIe et XVIIIe siècles." *Revue d'histoire moderne et contemporaine* 24 (1977): 497–523.

Girard, Sylvie. *Histoire des objets de cuisine et de gourmandise.* Paris: Jacques Grancher, 1991.

Goldstein, Jan. "'Moral Contagion': A Professional Ideology of Medicine and Psychiatry in Eighteenth- and Nineteenth-Century France." In *Professions and French State, 1700–1900*, edited by Gerald L. Geison, 181–222. Philadelphia: University of Pennsylvania Press, 1984.

Goodman, Dena. *Becoming a Woman in the Age of Letters.* Ithaca, NY: Cornell University Press, 2009.

———. *The Republic of Letters: A Cultural History of the French Enlightenment.* Ithaca, NY: Cornell University Press, 1994.

Guadet, Julien. *Élements et théorie de l'architecture.* Paris: Aulanier, 1904.

Guégan, Bertrand. *Le Cuisinier français, ou les meilleurs recettes d'autrefois et d'aujourd'hui.* Paris: Befond, 1980.

Hafter, Daryl M. "Female Masters in the Ribbonmaking Guild of Eighteenth-Century Rouen." *French Historical Studies* 20, no. 1 (Winter 1997): 1–14.

———. *Women at Work in Preindustrial France.* University Park: Pennsylvania State University Press, 2007.

Hecht, J. Jean. *The Domestic Servant Class in Eighteenth-Century England.* London: Routledge & K. Paul, 1956.

Hill, Bridget. *Servants: English Domestics in the Eighteenth Century.* Oxford: Clarendon Press, 1996.

Hufton, Olwen H. *The Poor of Eighteenth-Century France, 1750–1789.* Oxford: Clarendon Press, 1974.

Hyman, Philip, and Mary Hyman. "Les Livres de cuisine imprimés en France du règne de Charles VIII à la fin de l'Ancien Régime." In *Livres en bouche: Cinq siècles d'art culinaire français*, edited by Sabine Coron, Bibliothèque de l'Arsenal, 55–73. Paris: Bibliothèque nationale de France; Hermann, 2001.

Jones, Colin. "The Great Chain of Buying: Medical Advertisement, the Bourgeois Public Sphere, and the Origins of the French Revolution." *American Historical Review* 101, no. 1 (February 1996): 13–40.

———. "'Professionalizing Modern Medicine' in French Hospitals." *Medical History* 26 (1982): 341–349.

———. "Pulling Teeth in Eighteenth-Century Paris." *Past & Present*, no. 166 (February 2000): 100–145.

Kaplan, Steven Laurence. "Social Classification and Representation in the Corporate World of Eighteenth-Century France: Turgot's 'Carnival.'" In *Work in France: Representations, Meaning, Organization, and Practice*, edited by Steven Laurence Kaplan and Cynthia J. Koepp. Ithaca, NY: Cornell University Press, 1986.

Larson, Magali Sarfatti. *The Rise of Professionalism: A Sociological Analysis.* Berkeley: University of California Press, 1977.

Lehmann, Gilly. "Les Cuisiniers anglais face à la cuisine française." *Dix-huitième siècle* 15 (1983): 75–85.

———. "Politics in the Kitchen." *Eighteenth-Century Life* 23, no. 2 (1999): 71–83.

Lewis, Gillian. "Producers, Suppliers, and Consumers: Reflections on the Luxury Trades in Paris, c.1500–c.1800." In *Luxury Trades and Consumerism in Ancien Ré-*

gime Paris: Studies in the History of the Skilled Workforce, edited by Robert Fox and Anthony Turner. Brookfield, VT: Ashgate, 1998.

Martin, Morag. "Il n'y a que Maille qui m'aille: Advertisements and the Development of Consumerism in Eighteenth-Century France." In *Proceedings of the Western Society for French History*, 23:114–121, 1996.

—————. *Selling Beauty: Cosmetics, Commerce, and French Society, 1750–1830.* Baltimore: Johns Hopkins University Press, 2009.

Maza, Sarah C. *Private Lives and Public Affairs: The Causes Célèbres of Prerevolutionary France.* Berkeley: University of California Press, 1993.

—————. *Servants and Masters in Eighteenth-Century France: The Uses of Loyalty.* Princeton, NJ: Princeton University Press, 1983.

Mennell, Stephen. *All Manners of Food: Eating and Taste in England and France from the Middle Ages to the Present.* Oxford: Basil Blackwell, 1985.

—————. *Lettre d'un patissier anglois et autres contributions à une polémique gastronomique du XVIIIème siècle.* Exeter, UK: Exeter University Press, 1981.

Middleton, Robin. "Introduction." In Nicolas Le Camus de Mézières, *The Genius of Architecture; or, The Analogy of That Art with Our Sensations*, translated by David Britt. Santa Monica, CA: Getty Center for the History of Art and the Humanities, 1992.

Mignot, Claude. "De la cuisine à la salle à manger, ou de quelques détours de l'art de la distribution." *XVIIe siècle*, no. 162 (1989): 17–35.

Muchembled, Robert. *L'Invention de l'homme moderne: Sensibilités, mœurs et comportements collectifs sous l'Ancien Régime.* Paris: Fayard, 1988.

Owen, Joan Hildreth. "Philosophy in the Kitchen; or Problems in Eighteenth-Century Culinary Aesthetics." *Eighteenth-Century Life* 3 (March 1977): 77–79.

Pagden, Anthony. *Lords of All the World: Ideologies of Empire in Spain, Britain and France c. 1500–c. 1800.* New Haven, CT: Yale University Press, 1995.

Pardailhé-Galabrun, Annik. *The Birth of Intimacy: Privacy and Domestic Life in Early Modern Paris.* Translated by Jocelyn Phelps. Oxford: Polity, 1991.

Pennell, Sara. "'Pots and Pans History': The Material Culture of the Kitchen in Early Modern England." *Journal of Design History* 11, no. 3 (1998): 201–216.

Petitfrère, Claude. *L'Oeil du maître: Maîtres et serviteurs de l'époque classique au romantisme.* Brussels: Editions Complexe, 1986.

Pinkard, Susan. *A Revolution in Taste: The Rise of French Cuisine, 1650–1800.* Cambridge: Cambridge University Press, 2008.

Poovey, Mary. *A History of the Modern Fact: Problems of Knowledge in the Sciences of Wealth and Society.* Chicago: University of Chicago Press, 1998.

Portalis, Roger, and Henri Béraldi. *Les Graveurs du dix-huitième siècle.* 3 vols. New York: Burt Franklin, 1970.

Pratt, Vernon. "System-Building in the Eighteenth Century." In *The Light of Nature: Essays in the History and Philosophy of Science Presented to A. C. Crombie*, edited by J. J. Roche and J. D. North, 421–431. Boston: Kluwer Academic Publishers, 1985.

Ramsey, Matthew. *Professional and Popular Medicine in France, 1770–1830: The Social World of Medical Practice.* Cambridge: Cambridge University Press, 1988.

Revel, Jean-François. *Culture and Cuisine: A Journey Through the History of Food.* Translated by Helen R. Lane. Garden City, NY: Doubleday, 1982.

Richard, Henri. *Du Louage de services domestiques en droit français.* Angers: A. Burdin, 1906.

Roche, Daniel. *A History of Everyday Things: The Birth of Consumption in France, 1600–1800.* Translated by Brian Pearce. Cambridge: Cambridge University Press, 2000. Originally published as *Histoire des choses banales: Naissance de la consommation dans les sociétés traditionelles (XVIIe–XIXe siècle)* (Paris: Fayard, 1997).

———. *The People of Paris: An Essay in Popular Culture in the 18th Century.* Translated by Marie Evans. Berkeley: University of California Press, 1987.

———. "Le Temps de l'eau rare du Moyen Age à l'époque moderne." *Annales: Economies, Sociétés, Civilisations* 39, no. 2 (1984): 383–399.

Rosenblatt, Helena. "On the 'Misogyny' of Jean-Jacques Rousseau: The Letter to d'Alembert in Historical Context." *French Historical Studies* 25, no. 1 (2002): 91–114.

Sabattier, Jacqueline. *Figaro et son maître: maîtres et domestiques à Paris au XVIIIe siècle.* Paris: Librairie académique Perrin, 1984.

Sargentson, Carolyn. "The Manufacture and Marketing of Luxury Goods: The Marchands Merciers of Late 17th- and 18th-Century Paris." In *Luxury Trades and Consumerism in Ancien Régime Paris: Studies in the History of the Skilled Workforce,* edited by Robert Fox and Anthony Turner, 99–137. Brookfield, VT: Ashgate, 1998.

———. "Markets for Boulle Furniture in Early Eighteenth-Century Paris." *Burlington Magazine* 134, no. 1071 (June 1992): 363–367.

Schiebinger, Londa L. *The Mind Has No Sex? Women in the Origins of Modern Science.* Cambridge, MA: Harvard University Press, 1989.

Schroder, Anne L. "Genre Prints in Eighteenth-Century France: Production, Market, and Audience." In *Intimate Encounters: Love and Domesticity in Eighteenth-Century France,* edited by Richard Rand. Princeton, NJ: Princeton University Press, 1997.

Sedgwick, Romney. "The Duke of Newcastle's Cook." *History Today* 5, no. 5 (1955): 308–316.

Sewell, William H. "Etat, Corps, and Ordre: Some Notes on the Social Vocabulary of the French Old Regime." In *Sozialgeschichte Heute: Festschrift für Hans Rosenberg zum 70. Geburtstag,* edited by Hans-Ulrich Wehler, 49–68. Göttingen: Vandenhoeck & Ruprecht, 1974.

———. "Visions of Labor: Illustrations of the Mechanical Arts before, in, and after Diderot's Encyclopédie." In *Work in France: Representations, Meaning, Organization, and Practice,* edited by Steven Laurence Kaplan and Cynthia J. Koepp. Ithaca, NY: Cornell University Press, 1986.

———. *Work and Revolution in France: The Language of Labor from the Old Regime to 1848.* Cambridge: Cambridge University Press, 1980.

Sgard, Jean. "L'Échelle des revenus." *Dix-huitième siècle* 14 (1982): 425–433.

Sgard, Jean, and Jean-Daniel Candaux. *Dictionnaire des journaux, 1600–1789.* 2 vols. Paris: Universitas, 1991.

Shapin, Steven. *A Social History of Truth: Civility and Science in Seventeenth-Century England.* Chicago: University of Chicago Press, 1994.

Sheridan, Geraldine. *Louder Than Words: Ways of Seeing Women Workers in Eighteenth-Century France*. Lubbock, TX: Texas Tech University Press, 2009.

Sherman, Sandra. "'The Whole Art and Mystery of Cooking': What Cookbooks Taught Readers in the Eighteenth Century." *Eighteenth-Century Life* 28, no. 1 (2004): 115–135.

Simon, Jonathan. *Chemistry, Pharmacy and Revolution in France, 1777–1809*. Science, Technology, and Culture, 1700–1945. Brookfield, VT: Ashgate, 2005.

Smets, Josef. "À la table d'un seigneur languedocien en 1766." *Revue d'histoire moderne et contemporaine* 48, no. 4 (December 2001): 32–49.

Smith, David Kammerling. "Learning Politics: The Nimes Hosiery Guild and the Statutes Controversy of 1706–1712." *French Historical Studies* 22, no. 4 (Autumn): 493–533.

Sonenscher, Michael. *The Hatters of Eighteenth-Century France*. Berkeley: University of California Press, 1987.

———. *Work and Wages: Natural Law, Politics, and Eighteenth-Century French Trades*. Cambridge: Cambridge University Press, 1989.

Spang, Rebecca L. *The Invention of the Restaurant: Paris and Modern Gastronomic Culture*. Cambridge, MA: Harvard University Press, 2000.

Spary, Emma. "Making a Science of Taste: The Revolution, the Learned Life and the Invention of 'Gastronomie.'" In *Consumers and Luxury: Consumer Culture in Europe 1650–1850*, edited by Maxine Berg and Helen Clifford, 170–182. Manchester: Manchester University Press, 1999.

Steedman, Carolyn. "Service and Servitude in the World of Labor: Servants in England, 1750–1820." In *The Age of Cultural Revolutions: Britain and France, 1750–1820*, edited by Colin Jones and Dror Wahrman, 124–136. Berkeley: University of California Press, 2002.

Theophano, Janet. *Eat My Words: Reading Women's Lives Through the Cookbooks They Wrote*. New York: Palgrave, 2002.

This, Hervé, Robert Méric, and Anne Cazor. "Lavoisier and Meat Stock." *Comptes Rendus Chimie* 9, no. 11 (2006): 1510–1515.

Thomas, Keith. "Numeracy in Early Modern England." *Transactions of the Royal Historical Society* 37 (1987): 103–132.

Thompson, Grahame. "Is Accounting Rhetorical? Methodology, Luca Pacioli and Printing." *Accounting, Organizations, and Society* 16, no. 5 (1991): 572–599.

Troyansky, David G. *Old Age in the Old Regime: Image and Experience in Eighteenth-Century France*. Ithaca, NY: Cornell University Press, 1989.

Trubek, Amy B. *Haute Cuisine: How the French Invented the Culinary Profession*. Philadelphia: University of Pennsylvania Press, 2000.

Vardi, Liana. "The Abolition of the Guilds During the French Revolution." *French Historical Studies* 15, no. 4 (Autumn): 704–717.

Weigert, Roger-Armand. "Sur les Larmessin et les costumes grotesques." *Nouvelles de l'estampe* 4, no. 2 (1969): 67–75.

Wellman, Kathleen Anne. *La Mettrie: Medicine, Philosophy, and Enlightenment*. Durham, NC: Duke University Press, 1992.

Wheaton, Barbara Ketcham. *Savoring the Past: The French Kitchen and Table from 1300 to 1789*. Philadelphia: University of Pennsylvania Press, 1983.

Wigley, Mark. "Untitled: The Housing of Gender." In *Sexuality and Space*, edited by Beatriz Colomina, 327–389. New York: Princeton Architectural Press, 1992.

Wrangham, Richard. *Catching Fire: How Cooking Made Us Human*. New York: Basic Books, 2009.